Playing for Profit

Upside Books examines events in business and management through the lens of technology. *Upside Magazine* is the preeminent magazine for executives and managers eager to understand the business of high tech.

Published

High Tech, High Hope: Turning Your Vision of Technology into Business Success, Paul Franson

Risky Business: Protect Your Business from Being Stalked, Conned, or Blackmailed on the Web, Daniel S. Janal

Web Commerce: Building a Digital Business, Kate Maddox

Managing Telework: Strategies for Managing the Virtual Workforce, Jack M. Nilles

PLAYING FOR PROFIT

HOW DIGITAL ENTERTAINMENT IS MAKING BIG BUSINESS OUT OF CHILD'S PLAY

Alice LaPlante
Rich Seidner

John Wiley & Sons, Inc.

New York • Chichester • Weinheim • Brisbane • Singapore • Toronto

Published by John Wiley & Sons, Inc.
Published simultaneously in Canada.

Library of Congress Cataloging-in-Publication Data:
LaPlante, Alice, 1958–
    Playing for profit : how digital entertainment is making big
business out of child's play / Alice LaPlante, Rich Seidner.
       p.   cm.
    Includes index.
    ISBN 0-471-29614-7 (cloth : alk. paper)
    1. Electronic games industry.   2. Television supplies industry.
3. Computer industry.   4. Electronic industries.   5. Digital
electronics.   I. Seidner, Rich.   II. Title.
HD9993.E452L37   1999
338.4'77948—dc21   98-33166
                             CIP

For Rosalba Barron de Lopez, who made the writing of this book possible.

And especially for Sarah, who makes everything worthwhile.

Contents

Preface

"There's Gonna Be a Revolution"

"The passive ways of being entertained via television, movie pictures, and radio—with comedy shows, dramas, and football, and all the rest—will stay the same. But we're going to see a different form of entertainment that is a combination of what already exists and the interactive world of the Internet. It will be a completely new medium. We think a revolution is coming. We're certainly investing as though it is."

—MICHAEL EISNER, chairman and CEO,
Walt Disney Co., April 28, 1998

On October 17, 1989, a 7.3 temblor shook up residents of the San Francisco Bay Area. As earthquakes of this magnitude go, us locals got off easy. It lasted only 23 seconds. It caused half a billion dollars in damage to roads and buildings, but the Northridge earthquake in Southern California cost almost 10 times that. Astonishingly, only 88 lives were lost, despite the fact that the earthquake hit during rush hour—at 5:08 P.M. on a Tuesday evening—and that one of the more spectacular effects was the collapse of a major highway interchange.

In fact, most residents still marvel at how little they were affected by the event. About 85 percent of Bay Area residents lost electricity, but most of them were able to turn on lights, fire up televisions, and pop pizzas in their microwave ovens within 36 hours of feeling the first tremor.

Still, an interesting statistic resulted from this relatively small disruption in power: Approximately nine months later, the birthrate for the region was booming. The pundits had a field day chortling about what must have happened when the lights were out. Of course. But the fact remains that, statistically speaking, a lot of people were left at loose ends. They were left bereft of the primary ways they were accustomed to entertain themselves, which is to spend a whopping average of nine hours a day on so-called consumer media: television, recorded music on CDs or vinyl, and for those who hadn't had the foresight to have spare batteries, even radio was unavailable. Once the power was available again, the local energy supplier, PG&E, saw a marked jump in usage over the next two weeks. As if everyone was so relieved to get back to normal that they overdosed on the things they'd previously taken for granted. "Normal" is a relative term, of course.

Imagine—if you're able—what it was like to live a century ago. More specifically, imagine how you might have spent your leisure time, which is how Bay Area residents had to live for just a short period: without television, cable, computers, video games, and recorded music. Much of what we take for granted in our lives today simply did not exist back then.

In terms of human history, 120 years wasn't that long ago. Yet, there has been a revolutionary change in the way we spend our time, our money—our lives. And it is all due to an intense explosion of technical innovation. The telephone was introduced as recently as 1876, the phonograph in 1877. The kinetoscope that displayed primitive motion pictures didn't start making the rounds of state fairs and other venues for displaying oddities until 1890. It wasn't until 1901 that Reginald Aubrey Fessenden successfully broadcasted music and speech via his new-fangled invention he called "the wireless." And television? The earliest experiments in the transmission of images weren't conducted until 1907.

Well, it's déjà vu all over again. A new revolution, one almost as profound as the one engineered a century ago, is about to erupt again. And this time it won't take a century before it fundamentally reshapes virtually every form of entertainment we know.

■ TRANSFORMATION OF THE FITTEST

In truth, we've been in a sort of entertainment stasis for almost a century. Certainly, we've seen LP records become compact discs; we've seen black-and-white televisions replaced by color ones and 15-inch monitors replaced by wall-sized screens. We can listen to radio transmissions from our homes, our automobiles, or even while hiking in the wilderness. We see movies augmented by spectacular computer-generated special effects. We play games on our PCs or game consoles. But there hasn't been a real revolution. Not yet. With the emergence of new digital technologies, however, we're about to take another huge leap forward, and we are already seeing small signs of this.

For instance, we contact our satellite TV provider to request the specific movies we'd like to view, and when. The computer games we play are becoming more immersive, more sophisticated, and can involve more people in simultaneous play. We can communicate with people around the world via the Internet. We're forming on-line communities on the World Wide Web that transcend geographic and temporal boundaries.

What do all of these activities have in common? Two small words with enormous consequences: *interactivity* and *Internet*. Interactivity, as enabled by the Internet (and other emerging digital technologies), is beginning to rewrite all rules, explode all assumptions, and level all playing fields in virtually every entertainment medium we know.

It will also blur the traditional boundaries between the various categories of amusement as we now experience them. And it will invent some new categories we can't yet imagine. After all, is it still called a movie when *you* con-

trol how the characters on the screen behave in response
to various dramatic events? Is it still radio if you are listening to music via your computer, and it's not just audio,
but visual, in nature? Where you can click on an on-screen
icon and download additional information about the particular subject Howard Stern is ranting about today? Is it
still called a game when you are not shooting aliens, or
chasing enemy aircraft, but creating a new virtual universe with the help of scattered comrades from around the
world—who might not even speak the same language as
you, much less share cultural assumptions?

In this book, we explain the massive changes in technology, entertainment, and culture that are forcing this
revolution. We show how the entire entertainment industry will be redefined and look at how it will impact the current business models found in traditional radio, recorded
music, television, and computer games segments.

First, we'll look at how a massively different playing
field is being created for existing entertainment giants. Digital entertainment began with video games, of course. But
we'll see how game designers and publishers are only now
finding their feet in the *digital age*. Despite their familiarity
with the technology, and their well-deserved reputation for
innovation (if not chutzpah), the games industry is only
now emerging from a creative and financial slump, and
only now seeing the possibilities of building games for a
market that appeals to more than teenage boys.

Read on and you'll see how, as radio and television stations begin broadcasting over the Web, as record companies forge direct (and personal) relationships with
individual consumers, and as brick-and-mortar entertainment providers and retailers devise more creative—and
fun—ways to bring customers into their physical locations, new market structures and opportunities will inevitably evolve.

In Part 1, we'll see how all of this puts everything literally *and* virtually up for grabs throughout the entertain-

ment industry. There will be new rules, new players, and bigger jackpots. Will computer games break the on-line barrier and finally figure out how to make money on the Internet? Or, will interactive radio stations beat them to the promised land of on-line advertising revenues? Will there be a Tower Records if we can have any recording we want delivered to us wherever we are? What happens when we truly have radio without waves, television without schedules, and computer games for the rest of us?

In Part 2, we'll look at the ways technology will drive changes in every entertainment industry. In every media segment, rapid and powerful changes are shaking up the status quo. In the music business, for instance, recording artists are starting to act like *they* are the labels; the labels are beginning to act like broadcasters and direct-to-consumer retailers; retailers are becoming on-line performance venues; and broadcasters are attempting to move into everyone else's territory.

In Part 2, we'll also examine how the computer games industry is finally growing up. Not only are they creating games that interest—and satisfy—former niches deemed untouchable (e.g., girls, adult women, etc.), but they are forging ahead into new venues for game playing—in cyberspace as well as in your neighborhood.

Finally, in Part 3, we'll look at certain inevitable forces of evolution for all entertainment providers; at what advertising's shifting role will be in digital fun; at how the various telecom networks are scrambling to be the ones delivering the entertainment to your home; and at how our desire for intellectual and physical challenge, for excitement, for storytelling, and, of course, for interaction with others will play into the entertainment offerings of the future.

In short, we will be pushing the limits—and redefining the very essence—of what we call "entertainment." There *is* going to be a revolution. Prepare to be entertained as you've never been entertained before.

Part One
Everything's Up for Grabs

Why There Will Be New Rules, New Players, and Much Bigger Jackpots in the Digital Age

Nothing less than the birth of an entirely new form of entertainment. One that will incorporate elements from all existing forms, but in powerfully surprising new ways.

Chapter 1

What's Going On?

"The innovator has for enemies all those who have done well under the old conditions, and lukewarm defenders in those who may do well under the new. This coolness arises . . . from the incredulity of men, who do not readily believe in new things until they have had a long experience of them."

—NICCOLÒ MACHIAVELLI, *The Prince*

"The reasonable man adapts himself to the world; the unreasonable one persists in trying to adapt the world to himself. Therefore, all progress depends on the unreasonable man."

—GEORGE BERNARD SHAW, *Man and Superman*

"It's good enough to criticize."

—ROB GLASER, webcasting pioneer

Grab your pencils. It's time for a pop quiz that examines some prevailing assumptions about entertainment—and what the future (or nonfuture) of traditional media looks like when mated with emerging technologies.

Are the following statements true or false?

- ☐ Television is something you play.
- ☐ Newspapers are something you listen to.
- ☐ Television is something that watches *you*.

☐ Radio is something you watch.

☐ It is now possible to build an entire broadcast network without dealing with the FCC or any other government agency.

☐ It is now possible to offer an unlimited number of radio and/or television channels without having to change the laws of man or nature.

☐ Eventually, it will be possible to have personalized versions of favorite mass entertainment media products delivered directly to you—versions no one else will necessarily see, hear, or experience.

☐ Eventually, media advertisements will be another form of retail—a place you buy products, not just watch, listen, or ignore.

☐ Eventually, you'll be able to throw away your CDs and CD players (not to mention your VCRs and videotapes), yet still get every music recording or every movie you like—whenever you want it.

☐ Much of the above will be given to us absolutely free, if we choose.

☐ Often, we'll choose to pay for entertainment even when it's optional.

☐ Computer games are a niche market for hobbyists and boys (of all ages); most of us will never be interested in using our PCs to play games.

☐ Technology is a socially limiting, isolating sort of plaything—the more we depend on computer-based fun, the less we will interact with other people.

☐ For most consumers, cable will remain a vehicle for delivering broadcast and cable TV channels; the telephone will primarily be a mechanism for making phone calls and providing Internet access; and the television will always be best suited for passive entertainment.

This book will help you understand the answers to these, and other questions. (For your information, all of the preceding can be answered "true" except the last three statements.)

■ WHY EVERYTHING'S UP FOR GRABS

Ken Rutkowski, standing six feet two inches tall in his socks (he hates wearing shoes), as fit as a marathon runner (which he is), and sporting a three-day beard, is on his fifth conference call of the day. This one is to Melbourne, Australia, where his technology correspondents Down Under are planning new shows to syndicate.

It's a cloudy Tuesday morning on the South Side of Chicago, and what's on Rutkowski's mind is whether the time is right to move from broadcasting shows that focus on technology to a broader, more interesting—and more lucrative—selection of music, talk, or other mainstream entertainment content. The weather is typically muggy for August, but Rutkowski won't notice until he goes out for a quick run at 2:00 A.M. tomorrow morning. It's only 5:00 A.M. now, and Rutkowski is pacing about his office— well, kitchen—simultaneously working his three phone lines, his satellite uplink, and four computer workstations. He'll wrap up another 50 or so conference calls before his workday ends after midnight. Then, he'll grab a quick snack before his daily (nightly?) run, and finally, some sleep. However, if he could, Rutkowski would cut out the eating and sleeping stuff. It wastes too much time. He's on a mission.

Rutkowski is one of the pioneers currently defining the future of entertainment. A prototypical techie-turned-entrepreneur, what he's building will change the world of broadcasting forever. His company, PlusMedia, is about to launch a new kind of network. It's not radio, not televi-

sion, not a newspaper, nor a magazine; however, it will incorporate all these various ways of getting entertainment
and information to the masses. In fact, what Rutkowski is
doing is hard to classify because it crosses the boundaries
of all traditional entertainment media. (He wanted to use
the more appropriate name CrossMedia, but it had already
been snapped up by some other techno-savvy entrepre-
neur.)

In many ways PlusMedia is just like any other broadcast network, delivering programming content to satellite
uplinks, cable head-ends, and radio transmitters around
the country. But every one of the programs it delivers to its
affiliated radio, satellite, and cable operators differs fundamentally from anything that has ever been broadcast
before. No, it's not because of excess violence, or sexual
content, or any of the usual ways that media conglomerates try to shock prospective audiences to tune in. And, it's
not just because PlusMedia broadcasts the material via
the Internet. What makes what Rutkowski is doing so
unique? His programs are fully interactive in a way that
broadcasting has never been before. When PlusMedia is
fully operational, anyone located anywhere in the world
will be able to make a local phone call to appear live on
his shows. When PlusMedia is broadcasting a hot new
band, let's say live from a popular dance club in Santa
Cruz, California, the worldwide audience gets the live
video broadcast as it's happening (or later, if they're
watching a copy of the show that has been archived on the
web site)—just like any live broadcast. But what's more,
anyone in the audience can make a local phone call—
from wherever they are in the world—and talk to the
club's host about the concert and talk with the band during breaks. If anyone is in the mood, it's only a few clicks
away to buy the band's CD, to check out the really cool
posters and T-shirts, or to sign up for the club newsletter
and e-mail updates on the band's next gig. Or, they can
simply applaud loudly with the live club patrons when

the song is over. It will create, in short, a total free-for-all in the live broadcast audience.

➤ Pay Close Attention Now

Why what Rutkowski is doing should matter to anyone, let alone to the established and profitable companies (i.e., the massive conglomerates such as Disney, Sony, Time Warner Turner, Universal, and Viacom) who currently dominate the entertainment world, is at the heart of this book.

The major companies in each entertainment segment, including television, radio, recorded music, and movies, have been acutely aware that changes in technology are driving enormous economic and regulatory changes in their respective businesses. But, most of them hadn't begun facing what an enormous change was in store—until now. Whether PlusMedia succeeds is not the issue for the majors; it's the very fact that similar broadcasters are springing up literally all over the globe. The future of broadcasting has already begun and nothing can stop it.

Everything is about to go up for grabs. In the United States alone, more than $100 billion in annual revenues is at stake, not to mention domination of the entertainment industries of the future. Here are the three main reasons why the current entertainment playing field is about to be leveled:

1. First and foremost, there's a new technology that has created a new kind of network—the Internet. Many of the laws of man and nature simply do not apply to this new network; with the old rules, the old limitations are also banished. It's the Wild, Wild West all over again.
2. Second, this new network is global in a way that no network or market has been before. It creates a sin-

gle market, one that anyone in the world can participate in. This market spans all national, cultural, and geographic boundaries. It's the biggest new market opportunity in history.

3. Finally—and most important—the Internet enables *interactivity*. Interactivity was made possible by the still-ongoing transition between analog and digital technologies, and it will create entirely new ways for people to relate to one another. As you'll see, this interactivity translates into new ways to efficiently enter new markets, new ways to entertain, new ways to generate profits.

Existing players will either adapt or die.

■ CALIFORNIA DREAMING

You would think you'd died and gone to heaven. David Kessel works at home, which just happens to be right on the beach in Pacific Grove, California. He's a few miles north of picturesque Carmel-by-the-Sea, a few miles south of historic Monterey, and literally just a stone's throw from the world famous Pebble Beach Golf Course. It's a mystery how anyone can concentrate on work in such a serenely beautiful setting, but Kessel manages quite successfully.

Five years ago, before the Internet phenomenon had reached the attention of the world at large, Kessel had already figured out how to change the music business using the Web. In fact, he sees more changes coming over the next two years than have been seen in decades. (And he knows the music business as well as anyone.)

To say Kessel has a strong background in music is an understatement. In his 25-plus years of working with Phil Spector Productions, Kessel has been involved in virtually every aspect of music production, publishing, songwriting, and management—not to mention his myriad performances as a session musician and background vocalist on countless recordings, including records for John Lennon, Bob Dylan, The Ramones, Cher, and Celine Dion.

If all this isn't enough to make anyone envious, he owns an independent record label, which has recorded co-productions with Brian Wilson of the Beach Boys and other famous artists. And now, Pacific Grove, the scent of Monterey pines, and the soothing sound of lapping ocean waves as he works on the *next big thing*—for Kessel, not surprisingly, this involves the Internet.

Five years ago, a few of his college buddies got together and founded the Internet Underground Music Archive (IUMA) to wrest control of the music business from the grips of the Big Five companies, who tightly controlled every aspect of the industry. (The Big Five include Universal, Sony, Warner, Bertelsmann, and EMI.) Soon after, Kessel joined IUMA as chairman.

IUMA was the first—and remains the largest—hi-fi music site on the World Wide Web. Tens of thousands of unique visitors a day keep IUMA one of the most popular places on the Web. At the center of the IUMA site are more than 1,000 independent bands from every corner of the world. Anyone with a basic Internet connection can hear CD quality songs, view images and text from the artists, and in most cases, get direct access to the artists themselves via e-mail. Through secure on-line sales of recordings as well as the truly revolutionary next step of digital distribution via the Internet, IUMA promotes and sells its artists' music to a global audience. In addition to its original band members and their related content, IUMA also provides sites for nearly 30 independent record labels, each one a complete web site unto itself. Just click to jump from IUMA to any of these exciting new global music ventures.

IUMA's mission is simple: it wants to empower the independent musician through a complete reinvention of the music industry. We're talking a revolution here. Because using the Internet is an affordable and universally accessible performance-and-sales space for musicians and their audiences to meet and interact, IUMA provides services and technologies that circumvent—and, therefore, have the potential to destroy—the traditional food chain of music creation, promotion, distribution, and sales. So, the creative artists themselves get to keep more of the profits. Not surprisingly, the major record companies hope this falls flat.

■ ADAPTING LIKE CRAZY

Here's another example. Evans & Sutherland, the staid Salt Lake City–based maker of high-end graphic systems and real-time simulators for military and commercial aviation customers, might seem an unlikely harbinger of the New World Order of mass market entertainment. Yet, that's what it hopes to be. In 1997, it founded its Interactive Theater Division, with precisely that in mind, and it brought together an impressive team of gurus from a variety of entertainment segments—film, computer games, theme park, live theater, and television industries, even Las Vegas—to make it happen. In December 1998, Evans & Sutherland debuted the first product from this venture at the Adler Planetarium in Chicago. And it offered a glimpse into the future of interactive entertainment in a way that few mainstream entertainment providers had yet to achieve.

So, just imagine: you're leaning back in a comfortable, padded chair. Above you stretches a 300-foot dome that provides you with a breathtaking 360-degree view of the star-studded night sky. But you're not just seeing a static picture, or even a film, but 3-D images generated in real time. Now you've left the earth and are flying over Mars. With the help of your fellow travelers, you navigate down into the surface of the planet. You spy an intriguing-looking canyon and decide to plunge into the abyss at breathtaking speed. You just miss the cliff edge and careen off into another crevice, then out again into the strato-sphere. You slow down, relax a bit, take some time to look around you. Wow, the solar system is truly a miraculous place!

Sound like a scene from the latest movie? It could be. The only differences are that it's happening in real time (it's not a canned film); it would be different each time you sat down in the chair; and, most important, you're not just a passive observer, but actually part of the experience. That's what Evans & Sutherland's StarRider Theater already does in Chicago, and what it promises to do for other venues, other kinds of entertainment.

Adler's visitors are no longer just being educated (yawn). Neither are they passively enjoying what is admittedly a spectacular show. They are part of the show. How? Buttons located in the armrest of each seat in the audience allow viewers to react to the program in real time. They can change direction as they move over the surface of Mars, select a different destination (let's dive into the rings of Saturn today), slow down, speed up, whatever they choose. At this point, audiences are, in effect, voting to come to a consensus on changes in direction, speed, and altitude.

But, as Stanley Walker, head of E&S's new Digital Theater Division, is quick to point out, this is just the first baby step in audience participation. What Walker and his team eventually plan to do is change the sort of mass-market entertainment experience we've come to expect—everything from TV to amusement parks to movies—from merely a passive, or even active-passive, experience to a truly interactive one.

What's the difference? Everything. In a completely passive experience, such as watching broadcast television, you merely sit and absorb. An active-passive experience means that a lot is being done to you: you are being hurled down a slope of a roller coaster or bombarded with extreme audio or visual stimuli, as in a large-screen 3-D IMAX theater, but nothing you do changes the nature of the experience itself. That is, although you can certainly react (yell, scream, laugh), whatever you do won't change the nature of the experience. The experience goes on exactly as planned, no matter what you do or say.

But with truly interactive entertainment, of which StarRider is an early sign, the audience affects the experience itself. This has long been the case with interactive digital entertainment, such as computer games. How you react in the game Myst to the various puzzles and sensory clues placed in your path will determine the outcome of the game.

What's different about what Evans & Sutherland is attempting to do, and what makes it worth special note, is that this interactivity is occurring within a group. "It's not an individual experience. It's a group experience," stresses Rick Hinton, the creative director, who brings a rich background in film production to the E&S team. And the biggest challenge resulting from this difference is that the success of an interactive entertainment experience—like the Adler one—built for a group, depends on "giving the individuals a sense of control and satisfaction even though they are acting as part of a group."

This is no mean feat. Although early interactive trials like the Adler one involve voting via individual keypads located in the chairs, voting is not the most fulfilling way to go, stresses Walker. His goal is a more sophisticated form of interactivity that gives the group "tasks" that they can only accomplish together, such as navigating a submarine through a lunar valley and successfully avoiding dangerous objects in that valley. In a hypothetical case like this, "A group would be working with each other, shouting to each other, trying to make this thing happen," says Walker. Voting won't do that—"It won't get you working cooperatively with the guy sitting next to you," agrees Hinton.

If this sounds hard, that's because it is; and this isn't E&S's first attempt at this. "Many many millions of dollars have been lost in pursuing so-called interactive entertainment, and Evans & Sutherland has been one of the big losers," admits Dean Fox, director of marketing for E&S's Interactive Theater Division.

A case in point was a virtual reality (VR) experience that E&S designed in the early 1990s for theme parks. Called "The Loch Ness Monster Experience," it involved a group of people donning VR headsets and working together in a virtual submarine in a virtual loch to help find and protect the eggs of Nessie before they were destroyed by predators. In theory, it was a great idea—people got to go someplace they wouldn't ordinarily go (the bottom of Loch Ness in Scotland) and do something they wouldn't ordinarily do (steer a submarine and hunt for monster eggs), and they got to do it in a social setting. That is, it was a group, not an isolating, experience.

Commercially, however, Nessie was a flop. Evans & Sutherland tried to sell it to theme parks, like Six Flags, and other entertainment sites, but managed to install only two versions. For starters, says Celia Pearce, an interactive media designer who worked on the project, it was prohibitively expensive, making it difficult for amusement operators to see a return on their investment.

Secondly—and this is the important reason, according to Pearce—"LBE [location-based entertainment] is not just a product business, it's a service business," she says. The attraction of places like Six Flags and Disneyland is not just the rides contained there, but the entire experience. "It's a complex business," she says.

Indeed it is, and Walker, for one, is confident E&S is now on the right track to infiltrate it. For starters, there's the mix of skills and expertise. Rather than depending on technicians or engineers, Walker has pulled together a staff that includes representatives from virtually every entertainment media segment. Fox spent years at game manufacturer Atari; Walker himself comes from Universal Studios; Clifford Hay, program director for the Digital Theater Division, hails from the glitzy corridors of Las Vegas. And under these senior executives are scores of other writers, actors, theater and film directors, game designers, and theme park ride experts. "You need this spectrum of talent if you're trying to define entertainment in the digital age," stresses Walker. And his job over the next 12 months is to *evangelize*, to explain E&S's vision to players throughout the entertainment and technology world.

One possible application of the E&S technology is in live theater. Actors (yes, live ones) will interact both with the audience and with the environment, maintaining a sense of artistic integrity and plot while allowing the experience to be molded according to the audience's wishes.

The balance between a linear story and an interactive entertainment experience is a delicate one. We devote an entire chapter to this topic (Chapter 12). Fox is quick to point out that dabbling with this new interactive entertainment media is still a primitive art. "Look how long it took us to understand the new media of film," says Fox. "It took 20 years that you could get better effects by moving the camera." It's the same thing with interactive entertainment: it will take time before we understand it, according to Walker.

At the time the book went to press, Walker was in negotiations with a major entertainment provider that had plans for a mass-market interactive television product. That is, a form of entertainment that would be broadcast into homes but that was truly interactive in nature.

How would this work? (As we'll see in Chapter 7, previous attempts at so-called interactive TV have failed miserably.) Walker wasn't free to say, other than, "until I heard the details, I was pretty skeptical myself. Interactive in the context of TV usually means viewers are able to respond to advertising." But, if this project works out, he says, the truly interactive nature of entertainment as experienced within the context of broadcast TV "will be truly revolutionary."

■ IT'S HARD TO SEE WHAT'S COMING WHEN YOU'RE FOCUSED ON THE PAST

It's hard for most people to imagine that something new is truly new—that it's not just a more powerful, more jazzed-up, more feature-ridden version of what we're already quite familiar (and comfortable) with. That is how movies got their name: they were, at first, simply *moving pictures;* they were not something completely new, with completely new possibilities, but simply something we were already comfortable with—pictures—that also happened to move.

Of course, it's never easy to predict the future; there's a particular challenge in recognizing the potential effect of technologies still in their infancy. Many people took a long time to comprehend the importance of the personal computer; even a decade after the introduction of the first PC, it was still considered a toy by an astonishing number of otherwise very savvy businesspeople. Today, it's unthinkable to do business without a computer and an e-mail address. Intel and Microsoft understood right away; however, IBM took more than a decade to see this— an oversight that put the entire company at risk. Still, you hear the same sorts of things today:

➤ The PC will never be any good for entertainment— it's a business and information access tool only.

➤ The TV is good only for *passive* entertainment.

➤ The Internet won't ever become a mass medium for entertainment, in the way that broadcast TV and radio are.

Granted, these are quite reasonable assumptions held by successful people, already at the helm of thriving businesses, who have seen the litter of corpses of those who have tried to circumvent or contradict them.

But, this is *not* the attitude taken by the people spotlighted in this book. Some of them are already quite big names in their field: Douglas Adams, Mark Cuban, Michael Eisner, Rob Glaser. Others are currently nobodies—they may remain so, or they may become the spearheads of a new revolution.

Rob Glaser had it right when he referenced Alan Kay's remark about the 512K Macintosh computer when discussing the current state of web-based entertainment. Although not the first version of the now-famous user-friendly interface, it was, nevertheless, finally "good enough to criticize," Glaser reminded us. This means that not only were they worth *not* ignoring, but they showed significant promise. And, indeed, the Apple Macintosh changed the history of computing, and though Apple Computer was not the main beneficiary of that success (Microsoft was), it pushed out into the world the concept of the *graphical user interface,* now used in hundreds of millions of PCs worldwide.

The point of Glaser's remark is that the same is true of today's emerging entertainment media technology, called *streaming.* It's good enough to criticize. As we'll learn, it's not there yet—you can't watch *Seinfeld* via even the fastest Internet connection today. But soon you will. For today, it's enough that entertainment media on the Internet is (finally) good enough to criticize.

This book is about the people who see and understand this concept and the opportunities they're pursuing—like David Kessel, who sees a way to revolutionize the recorded music business, or Rutkowski, out to shake up broadcasting. As far as the naysayers who don't believe that big changes are coming, Evans & Sutherland's Walker says there are enough signs—everywhere about us—for people in all entertainment segments to begin paying close attention. "True, the increments of change are so small that at the time you might not be aware of the eventual implications," says Walker. "But they're coming."

During the biggest landgrab
in history, the sheriff decides
to leave town. And hordes
of newcomers are prospecting
for gold.

Chapter

The Wild, Wild West

"We said the following radical thing: How about if we don't have any rules that limit the way people develop this technology? And it's driving everybody nuts."

—REED HUNDT, former FCC chairman[1]

Game developers are cowboys. They don't care about the rules; rather, they pay attention to the rules long enough to figure out how to break or circumvent them—anything to win. Game developers especially don't like the limitations placed by the current state of technology—whatever that happens to be. Everything is too slow: microprocessors, graphics, networks, CDs, multimedia, you name it. It's *always* too slow for what they want to do. Which is why, if you want to see where the future of technology is going, you look to gamers. They're the ones on the bleeding edge.

Back in 1989, Nintendo approached a small developer in London, Argonaut Software, to create a game for their new system with breakthrough 3-D graphics. The problem was the so-called Super Nintendo System wasn't super enough to do the job. No problem, said Argonaut, and they promptly designed a 3-D graphics chip that would go into every Nintendo game cartridge. As it happens, StarFox sold over 4 million copies and is one of the most successful video games of all times. And the SuperFX chip ended up in more than 10 million game cartridges. *Gamers hate limits.*

Today's personal computer owes much of its pizzazz to game technology pioneers. Three-dimensional graphics, the 3-D surround-sound audio, and advances in reducing network latency started out as designs in some game developer's laboratory.

Here are some examples of technology that was originally seen as not-fit-for-prime-time, and that has now become standard in every PC shipped by IBM, Compaq, Dell, or Gateway. What do these features have in common? They're what game aficionados installed on their machines eons ago (well, five years ago, which in Internet years is eons): sound cards, 3-D graphics accelerators, video cards, microphones, joysticks. And guess what? These features now make the standard PC ready to be an entertainment box for the rest of us. Think about what you can now do with a bottom-line PC (as of press time, they were shipping for less than $600): listen to radio broadcasts from anywhere in the world, watch a movie trailer, and/or download the latest CD from top musical artists.

So game developers are pioneers. They have to be; otherwise, they'd still be playing Pong or Pac Man in dimly lit arcades. Furthermore, other entertainment segments have learned that if they want to see what's possible, look at what gamers are doing. "People who have designed computer games know how to engage people, draw them in, get them to act in a meaningful way," says Stanley Walker, vice president and general manager of Evans & Sutherland's Digital Theater Division, who has gone on a hiring spree at game companies to staff up his recently formed division, which intends to tap into the commercial promise of interactive entertainment.

True to form, gamers saw the potential of the Internet very early. By 1995—around the time that Netscape went public, and before Bill Gates got serious about the Web—most new games under development were pitched with this supposedly lucrative (and just-around-the-corner) multiplayer networked market in mind. Everyone jumped on this particular bandwagon. Traditional game developers, such as Electronic Arts, Sierra Online, Sega, Microsoft, and

Acclaim, all announced exciting new on-line games that would be delivered by Christmas (prime game-selling season). Major on-line service providers, such as America Online, Prodigy, and CompuServe, launched primitive game sites for subscribers. And several new, game-only on-line services were launched, notably Total Entertainment Network (TEN), Mpath, and the Imagination Network (later acquired by America Online and dubbed WorldPlay service). This was going to be the great new market for games. Analysts rubbed their hands together and gloated about the $10 billion market that was soon to be. Existing players and wanna-bes alike scrambled so as not to miss out.

If you think in terms of *interactivity,* as we discussed in Chapter 1, this evolution was a no-brainer. Surely, it would be a lot more fun for people to play against other people than against computers. Surely, the game experience would be richer, more challenging, more unpredictable, more fun—more of everything we want from entertainment. "It's one thing to play against a computer, which can be lots of fun, but that's nothing compared to the wild strategies and unexpected surprises you get when you're playing live against a friend," says Jez San, the founder of Argonaut, who wrote his first best-selling game at the ripe old age of 15. Add lots of friends to the equation—as allowed by the Internet—and "it gets even wilder, and even more intense," he says.

As it turned out, a lot of fuss but precious few revenues were generated by early on-line gaming efforts. Several online services have already folded their subscription game services (Prodigy, CompuServe). A few companies are achieving modest growth, hoping to survive until the online market *does* explode (and by the end of 1998, it finally seems to be on the verge of taking off). But most developers agree with Terry Bratcher, a board member of the Computer Game Developer Association, when he said in early 1998, "online games have been a complete disaster."

But here's the interesting part. Even as the renegade cowboys—the gamers—were struggling to figure out how to profitably play on the Internet, the profitability question didn't stop other entertainment providers from join-ing the fray. Just think about this:

> ➤ Every major record company has moved into direct sales on-line, and has begun to distribute samples of hot new releases over the Internet. You're more likely to be able to download a portion of Madonna's latest hit from the Web before the album is available from Tower Records.

> ➤ Every major radio station has begun broadcasting its shows over the Internet. Not incidentally, radio stations that formerly derived most of their rev-enues from local ads are now finding a broader— and more lucrative—list of prospective advertisers.

> ➤ Every major movie studio is offering on-line pre-views for all their latest releases, and are merchan-dising the hell out of everything.

> ➤ Every major television broadcaster (including cable and satellite providers) is eyeing Internet access and service as the single most significant new rev-enue opportunity ahead. And—as Michael Eisner said—that's what they're investing in.

What's going on here is something basic. Entertain-ment industries that have, until now, been heavily shackled with cumbersome regulations have discovered the Wild, Wild West of the Internet—where no rules apply (not yet, anyway), where the sheriff (the FCC) has decided to turn its back, and where anyone with a bright idea and a modem can pan for gold. Whereas the original digital entertain-ment providers—computer gamers—had traditionally been held back solely by the limitations of the technology itself, their rivals in other entertainment segments were handi-capped largely by governmental restrictions.

This book examines how, now that the competitive and creative landscape is more level, the convergence of tech-nology and entertainment will progress at startling speed.

We recommend buckling your seatbelts. We predict it's going to be a turbulent and exciting ride.

■ NET WORTH

Mark Cuban's net worth increased almost $250 million the day his company went public in 1998. The market capitalization of Broadcast.com (as its name implies, an Internet-based broadcasting company) went from 0 to over $1 billion dollars in a matter of hours. *Net* worth, indeed. Not bad, considering the fledgling Internet start-up had yet to generate a penny of profits. But what is most remarkable about Broadcast.com is not that it established its considerable valuation so quickly and in the absence of tangible financial assets—after all, a number of Internet companies have soared to stardom on Wall Street in a similar way—but that it has established a broadcasting business in a truly revolutionary fashion—and without a broadcast license!

That's right. Cuban was able to construct an entire broadcast network, encompassing hundreds of channels and tens of thousands of programs, without obtaining any government licenses or submitting to any regulatory intervention. Traditional broadcasters were weeping with envy. "Broadcast.com's stunning IPO should help put to rest the idea that webcasting is a niche product and is likely to remain so for many years," says George Bundy, president of BRS Media.

This was the first time that such a thing had happened—that a broadcast network could be born without the minute, even excruciating, midwifery of the federal and local agencies that exist for precisely that reason: to regulate broadcasting and telecommunications in the public interest. This translates into their two main goals: to prevent monopolies from either limiting the freedom of expression or competition.

What this meant, specifically, for Cuban, was:

➤ Broadcast.com didn't have to apply for a single broadcast license.

➤ Broadcast.com didn't have to worry about owning too many of the stations reaching specific markets.

➤ Broadcast.com didn't have to conform to any of the literally thousands of detailed rules that govern traditional broadcast operations.

In fact, most of the entertainment industries we know have been chained virtually since birth. Radio and television broadcasting, recorded music, motion pictures, gambling, and even newspapers had to conform to a multitude of local and federal regulations. And these regulations have fundamentally shaped these industries. For example, movie studios don't own movie theaters, cable TV broadcasters don't own radio stations, and the record industry has to be very careful in all its dealings with the radio industry—and does so via intermediaries.

But now, for the first time in their relatively short history, a new playing field has been created. If not completely level, it's as close to that as is possible in this world.

This lack of regulation on the Internet is already dramatically affecting a broad range of media and entertainment players. So, in addition to Mark Cuban, Webcaster renegade extraordinaire, we have gambling that is no longer limited to Las Vegas, Atlantic City, or Native American tribal lands. Take a look at CasinoLand, which operates virtual casinos that exist only on the Internet. The computers running these casinos are located in the tropical paradise of Belize—to circumvent U.S. criminal penalties? Yes, CasinoLand's business is gambling. True, Internet gambling is illegal in the United States. But although the company is officially based in Las Vegas, and because none of its customers are U.S. citizens who use Casinoland's services within U.S. borders, it's all legal. And, says Sue Schneider, president of Rolling Good Times Online, and chairwoman of the Interactive Gaming Council, "legal questions will remain until these new laws are tested in the courts." What is decidedly *not* in question is that if the U.S. government decides to prohibit on-line gambling, other countries will be happy to leap into the void. After all, there are potentially huge sums to be reaped in gambling—$100 billion annually worldwide, to be precise.

And here's another example. The radio broadcast industry is already in a frenzy of acquisition and merger activity due to deregulation. All because of substantial deregulation of ownership rules. Previously, station ownership was strictly limited within any local (geographically defined) market. Just five years ago, the top 10 radio station owners controlled less than 1 percent of the more than 10,000 commercial radio stations in the country. Today, the top 10 station owners control more than 20 percent of all the stations. Deregulation lead directly to industry consolidation. It won't be long before radio is truly an oligopoly, just like every other entertainment industry; and that's not even counting the effect the Internet will have on radio.

The television industry is also being dramatically affected by the lawless state of the Internet. For starters, although most consumers don't realize it, the television networks use broadband telephone connections and satellite communications to distribute their programs. And the fundamental economics of this distribution are currently being radically reshaped by the creation of the functionally equivalent, but totally unregulated, telecommunications services available on the Internet. For example, if you were to pick up your telephone and place an international phone call, you would pay, in addition to the telecommunications cost, all sorts of tariffs determined by a host of international treaties that control virtually every technological aspect of the transaction. Unless, of course, you are one of the growing number of people who are using the Internet for cheap long-distance telephone calls. Companies such as VocalTec (an Israeli high-tech start-up), Lucent Technologies (the AT&T spin-off), and NorTel (formerly Northern Telecom) already sell Internet telephones and services to consumers and businesses around the world—who then pay less than one-third of what they would pay if using Ma Bell or Sprint. Same telephones, same callers, same destinations—yet, a completely different set of rules and, therefore, costs—are in effect.

What this means to every broadcaster (radio, television, cable, satellite), is that there's a new way to create and distribute content that is far less expensive—and completely free from government involvement. "All attempts to deregulate broadcast spectrum have failed, and will always fail," says Rob Glidden, a former FTC lawyer, explaining why not regulating the unlimited shelf space of the Internet is key. "The Internet is providing an opportunity for true deregulation for the industry. It is the future of broadcast."

Other entertainment industries that will be affected include recorded music and film. Because of these changes in telecommunications costs alone, it will eventually be economically attractive to distribute music and movies over the Internet. Radical changes, indeed.

It is no surprise, then, that the major telephone companies are thinking about creating wholly owned subsidiaries, *to act as their own competitors in their own territories,* just to avoid regulation. At an open FCC meeting in mid-1998, Joseph Zell, president of U.S. West Interprise Networking Services, said his firm planned to do exactly that—once the regulations were changed to permit it.

■ THE SHERIFF TAKES A HOLIDAY

The regulatory free-for-all on the Internet is utterly unique in entertainment media history. In the United States, the Federal Communications Commission (FCC) has always controlled every aspect of broadcast and communications. That's its job. Yet, for reasons that will shortly become clear, the FCC is now leading the way toward *not* regulating—or at least deregulating—similar activities that take place on the Internet. Most other governments throughout the world seem to be following the United States' lead. Notably, most nations have already banned taxing any commerce on the Internet, at least for the next several years.

To understand the reasons for this, it's necessary to undergo a brief history lesson: In 1919, the Radio Corporation of America (RCA) was incorporated and soon became the de facto monopoly of radio broadcasting. It was created specifically to wrest control of American Marconi from its British owner, British Marconi—supposedly for reasons of national security. (It wouldn't have done to have such an important technology in the hands of a non-American.) RCA's major investors included some of the most powerful corporations in America at that time: General Electric, AT&T, Westinghouse, and United Fruit. RCA was a true monopoly. It controlled virtually all relevant technology patents. It possessed vast cash reserves and—through its chief investors—power to dominate a broad spectrum of industries. It even had U.S. government support, as per its stated importance to national security.[2]

But in the 1920s, the courts became increasingly involved in the legal disputes of RCA, its owners, and their competitors. As Erik Barnouw explained in his wonderfully entertaining history of the broadcast industry: "The result was an ether free-for-all, a fantastic jumble—and pleas to Congress to restore order. For the first time, said Secretary of Commerce Herbert Hoover, an industry was begging to be regulated."[3]

The Radio Act of 1927 mandated the formation of the Federal Radio Commission (FRC), and the FRC began to manage—micromanage, some might say—every aspect of radio broadcasting. Among other things, it began to license frequency spectrum for radio stations, to control ownership of broadcast and newspaper within every defined U.S. market, and to control every technical aspect of radio operations.

This was the first time that the U.S. government attempted to regulate the industry. But it wouldn't be the last. Later, the Communications Act of 1934 expanded the FRC's role into the larger telecommunications segment, and the FCC, as we know it, was born. Although—as repeatedly stated—regulation is in the interest of the "public good," much of this "good" was never spelled out. Instead, decisions about content and business rules were left to the discretion of the courts and the commissioners.

One of the main evils the FCC has guarded against over the years is to prevent another monopoly along the lines of RCA. Diversity of choice is at the heart of why—and how—the FCC regulates television broadcasts, radio broadcasts, cable and satellite services, and just about every kind of telephone service.

There are also rules in place that govern the ownership of media companies across different industries. For example, newspapers and cable companies are forbidden to own television and radio stations within the same community; a single company is prohibited from holding two broadcast properties in a given market; and foreigners are limited to ownership of less than 25 percent of a company with broadcast licenses.

It makes sense. The freedom of choice is as powerful as the freedom of speech. In fact, some would argue that without choice, there is no freedom of speech. Adam Clayton Powell, III, a vice president of the Freedom Forum, explains it with a question: "What's the freedom to choose worth, if there's no choice? Without an informed debate— with all sides able to present their points of view—there's no true debate. And if anyone can limit the discussion, prevent minority views from being expressed, they have directly limited freedom of speech—and democracy. Censoring choice is, by definition, a limitation on freedom, so it should only be done sparingly and for the most compelling reasons."

If a media mogul like Charles Foster Kane (the fictional protagonist of the film *Citizen Kane*) could control all of the news and broadcast outlets in your community, you might not have access to the whole story (and you might get tired of watching the Rosebud Channel). There's a technical reason why a single entity could easily control everything. It's key to why the Internet is *not* being regulated. Broadcasting channels are a limited resource. Because television and radio (and cable and satellite) are transmitted as electromagnetic waves (within a licensed frequency range), there's only so much usable bandwidth available, only so much channel space available. It's like limited shelf space in a store: someone has to decide what gets displayed prominently, what gets displayed a little less prominently, and what is destined to remain out of sight in the back stockroom. The FCC exists to make sure that some media bully with deep pockets can't buy up all the shelf space. This is why Robert Murdoch was having so much trouble trying to sell his PrimeStar satellites to the cable industry; the FCC doesn't want the cable industry to own, and possibly undermine, its satellite competition.

Of course, the FCC has always allowed itself to be affected by political and social pressures of the times. For example, early during the Cold War, FCC commissioners caved in to pressure from J. Edgar Hoover, director of the FBI, to help ferret out any Communists in broadcasting, and they made it rather impossible for anyone on the rather questionable list of "Reds" to obtain broadcast licenses. This was not the only time the FCC got involved in social causes, or made dubious decisions regarding the media under its jurisdiction. In the 1950s, there was blatant racial discrimination within broadcast industries, but when appealed to, the FCC did nothing about the fact that only certain jobs were available to certain minorities. So much for the public good. All of which makes it even more fascinating that the FCC has now decided that it can best fulfill its mandate—and thereby promote public interest—by meddling a lot less, and in some cases, not at all.

Kevin Werbach, the FCC's counsel for new technology policy, has turned out to be an outspoken advocate for keeping the Internet free. In his paper, *Digital Tornado: The Internet and Telecommunications Policy,* he lays out the economic, technological, and eminently practical reasons that the best government policy for the Internet was to remain as hands-off as possible. "The FCC today is moving rapidly to deregulate existing services rather than to expand the scope of its regulatory ambit," wrote Werbach. It's simply breathtaking to hear a government lawyer with such an enlightened policy attitude.

■ THE BIGGEST LANDGRAB EVER

There's no limit of virtual shelf space on the Internet, and that's one of its most important and inescapable attributes: that there are no equivalent physical limits on distribution as in the traditional broadcast markets. The reason is technical: because the Internet is a loosely conglomerated hierarchy of networks, and there is no limit to the number, or kind, of devices that can be added to this network. So, if there's no limit on Internet shelf space, there's no reason to regulate *for that reason;* however, there are always other reasons the government might see fit to regulate.

That's the key. That's why it's all up for grabs, and that's why what's happening is even possible. If you want to be a landowner, all the virtual land in the world is available. Werbach put it this way, sounding a lot like a parent talking lovingly about their child: "The Internet is a fluid, complex entity . . . It overcomes any boundaries that can be drawn, whether rooted in size, geography, or law. Because the Internet represents an ever-growing interconnected network, no one entity can control or speak for the entire system."[4]

Not incidentally, there is no significant cost barrier to entry to providing Internet entertainment, either. In addition to eliminating the expense of operating in a heavily regulated environment, almost anyone who can afford to access the Internet (a number that is growing daily as the cost of technology goes down) can create "entertainment content" to publish and broadcast on the Internet. It will be as easy as making a telephone call. That's why it has been possible for Mark Cuban's Broadcast.com, Ken Rutkowski's

PlusMedia, and thousands of other companies (big and small) and individuals around the world to become broadcasters on the Internet. No one was there to stop them.

Of course, this low barrier to entry means you also end up with a lot of junk, including 24-hour access to the activities of a 20-something woman, Jennifer Ringley (on her video-based web site, the JenniCam), who broadcasts everything she does from her home. You can find thousands of web sites broadcasting images of everyday objects like coffee pots or street corners. People are (naturally) providing copies of their home videos to the world at large.

What will determine whether the legitimate new media companies like Broadcast.com succeed—that is, make money—depends on their ability to capture an audience, and convince advertisers that they should pay to communicate with that audience, just like the challenges faced by any fledgling broadcast network. This is why Peggy Miles, president of Intervox Communications, calls Mark Cuban "the Ted Turner of the Internet."

Broadcast.com began when Cuban and a college buddy, Todd Wagner, decided to make a business out of their joint love of sports and broadcasting. The first content they acquired for their emerging network was sports. Local sports—college baseball and basketball games that were being broadcast over the college radio stations. Broadcast.com (then called Audionet) started to make deals with the college radio stations. They'd pick up the local radio transmission, and using mostly off-the-shelf tools, created Internet transmission (live and on-demand) of the games. They slowly built an audience of fans and sold advertising space on their web site. And as they built their audience, they expanded into other subject matter, including talk and music radio, television, business events, full-length CDs, news, commentary and full-length audio books. They now serve an average of over 400,000 individual users per day. That's a lot. Enough for advertisers to shell out $4 million in revenues annually. In fact, today, the amount of content broadcast over Broadcast.com rivals the largest television and cable networks. It includes live continuous broadcasts of over 345 radio stations and networks, broadcasts of 17 television stations and cable networks, play-by-play game broadcasts of more than 350 college and professional sports teams, on-demand music from the CD jukebox with over 2,100 full-length CDs, live and on-demand special-interest shows and Internet-only webcasts, and more than 360 full-length audio books.

Broadcast.com has also distributed some of the largest sporting events in Internet history, such as Super Bowls XXX, XXXI, and XXXII, World Championship Wrestling, NCAA Final Four, NHL season games, and Stanley Cup Play-offs. Broadcast.com has also provided webcasts for many high-profile media and entertainment events, including the Hong Kong Handover Ceremony, Blockbuster Rockfest '97, premieres for movies such as *Flubber* and *Titanic,* backstage interviews from the 1998 Academy Awards webcast, and concerts with stars such as Travis Tritt and Leann Rimes.

None of this would have been possible with either traditional broadcast regulations or traditional broadcasting costs. Broadcast.com needed no FCC licenses, and was built from the ground up by two believers.

■ A DIFFERENT KIND OF NETWORK, A DIFFERENT KIND OF PERSON

The kind of people moving into Internet entertainment are, like early computer game designers, pioneers—outlaws, even. Without the dual crushing constraints of regulation and cost, they're making it up as they go along. And one of the main things they've made up is a complex bartering system that helps them bootstrap their way into promising enterprises.

Take Ken Rutkowski. His PlusMedia network is being built on a shoestring budget. In fact, he probably had to borrow the shoestring. And although his network spans every kind of broadcast—Internet, radio, cable and satellite TV—he's creating this uniquely new kind of entity without having to raise significant investor funding. "It's all about relationships," he says. Indeed. Rutkowski started by himself, in his kitchen, building an audience that was interested in technology news and analysis (a natural sort of audience to find on the Internet). His listeners didn't know where the broadcasts came from; they simply liked Rutkowski's style, enthusiasm, quick wit and insight into what mattered—and why—in breaking technology news.

Rutkowski slowly created a team of correspondents located around the world (Australia, Europe, Hong Kong, Japan, New Zealand, South Africa, and the United States), all of whom also work from kitchens, basements, bedrooms, and home offices. And when he'd built a large enough Internet audience, Rutkowski made his move—to change the world of broadcast entertainment.

He wanted to create a new kind of programming experience, and with nothing but a terrific idea, he was able to create barter relationships with technology companies to accomplish just that. Webley Systems contributed a new telephony product that allowed Ken's listeners to call in from anywhere in the world with a local phone call. Cisco Systems provided networking hardware. And EchoStar, the second largest digital satellite broadcaster in the United States, provided the broadcast bandwidth for seven TV channels. It wasn't long before Rutkowski was making deals with performers and producers in the entertainment business. Performers like Todd Rundgren, The Captain and Tennille, and top music industry executives like Ted Cohen and David Kessel, local TV personalities like Chicago's Aaron Freeman. It was a quid pro quo: they had material they wanted to promote; he had an audience and all the broadcast space he needed. All of this was done without spending a penny, and without making even a single call to a single government agency.

How interactivity will
transform the business
relationships between
entertainment providers
and consumers.

Chapter

Let's Get Personal

"On the web, fans can buy songs direct from the artists. So the record industry is asking itself the obvious question: who needs the labels anymore?"

—DAVID KESSEL, chairman, Internet Underground Music Archive

"Advertisers just hope and pray that you see their TV ads and billboards. But with interactive TV, we'll just click on our TV sets to 'buy now', and advertisers fondest dream (and worst nightmare) will have come true. They'll finally know what works and what doesn't."

—ANDY BOURLAND, CEO, ClickZ Online Advertising

If you're a Generation X–type guy or gal looking for some wired fun, then Bo Peabody wants you to drop by and join him and 350,000 of his closest friends. Log onto www.tripod.com and you'll be treated to on-line entertainment ranging from games such as Final Fantasy VII, to previews of the latest movies and records, to chat rooms on subjects ranging from safe sex to saving for retirement. If you choose to become a member, not just a visitor, you get special privileges, like an Internet e-mail address and Internet access, plus special features reserved only for Tripod members. You can create and post your own home page, for example. (Indeed, the tens of thousands of quirky and entertaining home pages created by the members is one of the chief attractions of Tripod.) And it's all free—such a deal.

Even though it takes Peabody's 50-plus employees to keep this virtual community humming along 24 hours a day, 365 days a year, you don't pay a cent. Compare this with steadily rising charges by other Internet service providers, and you can see why Tripod is such a popular place for wired Gen X types.

We've seen in previous chapters how the interactivity inherent in traditional video games is insinuating itself into other kinds of entertainment. We see how digital interactivity is creating new forms of entertainment, such as Peabody's on-line community, along with myriad other on-line entertainment communities that are growing on the Internet (see Chapter 8)—all new, exciting, and fun—and mostly being handed to us gratis. What's not to like?

Well, as we're about to see, there's a Faustian bargain that comes along with these new forms of digital entertainment. There are rules, addenda, and quid pro quos—some of them stated up front, some hidden. But this quid pro quo is key to why the digital age is reinventing how the *business* of entertainment works. There's a cost to entering the Tripod community. You don't pay in dollars; you pay with personal information (your full name, zip code, e-mail address, and a list of the things you're interested in). And Peabody takes the very attractive demographics of his community to Madison Avenue to garner big ad bucks from the likes of Fidelity, Sony, and Ford—in 1997, $50 million worth of advertising—which more than pays for Tripod's operations. In fact, Tripod was one of the few on-line businesses to be actually profitable by the end of 1998.

Advertisers benefit because the type of Internet users who congregate at Tripod are very attractive demographically. "They have lots of money, use technology, and they like to buy—on-line and off," said Rob Frankel, president of Frankel and Anderson, an advertising agency specializing in placing new media ads.

■ DON'T LOOK NOW

Let's examine this quid pro quo even more carefully. If you were one of the 400,000 households who had signed up for a WebTV subscription by the end of 1998, *your television is already watching you.* WebTV Networks is a new kind of Internet service provider (ISP). Subscribers pay WebTV for Internet access (just as they would any ISP), but surf the Web on a standard TV set, not on a PC. Most significantly, they can watch broadcast and cable TV shows at the same time they're surfing the Net—flip back and forth between Monday Night Football and their favorite Web sports statistics page.

Eventually, of course, the two kinds of entertainment offerings will be closely linked: you can easily get from the latest network hospital ER drama to a web site that gives you in-depth information about the actors, the characters they play, and the specific medical emergency being dramatized in this week's show by just pushing a button.

Purchased by Microsoft in 1996, WebTV's subscriber count should top the half million mark somewhere in 1999. This is a lot less than America Online's 13 million subscribers—and a hell of a lot less than the 25 million people who tune in to watch *Frasier* every week—but with Microsoft's deep pockets and tenacious competitiveness, it's a force to be reckoned with.

But think about this: Say an advertisement for a new automobile comes on during a break in your favorite sitcom. You find it alluring. You click on the WebTV button to get more information about that car, that maker, that leasing deal—whatever caught your eye. It's displayed on your screen immediately. Cool. Helpful even. And depending on how interested you *really* are, you either spend a little time with the additional information, or you click back to the show you were watching.

But here's the part that's a little different. WebTV is not only happy to provide you with more information directly related to that advertisement, it will also automatically forward you to the web site of the auto dealer located nearest you. Located *physically* near you, in the real world. No, you haven't entered your address, or phone number, or even indicated that you wanted to get dealer-specific info. You had just been mildly interested in a standard television advertisement. Whether this delights or alarms you is largely a function of your state of mind. It's that Faustian bargain again. You're paying for the convenience of having additional information available at the click of a button by allowing WebTV to observe you perhaps more closely than you might feel comfortable with. As when joining the Tripod community, you're paying for things (more and quicker access to information and services) not with dollars, but by providing information *about yourself.*

■ IT'S ALL ABOUT RELATIONSHIPS

Every entertainment business will now have the means to engage each of its customers personally, on a long-term basis, electronically, and interactively. Sometimes we'll pay an up-front fee for the entertainment ($2.99 to watch *Flubber* on Pay-Per-View). Sometimes we'll be subscribers ($9.95 for a month of unlimited game play on the Total Entertainment Network, an on-line gaming service). Sometimes we'll accept a so-called free offering—with varying degrees of awareness of who's picking up the tab, and why.

Over time, each entertainment segment has evolved its own method for gathering revenues. Table 3.1 shows how it looked in 1998. It's generally accepted wisdom in entertainment economic circles that these models took a long time to evolve—and that they change slowly, and reluctantly. And here is where the economic shake-up is going to occur in every entertainment industry segment. Within just a few short years, this chart will look completely different: every industry segment will be generating signifi-

TABLE 3.1   How the Entertainment Segments Gathered Revenue in 1998

	Advertising	Sales	Subscription
Movies		100%	
Radio	100%		
TV	100%		
Cable TV	50%		50%
Records		90%	10%
Games		100%	
Gambling		100%	
Magazines	55%	20%	25%
Newspapers	80%	10%	10%
Books		90%	10%

Sources: Adapted from Veronis, Suhler & Associates, *Communications Industry Forecast 1997–2000,* and Silicon Valley Virtual.

cant revenue more equally across all of the columns. What this really means is that the relationship each industry has with the customer will shift.

Here's another way to think of it. When a revenue source is sales, it implies a very direct, and probably short-term, relationship between the entertainment provider and consumer. You buy the book, or CD, or pay at the movie box office, and you're out of there. Of course, there is such a thing as loyalty in this situation: if you are pleased with the entertainment product you've received, you'll return and buy another. But no long-term relationship is *guaranteed* by the direct sale.

Here's where subscriptions come in. When revenues come from subscription or membership, you've got a long-term (or longer-term) relationship, contractually. You buy season tickets to the Chicago Bulls. You subscribe to *Rolling Stone* for two years. And you get benefits from making these sorts of commitments: you get guaranteed access to a scarce resource (I don't necessarily want to see every performance at the Metropolitan Opera, but if I don't subscribe, I probably won't get tickets to any), or to lock in a discount (two years of *Newsweek* is cheaper, per issue, than six months), or special services (if I join a frequent flyer club, I get free trips). Loyal, repeat customers are the heart of the video rental business. Stuart Skorman makes the economics clear: "First run movies cost us $10 a week, everything else costs us 5 cents a week. Repeat business is the key to success." In the case of WebTV, the monthly subscription fee is either $25 for the full service or $15 if you use another ISP for the basic Internet access.

When revenues derive from advertising, it means that businesses are paying to capture the eyes (or ears, or noses) of the consumers. The consumer, in such cases, pays less than he or she would if there were no advertisers, and in some cases (network television and radio), pays nothing at all.

That's why everyone in entertainment is eventually going to be messing around in everyone else's business. They will be switching from direct sales, to subscriptions, to advertising-based revenues—and every possible combination of the three. As you read about each industry in Parts 2 and 3, you'll see how each one is changing its relationship with consumers and, therefore, changing the source of revenues. What this means, incidentally, is that they find themselves competing in ways they never dreamed of for the consumers' advertising dollars. Stay tuned.

➤ Buy Now—While Supplies Last—Don't Delay

"Buy now" is the slogan of short-term relationships. *Buy. Now.* But in fact, many entertainment providers would just as soon capture your long-term business. Buy now, for later. Churn rate, the rate at which subscribers sign up and later drop their subscriptions, is a key success factor (and competitive measure) in the telephone, cable and satellite TV, newspaper, and magazine industries.

Thus, *branding* will be increasingly important, even in those entertainment industries that were formerly free of brand recognition issues. Although in the movie business, we may want to see Harrison Ford in the next Tom Clancy thriller, we usually haven't a clue as to which studio owns that property. Yet, as we'll see, the film studios and record companies are already learning how to use branding in new and profitable ways—by exploiting the interactive aspects of digital entertainment.

■ WOULD YOU WATCH MORE TV IF SOMEONE PAID YOU TO?

There's another way that interactive aspects of digital entertainment are infiltrating the broader world of entertainment: in the very near future, advertising will be virtually indistinguishable from the kind of computer games formerly found in arcades. CyberGold, located in the hills above the University of California, in Berkeley, California, typifies this new approach to advertising. For starters, CyberGold is an advertising agency that exists only in cyberspace. You can only get to them or their clients via the Web.

The second, and more notable, distinction is that CyberGold actually *pays* consumers to view its ads. That's right. Instead of the implied quid pro quo (i.e., you absorb an ad, you get a free radio or television program), CyberGold actually gives consumers cash, products, or services. After showing the advertisement in question, they always perform a quick test of the user's knowledge (this is part of the deal) to determine the consumers' level of interest in whatever is being sold.

This is extremely efficient from the advertiser's point of view—targeted right to the people who are most likely to be interested, most likely to actually buy, and cost effective when compared with all the traditional means of advertising. And it's not so bad for the consumer.

CyberGold's depth and breadth of knowledge of sales and advertising techniques is quite extraordinary. Its board of directors includes: Jay Chiat, the founder of the Chiat-Day advertising agency; Regis McKenna, the venture capitalist who helped create and launch many of the most influential technology companies; and Peter Sealy, who held just about every senior marketing position at Coca-Cola in his 24 years there. These guys understand sales, and they are at the forefront of exploring how interactivity will affect the sales techniques of the future.

But CyberGold is also doing groundbreaking trials using digital entertainment as bait in advertising. When they added a simple game to their web site, they experienced immediate increases in every aspect of their business: membership sign-ups, the number of ads viewed by members, and the number of clicks to view additional advertising information.

CyberGold, Tripod, and WebTV aren't alone, of course, in understanding that interactivity is a two-way street. As you provide entertainment for your audience, you can simultaneously be collecting information from them. This quid pro quo can be very profitable indeed.

In many cases, consumers knowingly and eagerly sign the contract. Like Tripod, WebTV is sensitive to privacy issues and does not release personal information directly to advertisers that would allow them to contact individuals outside of the WebTV environment. They can, however, certainly target any group within WebTV that conforms to certain specifications—interested in books (frequently visits the Barnes & Noble Online site) and foreign movies (ditto for the Internet Movie Database) and is vegetarian (similarly)—and flash targeted advertising at only those screens.

➤ "Where Would You Like to Go Today?"

Just look at MSN, the Microsoft Network, relaunched by Microsoft in late 1998. MSN is the virtual front door to Microsoft's on-line premises—it provides links to everything Microsoft and its content partners offer in cyberspace: news, weather, sports, travel, business, entertainment, shopping, Microsoft products and support, and all of Microsoft's network offerings (MSN, MSNBC). Perhaps the most engaging feature of MSN is the ability it offers every visitor to customize what they see whenever they enter—to make it personal, to make it theirs. If you will, the front door to Microsoft that you see is different from what anyone else will see. Your virtual welcome mat, for example, might have the latest business news, the weather in your community, the weather in your parents' retirement community (how are they doing today?), any breaking news on Princess Di's death, and absolutely, positively, no sports. In effect, MSN lets you create you own personal *Good Morning America,* or *USA Today,* or morning commute radio show. You get to pick whatever you want to know about local or national weather, news, sports, whatever. You don't need to know anything about media, publishing, or broadcasting; you just have to know what you like. Therein lies the mutually beneficial relationship— the quid pro quo. The consumer offers personal information to receive superior products and services. And the companies, trying to sell something to the consumer (products, services, advertisers), use that personal information to increase their return on investment—as a more efficient means to make sales.

■ SUCH A DEAL

So let's be very clear: Somebody always has to pay. We all know and accept this. When we buy a video game at Costco, we shell out cash or hand over a credit card. When we watch television or listen to the radio, we pay with a piece of ourselves by watching or listening to advertising commercials. More recently, we understand that to receive "premium" broadcasting, we need to pay for it directly, either through a cable subscription or a fee, as in pay-per-view. If we want to see a movie, or a play, we buy a ticket at the box office. Back in the sixteenth century, it was expected that the hat would be passed among the audience to pay for any performance on the village green.

But now something's different. The way we pay for our various entertainments is about to undergo a radical transformation, and interactivity is at the heart of it all. This is all made possible by digital technology, which is creating hundreds of new ways to enable the quid pro quo. To mention just a few:

➤ Fox Television News Online allows users to select the kinds of newsclips they want in their daily customized news reports. "Please include technology, my local weather, *Dilbert* and *Doonesbury,* but no sports please." So Fox and its advertisers know which ads you're most likely to be interested in, and which ads will most likely lead to an eventual purchase. If you're interested in baseball, they place ads for game tickets, sportswear, alcoholic beverages, and auto parts stores.

➤ Imagine Radio allows users to select any of the many live channels they broadcast on the Internet (and they only offer live channels), and the users can indicate how much they like any specific genre, channel, or specific program. Imagine Radio then uses that personal information to program a selection of content (music, news, whatever) that is different from literally everyone else's broadcasts (unless they indicate exactly the same preferences and survey results). The user can indicate what he or she is in the mood for right now: "I'm feeling sad today. Please cheer me up." If you select folk and country artists, they'll use that to choose which CDs to offer you for purchase. They won't place ads for rap artists with people who enjoy the mesmerizing quietude of New Age music.

➤ When you purchase books at Barnes & Noble Online, they suggest other books you might enjoy (as does Amazon.com, and reel.com for videos). If you like *The Woman Warrior* by Maxine Hong Kingston, you might like the *The Joy Luck Club* by Amy Tan. So, they offer you the same books on tape and video interviews with the authors. "And click here to buy a ticket for their next speaking engagement in your area."

➤ While you're booking your on-line air travel reservations at Microsoft's Expedia web site, they offer you specials on hotel accommodations and tours at your destination: "As long as you're going to Disneyland, would you like a family discount to the Universal Studios tour?" Not a new idea, by any means, but exceptionally effective when offered exactly at the moment you may be most receptive to the pitch.

➤ When you go to MovieFone Online to check out show times at nearby theaters, they collect information on the kinds of movies you like. That lets them offer you deals on future movie events, T-shirts and posters, CDs of the sound track, and more. They can also sell this information to film studios, who can market their on-line previews to people most likely to go see the film. The studios spend $50 million to market a major film, and the hardest bit is just capturing an audience to watch the previews. This is the cheapest way ever devised to get the preview to exactly the people who are most likely to attend. Massive cost savings are possible.

You get the idea. Either by explicitly expressing your preferences, or simply through your actions, the services who want to sell you something get a much better idea of what you'll actually buy. It's a lot more cost effective than most forms of traditional advertising—actually, getting closer to direct sales.

■ GREAT SERVICE KEEPS CUSTOMERS COMING BACK

Sometimes this exchange of personal information for free fun and games is completely above board. After all, there are two ways that a digital entertainment provider can make money off you: either by convincing advertisers that you are a valuable audience to flash ads at, or convincing you to directly pay for the entertainment goodies they are offering, or—increasingly—some combination of the two.

WebTV does both. It makes its money by selling you Internet access, and by selling the data they've collected about you to other companies. But many players in the on-line entertainment business are going the opposite route: they try to learn as much about you as possible to sell you more of the entertainment product *they* offer. It's the old idea of customer service and fostering loyalty, only backed up by huge electronic databases.

Late in the nineteenth century, Stuart Skorman's grandfather was a merchant in a small town in Ohio. His vision was to serve his customers, even if it meant sending them to a competitor down the street. To really help your customers is the best way to build a loyal customer base. Skorman learned that lesson well and built a video rental business (Empire Video) that was so successful—including the single most profitable video rental stores in the United States—it was purchased by Blockbuster Video, the largest video rental chain in America. His business vision is to deliver personalized service to best help each individual customer (quite a radically different approach than that taken by fast-food franchises).

Skorman took the proceeds from that Blockbuster Video purchase and founded reel.com. The vision was the same: personalized service for every customer. One of Blockbuster's competitors, Hollywood Video, acquired all of reel.com in 1998 and is a serious contender to become the Amazon.com of video rentals (Amazon.com being the common yardstick for measuring the success of Internet ventures).

Now, you may be wondering what's so personal about the video rental business, but if Skorman is right, and we think he is, then it's something you'll come to depend upon in the not-too-distant future. Here's what reel.com does today. When you're in either their on-line or brick-and-mortar stores, reel.com does everything it can to offer you useful advice about the movies you want to rent or purchase. Even before you do anything. If you're considering watching John Sayles' *Lone Star*, look at all the useful information that they've placed on the back of the video box:

➤ Close matches: *Matewan, City of Hope.* If you liked them, you'll probably like *Lone Star.*

➤ Creative matches: *Blood Simple, Tender Mercies, Do the Right Thing, Passion Fish.* If you liked them, our staff thinks it's possible that you'll like *Lone Star,* too.

➤ Critics' views: *The New York Times* rated it a 10, *Los Angeles Times* a 10, *USA Today* a 6, Roger Ebert a 10, on a scale in which 10 is best.

➤ Reel anatomy: action = 3, drama = 9, humor = 4, sex = 7, violence = 6.

➤ A pull-out slip listing the close and creative matches with more details on each is placed inside the video packaging. The insert is for you to keep.

Look at all the ways they've helped you evaluate the movie, and you haven't made a purchase yet. Once you become their customer, you can receive free information (via e-mail or post) about movies you might be interested in and what's going on in the industry, but customized to include only the kinds of movies you're interested in.

So here's the power—reel.com then combines their movie database with the information they keep about each customer's activities ("always rents thrillers and sci-fi, and anything with Tom Conti in it"), and does its best to enhance their video rental experience. They now know what kind of movies you'll rent and buy more than you do. They can, therefore, be very cost effective in what they market to you.

Every customer can also *volunteer*—this word is key— information on their personal preferences (which is never required), along with their mailing address and some other useful demographics. Advertisers drool with glee when they think of databases with this level of specific, personal information.

■ THE DARK SIDE OF THE FORCE

As mutually beneficial as this deal often is, it's just not for everyone. The problem is this: through your interactive selections, *they* can determine more about your buying habits than you might even be aware of yourself. This is scary stuff. For those who are inclined to be paranoid, this comes too close to George Orwell's novel *1984,* in which every room in every building was equipped with a big-screen TV—designed as much for watching the occupants of the room as to delivering somewhat mediocre (although continuous) entertainment content. So you may not be aware that you're lingering on the ad for new automobiles as you surf the Web, but someone is probably watching exactly how much time you spend and which items you interact with, and they can spot trends in your interest and buying patterns before you are aware of them. Common responses to this are: "I don't want them knowing so much about me," and "I don't trust them."

The issue of what constitutes personal privacy and how to protect it in the digital age is a complex matter, and it is already stirring passionate debate. It's also deeply entwined into the fabric of future digital entertainment offerings. The good news is that there are some big guns battling for your privacy rights. Several government agencies (most important, the FTC) are already working with interested industries (technology, network, medical, and financial) to attempt to make sure that your rights are protected, and that you actually understand the bargain before you eat that seemingly free lunch or watch that free show. The other good news is that technologies are being developed that will allow individuals to protect the privacy of their on-line activities and preferences, while still enabling the golden exchange of information that advertisers crave.

The bad news is that, like it or not, companies are going to make the most out of what they can find out about you anyway. "Bob's buying pattern is a lot like Mike's, and Mike just bought a new BMW, so . . . let's offer that information to BMW, Lexus, and Porsche dealers. And *Playboy* magazine."

Of course, sometimes we actually want our personal data to be distributed—to the right people. David Kessel, a pioneer in the Internet music business, says, "The Rolling Stones can have my credit card number forever. Whatever they ever want to sell me, I'll buy." Expect to see a lot more of this. Entertainment and e-commerce are merging. The future of the entertainment business is truly *personal,* in every way.

In the digital age (to paraphrase Shakespeare), the stage is rapidly turning into the whole world, which opens up a universe of money-making opportunities for entertainment providers.

Chapter

4

It's a Small World
after All

"Online has arrived. Advertisers are already seeing the benefits of it. Consumers are becoming dependent on it. . . . We are shifting to a true mass market."

—ROBERT PITTMAN, president, America Online

"It's largely the relationship between technology and cost that has shaped the external world."

—FRANCES CAIRNCROSS, author, *The Death of Distance*

"Most people's interests still lie within the general limits of the cities where they live."

—BARRY DILLER, chairman and CEO, USA Networks

It used to be that your entertainment choices depended on where you lived. If you were lucky enough to live in a major metropolitan area like San Francisco, you could have as many as nine daily local papers delivered to your doorstep. If you were a news junkie, you could also get your hands on dozens of other hot-off-the-press newspapers from around the world. With a decent outdoor TV antenna, you could easily get 15 television stations, containing both local and network content, and up to 75 channels from the local cable TV operators. Satellite broadcast services were also readily available, of course. From your car radio, you could get 89 stations (49 on the AM band, 40 on the FM band). You'd have a whopping 500 movie theater screens within reasonable driving distance; more than 250 video stores to rent movies from; and retail stores offering you shelves filled with thousands of video games; not to mention, of course, all the live venues for entertainment that would be available: clubs, concert halls, live theater performances, and more.

But if you resided in a community that was less populated—for instance, the middle of the American heartland, say Urbana, Illinois—your choices would be dramatically limited. Despite the community's being the home of a major university, you'd have just a fraction of the radio, television, cable, and movie options. You'd be largely dependent on the schedules of visiting performers in the arts, music, and theater to experience first-class entertainment—much like in the days of vaudeville, when Urbana was a major stop on the circuit (the Marx Brothers made their last live appearance together there in 1927 before heading to Hollywood). Of course, locals can always drive the two hours north to Chicago or the four hours south to St. Louis, but if you wanted to stay close to home on a Saturday night, you had limited resources.

If you were settled in Las Cruces, New Mexico, or Tahhina, Oklahoma, your choices would be more limited still.

Digital technology is rapidly changing this. Just as it's the Wild, Wild West (free of regulation) in terms of legal shackles, and just as it's interactive (providing a two-way dialogue between consumers and the businesses providing them with entertainment), so, too, it's expanding the various entertainment markets in an unprecedented way: by eliminating geographic and temporal boundaries. Not incidentally, this globalization of entertainment media requires a whole new way of doing business. And the fact that there are no geographic or temporal barriers to on-line communities is key. To put it another way, the Internet is turning what were already international businesses—more than 50 percent of movie, record, gambling, and video game revenues are derived from overseas sales—into *one* market. Is this an important distinction means in business terms? Yes. It's all the difference in the world.

■ *BAYWATCH* MEETS NIEMAN-MARCUS

Gregory Adams-Tait doesn't like to use the telephone, because he can't control it. There are too many variables. He could be calling at an unreasonable hour (because he's based in the United Kingdom and his business contacts are international). He could get a busy signal or a line that rings forever. Perhaps he can leave a message with a human (good) or a machine (better), but he is also taking the risk of getting stuck in an interminable and time-wasting conversation, when all he wants to do is impart information and *hang up.* So Adams-Tait uses e-mail. He controls what he wants to say, how he wants to say it, and when he wants to say it. And he doesn't have to worry about where, or in what time zone, the other person might be. It doesn't matter. They could be in the next room asleep or in Sydney, Australia, having lunch. And, of course, no one has to know where *he* is. He travels constantly, so unless someone explicitly pins him down, they have no idea whether he's at home in London, or at his office in another part of London, or in Paris or Brussels at a business conference. Which is just how it should be for someone who is launching a new Internet-based entertainment network that is an interesting (if sometimes tasteless) combination of the Home Shopping Network and *Baywatch,* which, incidentally, has proved to be the top U.S. entertainment export since *The Muppet Show.*

That's right, *Baywatch* attracts more viewers worldwide than any other TV program.

Adams-Tait's start-up, WowGlobal, is a 24-hour-a-day, 365-day-a-year global retailer that plans to sell just about anything to anyone just about anywhere in the world. Think of an all-night, multilingual, omnipresent Wal-Mart on steroids in which the clerks are bikinied babes, and you begin to get the idea. Well, paraphrasing W. C. Fields, no one ever got rich overestimating the intelligence of the American people. Only with the Internet, we'd have to amend that statement. We're now in a truly global village.

WowGlobal intends to build the world's first international network of digital television and Internet home shopping channels. In a sense, the business will do what traditional retailers have always done—find customers (as many as possible) and offer them goods and services at competitive prices. But it will do so by combining the television, the telephone, and Internet technology—and, perhaps most important, entertainment media—in a way that no one has ever done before. It won't care where its suppliers (both its content providers and merchandisers) are. It won't care where its customers (audiences) are. It will be happy to act as a matchmaker between the two on a global basis.

Let's try and define the increasingly blurred line between entertainment and retailing in the digital age. (It's getting harder all the time to distinguish the two.)

WowGlobal is definitely *not* your mother's Home Shopping Channel. It's more like your favorite soap opera than an infomercial. It has dialogue, it has lots of sex appeal (big surprise), and it's all about seducing the audience into acting now. Just click on your screen (if you have an interactive TV, or a WebTV), or pick up a telephone to place your order. Now, please.

What will be interesting is how this plays out culturally. The rules—we're talking about the social rules (what's politically correct and acceptable)—are different everywhere. Richard Hart, on-air host of *C-Net Central*, recalls the old joke about Singapore: "It's Disneyland, but with the death penalty." What you don't know *can* hurt you. Across the nations of the world, we have different ways of talking about sex (what's permitted, what isn't), we disagree about what's funny, we discuss other nationalities with sarcastic remarks (when the rules of those other cultures differ from ours), and so on. All media will have to adapt to this new world market. "I intend to revolutionize the web based retailing experience so that the Internet becomes the first choice for a large portion of the world's population," declares Adams-Tait. If that involves hiring 100 exotic dancers, so be it. If that requires dancing bears in tutus, no problem. That's the attitude that's needed to succeed in this new global market.

■ LOCAL WILL NOW MEAN GLOBAL, AND VICE VERSA

Not every form of newly digitized entertainment is going to go global in precisely the same way, of course. For most entertainment media segments (radio, for instance), the changes will be truly revolutionary, because going from a local to a global market completely upsets all previous notions.

In the games industry, the business has long been an international one. More than 50 percent of the video game business's $5 billion annual revenue is reaped from offshore customers. Language does not constitute a barrier for a game crossing international boundaries, because most games made for English-language speakers are purchased as is throughout the world (mainly because most of today's action-oriented games have little language content).

How will the global aspect of the Internet change this? In several ways. For starters, game players won't be limited by whatever titles their local retailer happens to carry. Go ahead and download any game title from anywhere. Also, as games become less focused on shoot-em-ups and twitching joysticks, language *will* become an issue to global appeal.

➤ Playing Midnight Poker with a Partner in Padua

So it's 2:00 A.M. and you're bored. You love playing poker, but your poker buddies went home hours ago. So what do you do? You go to your PC, log onto the Mplayer gaming network (www.mplayer.com) and find a wild and wooly poker session with precisely *your* kind of people that you can immediately join. Best of all, it's free—that's right: as long as you have an Internet connection, you've got a universe, not just of poker, but of backgammon, pinochle, mah-jongg, or chess partners, all just a mouse click away.

This means that once you're bored with the poker game (or the Australians and Japanese need to get to work), you can click your way over to the classical guitar room and either listen in to musicians (and music appreciators) from Spain, Portugal, Finland, and Peru, or pull out your guitar and strut your own stuff. Who's paying for this motley crew of international music lovers to get together and jam? A variety of advertisers—the ones who see the advantage of capturing the attention of this multilingual crew—is paying. These are major advertisers such as Pepsi, Nike, and General Foods.

As we'll see in Part 2, the rapidly growing on-line gaming community will allow us to play with newfound friends all across the globe, in a variety of venues. This opens up commercial possibilities for game makers and advertisers alike. Hal Vogel, managing director of SG Cowen Securities, says, "Demand for entertainment cuts across all cultural and national boundaries . . . most entertainment products have worldwide appeal and incremental revenues from international sources can be important."[1] And not only that, successful content can be rechanneled into other media. Nintendo's Donkey Kong resurfaced on cable's Fox Family Channel as Donkey Kong

Country, after its tremendously successful launch in Canada in 1998.

➤ Play Music for Me

The recorded music business has also long been global in scope, with a $40 billion annual worldwide business, only 35 percent of which comes from U.S. sales. Albums by many of the top artists sell equally well anywhere in the world (Sting, Phil Collins, The Rolling Stones, Celine Dion). And music lovers are increasingly interested in artists from other regions, hence the growing popularity of such "world music" artists as Ladysmith Black Mombazo and Enya.

Despite this global sophistication—and as you'll see in Chapter 6 ("It Ain't Groovy")—the current worldwide sales and distribution chain of recorded music is about to be dramatically reshaped by digital distribution. Think about it: as with video games, consumers will no longer be limited to the tastes and business judgments of the local record shop buyer.

The most important success of the Internet Underground Music Archive (IUMA), beyond the financial and artistic, is the opening it has created for literally thousands of acts—none of which had a chance whatsoever of being recorded by a major label, or being displayed in a bin at Tower Records, many of which now have loyal followings.

➤ How Do You Say "I'll Be Back" in Balinese?

More than half of the film business's $25 billion annual revenues come from offshore. U.S. movies play throughout the world. In fact, it's not uncommon for a film that is a commercial flop domestically to reach profitability through overseas distribution. *Godzilla, The Horse Whisperer,* and *The Postman* all come to mind.

Where the Internet will affect this already global industry is in aftermarket and cross-media possibilities. As we'll see, the very food chain of movie distribution will be changing—digital TV viewers may see first-run movies *before* they can rent them from Blockbuster Video. They'll get to see video clips, read the scripts, and participate in discussions about favorite movies with fans around the world.

And it's not just from the United States to the rest of the world. Sometimes, it's the other way around. French film studio Gaumont SA has already begun—*sacré bleu*—to produce movies in English. That's because it's hard to reach a big enough U.S. audience to interest film distributors, and even art film movie houses, with a film that's dubbed or has subtitles. Their film, *The Fifth Element,* was the most expensive European film ever made ($50 million), and it came in fifth worldwide in 1997 with $270 million gross. It was the most successful French-made film ever. They saw the global market and sold more than 50 million tickets abroad. If there will ever be a direct way to offer movies to U.S. consumers, let's say via broadband Internet access, they'll no longer have to worry about dealing with risk-averse distributors.

It's in television and radio entertainment, however, that we're going to see the truly revolutionary changes. These kinds of "entertainment content"—whether they are distributed via antenna, cable, or satellite receivers—are mostly *not* distributed worldwide. We'll go into the reasons in Chapter 5 ("Don't Make Waves"). There are a few notable exceptions, of course: *Baywatch,* as we already mentioned, and CNN, which broke new ground by seizing the attention of the world through its on-the-spot coverage of global happenings. But these are exceptions. Currently, international syndication remains less than 2 percent of revenue for U.S. television programmers (whether network or independently produced). A full 80 percent of radio advertising revenues currently come from local sources. But Internet entertainment pioneers are already upsetting traditional broadcasters with their renegade, and global, efforts.

One example is MTV. The music channel that started the music video revolution in the early 1980s launched an on-demand, on-line music channel (we can still remember Mick Jagger barking "I want my MTV"). Dubbed M2 Europe, it was Europe's first Internet TV station. According to *Webnoize,* the music industry insiders' publication, MTV launched the Internet version of M2 prior to the cable television channel with the same name to make a point. "We wanted to launch M2 on the Internet to really send a clear message that M2's website is an important part of the channel, rather than simply an afterthought," said Peter Good, managing editor of M2.[2]

And, though it's not the oldest leisure occupation, it's certainly a close second. We're talking about gambling, of course. And it's one of the most tightly regulated and local of all types of games. Most of gambling's $100 billion worldwide revenue is derived from local casinos, usually because of strict legal controls. But already there's tremendous competition heating up from virtual casinos, which can exist anywhere in the world, and reach any would-be high roller in the world.

And it's not chump change. Market forecaster Datamonitor predicts that worldwide, 15 million people will be gambling on-line by 2002. That's $10 billion in virtual gaming, as compared with industry estimates of just $1.4 billion for on-line games. And because U.S. legislation is likely to make on-line gambling illegal in the United States (for U.S. citizens), this lucrative market is moving offshore.

■ ACT GLOBALLY, THINK LOCALLY

But there's something important about the ways humans amuse themselves that *won't* be changing anytime soon. Because, in fact, people have a natural interest in what's happening close to them, that is, locally. In many cases, entertainment is highly focused in nature: focused on language, on local social expectations, and on local interests. It is not surprising that the mantra of television broadcasters, when TV went national, was, "Will it play in Peoria?" Tastes do differ from region to region; the new question may well be, "Will it play in *Pretoria?*" Most Americans are not going to be interested in hearing Italy's equivalent to Rush Limbaugh. So the new global entertainment market has some significant *content* challenges in addition to all the business opportunities.

And it's not just language that separates us; it's culture. In 1998, McDonald's (the hamburger people) launched a promotional giveaway in Hong Kong and the rest of the Far East, but not in Europe or the United States. They gave away Snoopy dolls dressed in the national clothing of each of 30 countries. It's not that kids elsewhere are not interested in dolls, national differences, or Snoopy. It was McDonald's marketing campaign that made Hong Kong residents feel left out and deprived if they didn't have the entire set of dolls. There was even a black market for the dolls. In Far Eastern cultures, people want to fit in and be indistinguishable from everyone else. *The nail that's up gets hammered.* But in the United States, we relish our personal differences, our individuality. A marketing campaign based on being like everyone else would never succeed in the United States.

Some content has global appeal, and some doesn't. *Star Trek* seems to cross all cultural boundaries: Klingon opera is Klingon opera, in New York or Australia. But whether Scott Adams' *Dilbert* will be appreciated outside the postindustrial, white-collar crowd, only time will tell. The point is simply that content has a chance to be enjoyed worldwide, and there is a new worldwide network that anyone can access.

Perhaps it's in the advertising arena that the global impact on entertainment will be most significant. Already, the amount of money spent on Internet advertising and on direct revenue from related sales and services is escalating. It's turning out that there are many surprising roads to advertising profit in the new global entertainment marketplace. For instance, just as Coke, BMW, Sony, and just about every international brand pay moviemakers to film lingering, tantalizing images of their products and logos, you should expect to see a lot more of the same in other media. Yes, this is paid advertising intruding into content, and it's not something we necessarily like. But get used to it. Video games built around kids' products (just as Nintendo's 1080° Snowboarding is built around Tommy Hilfiger snowboard products). If it's entertaining enough, it will drive audience size (thus advertising revenue), and retail (direct product sales).

The biggest change of all may be the move from advertising mainly to large-broadcast audiences (either local, regional, or national) versus the Internet way of selling to a much larger number of far smaller (niche) audiences—or in a word, *narrowcasting*. As we'll see in Chapter 9 ["Brought to You by . . . (Ads)"], that's something that advertisers are going to have to learn how to do, or lose to those who have the know-how and technology. And, in most cases, today's major broadcasters and advertisers will do both.

➤ Barry's Way

Barry Diller runs USA Networks, which reaches roughly 70 million U.S. homes via broadcast, cable, and satellite television. Diller knows more than most people in broadcasting about how to use television to generate sales revenue. Everything he's done is about how to generate advertising and sales revenue. He built the Fox television network; he then built the Home Shopping Network (and its QVC spin-off), which is now USA Networks and is jointly owned by the entertainment colossus, Seagrams.

Diller believes that *local* is what most people care about. So, he's combined local content (such as the on-line communities of his CitySearch subsidiary) with local services (like those offered by Ticketmaster, his entertainment ticketing subsidiary). But USA Networks is also, as its name implies, a national broadcast network, and Sea-grams (which owns a 45-percent stake in USA Networks) is in the movie, music, theme park, and television busi-nesses. So, it will focus on those interests as well, even when they're international. We'll see more of this local-versus-global balancing act in Part 2.

➤ Birds Do It, Bees Do It, Even Phone Monopolies Do It

Another approach to gaining worldwide customers is to partner with companies in your industry who operate in other countries. As we'll see in Part 3, we'll see how phone companies are increasingly going to provide the delivery systems for entertainment content. They may even become the companies we go to when we want entertainment. *My phone company is going to provide my television, cable, radio broadcasts, and my music service?* Possibly, yes. Possibly, it will even be more than that. AT&T's purchase of cable giant Telecommunications Inc. (TCI) will make AT&T an enter-tainment empire. This is a harbinger of what's to come.

This is why those in the entertainment business need to pay close attention to the telephone business's fevered urge to merge in 1998. AT&T has partnered with British Telecom to operate Concert, an offshore business provid-ing Internet-based services to enterprise. All of the U.S. Re-gional Bell Operating Companies (RBOCs, the incumbent local phone companies), have partnership arrangements with second- and third-world countries. Nippon Telephone and Telegraph [NT&T (Japan's AT&T)] has partnered with U.S. companies to enter our market. It's *the* big party, everyone has a date, and don't be surprised if it's the Telcos who end up supplying the band. Part 3 has the story. In short, the Internet is a new kind of world market, and every entertainment industry is going to have to learn new ways to profit, or partner with those who know how.

Part Two
New Tricks for Old Pets

How Technology Is Reshaping Every Media Segment

Radio was the first technology-based entertainment success story. A century later, it's again pointing the way toward the future.

Chapter

Stop Making Waves

"It ain't gonna happen. You will never find larger audiences on the web than for traditional radio broadcasts. The very diversity of the online community will prevent it."

—RICH WOOD, director, WOR-FM

"The Internet is the next platform for network radio"

—STEVE LEHMAN, president, Premiere Radio Networks

"We're diving deeper into the barrel of crap."

—DAVID LAWRENCE, host, Daily Online Update

The vice president of technology at the National Association of Broadcasters (NAB), Rick Ducey, calls the Internet "the Wild, Wild West." Composer/performance artist Lori Anderson calls it "a ghost town." As we'll discover, they're both right.

■ JUST IMAGINE

Not far from San Francisco's 3Com Park (which used to be Candlestick Park, but Silicon Valley money can overwhelm even the most entrenched home-team traditions), Brad Porteus and his young team—they're all in their 20s

and 30s—are in the process of recreating the radio business. Their baby, Imagine Radio (www.Imagineradio
.com), is a radically new kind of radio station, because it's
one that you can only receive via the Internet—and one
that provides its audience with a startling array of personalized choices.

Log onto Imagine Radio and you get the equivalent of
dozens of different stations of traditional radio, all broadcasting simultaneously. You want news? They have Associated Press Reports live, 24 hours a day. You want hip-hop?
Smooth jazz? Country heavyweights? Classic rock? Or, perhaps the London scene? Serious head-thumping rock and
roll? No problem, they have scores of different music
channels, broadcasting literally thousands of artists from
all around the world, with more coming on-line all the
time. You want talk? Name your topic: games (*PC Gamer
Hour*), technology (*Maximum PC Hour*), the Internet (*CyberWoman*), books (*Book Talk*), sci-fi cult (*I-Files*), and
more.

Sounds like an entire radio *network* rather than a station, right? But no. And, to be precise, describing Imagine
Radio using traditional radio terms such as *station* or *channel* does not do it justice. Because this is something completely new. This is a broadcaster where the DJ and
program director know *exactly* the kind of material you
like. They program it just the way *you* like it. You're no
longer at the mercy of the taste or whim of whoever is on
duty at the station. So you want to hear more Sting? More
Phil Collins? Absolutely no David Bowie? Sure thing. You
want to hear the latest hot rap releases, even from relatively new or unknown artists that Tower Records doesn't
yet carry? Here they are. You like a mix of slow and fast, of
tunes you can dance to intermixed with slow, dreamy love
songs? No problem.

So how does this work? Simple—you tell them. You rate
your interest in any of the thousands of artists that Imagine offers, and they mix the broadcast so it exactly
matches your personal choices. And, that's not all. As

you're listening to a song, they show you the CD cover art-work, the song title, and they link you to sites with more information about that artist. And, of course, there's a convenient button so you can buy the album now, with just a click of your mouse.

Don't like the current song? "Just click a button and go to the next selection," Porteus explains. Like what you're hearing? Tell them by rating the artist 5 on a scale of 0 (never play it again) to 5 (play a lot of this, and other selections like it). You can even customize their preprogrammed stations. They have DJs who program the material, just like any on-air DJ, *but* you can add or delete any artist from that mix. You're the program director of your personalized station. As one listener said excitedly, "It's like they're reading my mind, because I always get what I want." This is not your father's car radio.

"The Internet is the next platform for network radio," says Steve Lehman, president of the top syndicated radio network, Premiere Radio Networks. So how is this both the Wild, Wild West *and* a ghost town? It's the Wild West because in the real world of traditional radio broadcasting, no company can own 20 radio stations in a market. Heck, they wouldn't even get all the required broadcast spectrum. And, surprisingly, it's also like a ghost town; it's like listening to a station and not knowing if anyone else is listening with you. Even though you might be listening to the same *station* as a friend, you might actually be hearing different material at the same time, because you've customized your play list.

➤ What Do You Get When You Cross Radio Broadcasting with the Internet?

One cautionary note before you get too excited: the audio quality you can experience today depends almost entirely on the speed of your Internet connection. And, for most listeners today, that's a 28.8-K modem connection, which usually delivers acceptable AM-quality reception. And though you can sometimes get even better real-time audio quality over the Internet, it's sometimes a lot worse, too. Later on, we'll see why this is—and how it's soon going to get much better.

Why Internet radio is important, let alone even possible, is a story of visionaries, pioneers, and venture capitalists all engaged in a race for market dominance. A race that will eventually reshape the radio broadcast industry, if not all of digital entertainment. (When you don't work at the FCC, you can dramatize a bit.) So, even if fledgling start-ups like Imagine Radio don't end up leading the revolution, the first shots have been fired—and there will be no stopping the spectacular battles to come.

What does a radio station *do* on the Internet? Good question. You might have thought that a radio station, like any other business, would have a Web page that posted information for its audio listeners. And that's how it began. Figure 5.1 shows that as of June 1998, more than 5,500 radio stations from around the world had already constructed web sites that listed such things as station charter, location (both physical and on the broadcast spectrum), programming information, and data about personnel, just like any company's Web page, in fact. (Not surprisingly, about one-half of these web sites belong to U.S.-based radio stations.) But, the true harbinger of the fundamental changes ahead is the fact that a full 1,700 of these stations are already *broadcasting* over the Internet, as shown in Figure 5.2. That's right—stations are actually sending music, talk, and related advertisements over the Web. Again, approximately one-half of these broadcasting pioneers are from the United States.

The range of what's being broadcasted on the Internet today is sometimes literally out of this world. Just take a look:

➤ Live and on-demand broadcasts from NASA's Mars Rover and its other satellites

➤ Live and on-demand news from the BBC, *The Wall Street Journal,* Fox Television, and CNN

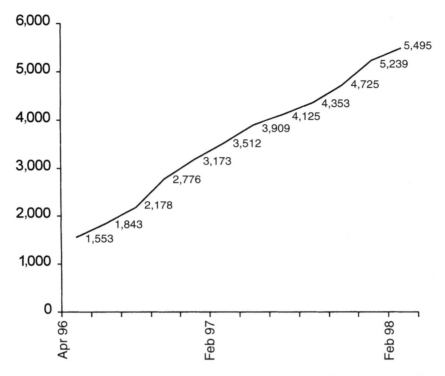

Figure 5.1 Radio stations on the Web, April 1996–April 1998.
Source: BRS Media, 1998.

➤ Live sports broadcasts for everything from baseball to football, soccer to mountain climbing

➤ Live music concerts from artists ranging from the Rolling Stones to Papa Doo Run Run (a California surf band)

➤ Live acts of stand-up comics from *Comedy Central*

➤ People talking about anything and everything, from politics, to sports, to sex

➤ On-demand audio of historical events (for example, the oral arguments presented to the U.S. Supreme Court in *Roe v. Wade*)

➤ The sound of the waves breaking on Maui's coast, as well as silly sounds (check out www.dailywave.com).

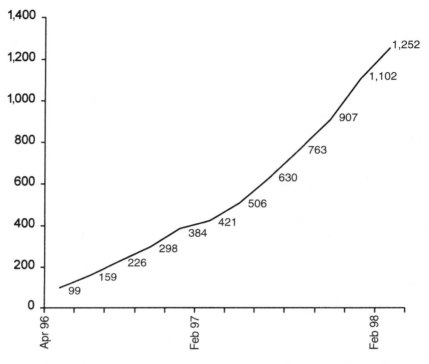

Figure 5.2 Webcasters on the Web, April 1996–April 1998.
Source: BRS Media, 1998.

In fact, it's not easy to think of a form of sound that *isn't* available somewhere on the Internet.

As it turns out, radio is leading the way over all other types of consumer media on the Internet. Radio is even beating out computer gamers, who got there first, but subsequently floundered.

So why is radio the first digital broadcast breakthrough? First and foremost, its demands on bandwidth are significantly less than what's required for video. But it's more than that. "Radio broadcasters—like other media players—have been debating how to go digital for a decade," points out Peggy Miles, president of Intervox Communications, and author of the most comprehensive book on webcasting.[7] But, she says, they've been stymied by "their inability to agree on standards that will meet the various regulatory requirements. On the other hand, when someone does something new and cool, everyone else quickly rallies around the new *de facto* standard." In other words, the same people who have been bickering for 10 years over how to do digital radio broadcast; which broadcast spectrum to use; what technology standards to back, always based on the current political mood at the FCC, don't have to wait any longer. Internet technologists simply invented a solution, deployed it for free, requiring no one's approval, and set out to create an enormous new market. More than 70 million personal computers can receive streaming audio broadcasts on the Web. Like the Nike slogan, they just did it. "The Internet is a fluid, complex entity . . . It overcomes any boundaries that can be drawn, whether rooted in size, geography, or law," concurs the FCC's Kevin Werbach.

■ SOMETHING'S COMING, SOMETHING BIG

At first you might be inclined to think that radio broadcast over the Internet is just like radio broadcast over airwaves. After all, KSFO Live is KSFO Live, no matter whether you are listening to it via your car radio, or via your desktop computer while working on a Lotus spreadsheet.

But, in fact, Internet radio is almost, but not quite, completely unlike the radio we've come to know and love. As we saw in Part 1, the Internet is not limited by regulations or geography. There are no limits on shelf space, no limits on how many stations can broadcast, no limits on ownership of broadcast stations, no geographic limits on markets. In short, none of the limits that have been instrumental in shaping the radio industry from its infancy until now apply. And this will make all the difference in (literally) the world.

Traditional radio broadcasters, for the most part, don't agree. They yawn when you talk about the Internet. They don't see how it relates to what *they* do. To understand why traditional broadcasters have decided to ignore, and not pursue, an opportunity that has quite a lot of other people excited, you need to remember that advertising revenue is the basis for the currently booming radio broadcast industry—*local* advertising revenue, which we listen to an average of three and a half hours per day per person in this country. That business, for traditional radio stations, is currently very good. Ask a typical radio station owner if it is likely that the mainstream radio audience would move over to a new broadcast medium (the Web), and he or she will laugh. For a business model to work, enough of an audience would have to move over for sufficient ad dollars to follow. Simply put, the revenue model for an entire industry would have to shift dramatically for traditional broadcasters to feel threatened. Of course, this dramatic shift is precisely what webcasters predict is going to happen. To see how this will play out—whether traditional broadcasters will ever have to go head-to-head against in-your-face webcasters—we need to take a deeper look at today's radio broadcast business.

➤ Radios Are Everywhere

In North America, every household owns an average of six radios. We listen to the radio for almost three and a half hours per person every weekday, and more than five hours on weekends. This adds up to roughly 1,100 hours a year for each of us. Naturally, we're not always paying attention; sometimes the radio exists only as background noise as we go about our commutes, household chores, work, and romance. But that's still a lot of background noise. Not surprisingly, this audience of roughly 200 million, each of whom listens to radio more than 1,100 hours each year, and which reaches 95 percent of consumers every week, is very appetizing to advertisers.

Radio was the first entertainment media to see the possibility of using advertising revenue to completely subsidize its product—or, how to deliver entertainment free to one group (consumers) by convincing another group (advertisers) to pay for it.

Radio is currently experiencing an economic boom. In 1996 alone, radio advertising topped a whopping $12 billion. Between 1991 and 1996, total radio broadcast industry revenue has been growing at a 7.7-percent compound growth rate (CGR). This is a faster rate than the 5.1-percent CGR at which the overall U.S. economy has been growing, and faster than the 7.0-percent CGR for all communication industry segments, during that same period. "The radio industry is incredibly healthy today," said Mark Fratrik, vice president and economist at the National Association of Broadcasters (NAB). The reason for this healthy state? According to Fratrik and other industry observers, this is largely due to recent deregulation.

➤ Big Fish Eat Little Fish

Over the last 15 years, the FCC has been gradually loosening ownership rules in radio to boost what was increasingly a sagging industry. The most recent (and most dramatic) effort in deregulation was the Telecommunications Act of 1996, which eliminated *all* national ownership limits. In markets with 45 or more commercial radio stations, a broadcaster can now own up to 8 stations; in markets with 30 to 44 stations, a single broadcaster can own 5 stations. (Previously, licensees were limited to owning 20 AM and 20 FM stations total nationwide.) Not surprisingly, a flurry of acquisitions took place upon passing of the Telecommunications Act: the number of radio station owners dropped to 4,507 from 5,105 in the eight months immediately after the Telecommunications Act passed in 1996, and the number continued to drop as this book went to press.

According to Veronis, Suhler, & Associates, a leading investment banker for the communications and entertainment industries that releases an annual report on the state of the businesses it covers, "the consolidation that followed deregulation meant that radio is able to deliver larger audiences to advertisers. As additional stations come under the umbrella of a single owner, there will be more efficiencies of scale in selling advertising, marketing program content, and managing inventory. This, in turn, will allow for diversification of formats, which will attract more listeners to radio." It may seem counterintuitive, at first, that consolidation is leading to diversification of formats, but that's what's happening. Here's what the FCC concluded: "Rather than concentrating on particular formats, owners are choosing to operate stations with a variety of formats . . . [that] allow the owner to appeal to more advertisers, and in particular to the advertiser who wants to reach a variety of different audiences."[2]

There's no better example of the effect of the deregulation of radio ownership rules than Chancellor Media. Run by Thomas Hicks, who started from scratch in 1994 with a $48 million investment and no stations, Hicks (through his firm Hicks, Muse, Tate, & Furst) has built a radio broadcasting empire that is currently first in both number of stations owned and annual advertising revenues. In three years, it has achieved a market capitalization of more than $7 billion. Charles Foster Kane must be turning over in his grave with envy. Chancellor has consistently doubled the operating margins of the stations it has acquired, achieved by the cost efficiencies of running multiple operations in each market, and through establishing a broad audience reach that is increasingly attractive to large advertisers. It is everything that the FCC predicted would happen when it began deregulating radio in the hopes of boosting a sagging industry.

Another radio player to thrive in the new deregulated environment is Premiere Radio Networks, a wholly owned subsidiary of Jacor Communications. Premiere is the second largest radio group (by station count); the third largest by advertising revenue. Through its 5,500 third-party affiliate stations, Premiere's syndicated programming reaches 99 percent of the consumers in the United States with nationally successful programs such as *The Dr. Laura Program, The Rush Limbaugh Show, The Dr. Dean Edell Show, Coast to Coast AM with Art Bell, The Jim Rome*

Show, The Michael Reagan Show, Entertainment Tonite on Radio with Leeza Gibbons—the list goes on and on.

Yet, despite the consolidation that resulted when the Telecommunications Act was passed—and which will continue to occur—the radio business remains highly fragmented. According to Katie Bachman, president of the Radio Broadcast Report, the top 5 radio groups accounted for just 30 percent of 1997 industry revenue; if you aggregated revenues from the top 50 radio groups, you'd still only account for half of 1997's total revenues. So there are still plenty of individual owners of individual stations, which assures format diversity—something that the FCC is anxious to promote. Says Bachman, "The radio business is a zoo parade. There's always something new and unexpected when I come into work every day." In fact, as much as deregulation did to encourage the growth of traditional radio, it's nothing compared with what the Internet promises to do.

First of all, there's the physical limitation of the broadcast medium, which will always exist in the real world (as opposed to the virtual world of the Internet). Most radio station transmitters are located at the top of towers, on good old terra firma, in the communities they serve. Of course, mobile radio transmitters are also located wherever they are used: in airplanes, boats, cars, trucks, and so on. But wherever radio transmitters are located, there are limitations in nature of just how far the signal can be transmitted. Depending on the frequency, and on the level of signal power, the distance that a radio signal can be received and clearly heard varies from tens to hundreds of miles. Not more. Without repeating the original signal, and/or retransmitting it via some other means (telephone, satellite, cable, wireless), radio transmission remains local. That's a basic truth, of fundamental importance to the radio broadcast industry.

Because the radio broadcast signal can only be received locally, it's not surprising that the business of radio is also local. Radio broadcasting is wholly subsidized by advertising revenue, and local ad spots account for 80 percent of the total industry revenue. Rick Ducey, senior vice president of research and information at the NAB, says that "as a national average, households spend almost 80% of their entire annual spending within a 20-mile radius of where they live." Radio suits local advertising perfectly. Local businesses reach out to their local customers. Later on, we'll see that some very smart broadcasters are learning how to benefit from a more national approach to ad sales.

But even deregulation—and the resulting consolidation that occurred—can't change the fact that there's only so much shelf space, or range of frequencies, suitable for radio transmission in any geographic area. (Indeed, this was the basic reason the government chose to regulate radio to "promote the public good.") To assure that all communities have a diversity of broadcast material to choose from, and to promote competition, the FCC regulates spectrum and ownership of stations for every one of the 210 market areas it defines in the United States. It's here that the Internet promises to do what no amount of government deregulation can do: unleash an avalanche of potential new players in radio.

■ IT'S GLOBAL—IT'S EVERYWHERE—IT REALLY *IS* A SMALL WORLD, AFTER ALL

Log onto www.comfm.fr and you'll be able to choose from a list of more than 1,430 live radio stations broadcasting from 78 countries. They're organized by country and by format. The site is all in French (you may remember, we *did* mention that the Internet is global), but don't let that stop you. Click on a country's flag, let's say *Grèce,* and you get a list of the 27 Greek radio stations broadcasting live over the Internet. Sports, news, weather, classical music, rock, Greek music. Click away, and your PC will begin to play the live audio. *Yasu!* Or, if you prefer your entertainment in English, you can click on *Grande-Bretagne* (that's French for Great Britain), and see their list of 40 live radio stations on the Internet, including several BBC channels and Virgin.Net's Radio. Or you can click on the list of *USA Live Radios* for a rather long list to choose from, organized by state, time zone, and format. Most of these Web pages, you'll be happy to hear, are available in English.

So listeners no longer have to be anywhere near the radio station to receive it. It's just as easy to listen to a broadcast from Hong Kong, London, or Johannesburg, as it is to punch in your favorite local traffic channel. Access is truly global and truly unlimited. (We couldn't get this book to press if we tried to give you an accurate number of Internet broadcasts, because it changes on a daily, if not hourly, basis.)

The global perspective also means dramatic changes in the *business* of radio. Take a quick jaunt to the sunny Bahamas, and listen to JAMZ (www2.100jamz.com), a Nassau radio station that plays a mix of traditional rock and what it calls "island" music, or, as JAMZ itself describes it, "Island/Urban." "Which consists of R&B, Hip-Hop, Reggae, Junkanoo, Dancehall, Soca and Calypso," as the web site proclaims. There are several interesting things to take note of at JAMZ, aside from the rather exotic nomenclatures for different categories of island music. And the most prominent one is that if you choose to go ahead and actually listen to the live broadcast from Jamaica (by clicking on the "listen" button), your browser takes you to a completely different web site. To Broadcast.com, to be exact. If you recall, Broadcast.com, introduced in Chapter 2, is a Texas-based webcaster that originally specialized in broadcasting sports news and events, but has since branched out.

And it's at the Broadcast.com site that you actually listen to the JAMZ broadcast. That may seem odd. Why would a radio station such as JAMZ, which is naturally interested in maximizing its advertising revenues (its sole source of income) send you to somewhere else to hear its own broadcast? Technically, JAMZ could easily broadcast its own music to anywhere in the world quite easily via the Internet. And if JAMZ sends all its Internet listeners to Broadcast.com, then Broadcast.com gets to display advertisements while the JAMZ music is playing—and Broad-cast.com gets to collect the subsequent ad dollars. (Internet advertising rates are calculated according to the number of "eyeballs" that see a particular ad, the number of "click throughs" that indicate specific interest in that ad, or some combination of the two.) And this turns out to be the point. Like most radio stations, JAMZ derives at least 80 percent of its revenues from *local* advertisers. Although JAMZ would be able, quite easily, to show you ads via the Internet from local business sponsors, it would be a largely futile exercise. Unless you're likely to be in the Bahamas soon, it isn't going to help you—or the advertisers—very much to see an ad proclaiming the best car servicing on the islands, or to hear about the best place in town to get fresh fish.

On the other hand, Broadcast.com has a sales force that specializes in selling *Internet* ads, which are inherently global in nature. So the two businesses hammered out an arrangement that allows both Broadcast.com and JAMZ to profit. The way it works is simple: all advertising derived from showing ads to an Internet "listener" sent to Broadcast.com by JAMZ is revenue split between the two sites. And, so you begin to see how new kinds of relationships between local radio stations, webcasters, and advertisers—who can be located anywhere in the world—begin to shape up.

Although there's cooperation and collaboration involved in the new business of Internet radio, there's also a bitter—and bloody—battle shaping up. How? These point-and-click relationships between web sites (where you get sent to one site from another, and the site owners share the benefits) are not going to be as free-form as the technology allows.

Here's another example: George Bundy has been eyeing the appetizing pie of Internet radio for some years now (yes, he was ahead of his time). Visit his web site at www.brsmedia.com, and you'll find a list of every radio station broadcasting on the Web. Nice. But, sometimes, when you click on one of the stations to listen in, the radio station's web site merely tells you that to listen to their station, you have to please move your browser to the Broadcast.com Web page. They won't let you listen from wherever you are. In short, webcasters such as Broadcast.com are setting themselves up as rather dictatorial gatekeepers to radio content that, technically, could be accessible to anyone, from anywhere. Ouch! The idea is that if they "own" the gateway to the content, then they "own" the eyeballs of the world-wide Internet radio audience, which means they can go to advertisers with an attractively captive audience. It's the old, old story of audience aggregation as the basis for revenue—something the television networks learned a long time ago. So, stay tuned as this particular war heats up.

Of course, there are also other challenges to this global-versus-local expansion: Global access to content also means that broadcasters can get sued, sent to jail, or otherwise face legal woes for breaking laws they might not even know about. Did you know that there are legal limits on how a radio station can broadcast music on the air? And that these laws are often different in different countries? In the United States, for example, a radio station playing music has to play a mix of at least 20 artists to be legal (to prevent someone from broadcasting all the music of one artist, and thereby undermining sales of that artist's records). Different rules for different territories are quite a challenge for webcasters like David Lawrence. "My show is heard in Nairobi, and 180 other countries," he says. "And we're finding we're ill prepared to cater to the global audience."

■ AN UNLIMITED SMORGASBORD

In addition to its global nature, there's another thing about Internet radio that is redefining the radio biz: the fact that there's no limit to the number of potential stations (although, as we said before, the station metaphor no longer holds in the Wild Wild West of the Internet). Do a quick search of BRS Media (www.brsmedia.com) and you'll find a list of 1,650 radio stations currently broadcasting on the Net. And this number is growing daily (see Figure 5.1). From a user perspective, this means aural information overload. Even now, we need mechanical and digital ways of keeping track of our favorite radio stations (at home or in the car) so we can immediately get to what suits us at any particular moment. We program buttons to our most frequently listened-to stations. We use the "seek" and "scan" buttons to help us more randomly search for programs of interest.

However, in the unlimited Internet age, you literally have a whole world of choices. At the time of this book printing, the Real Broadcast Network (RBN) was distributing more than 150,000 hours of live audio every week, and it had another 200,000 hours of archived audio material available at the click of a mouse—more than anyone has time for, even in several lifetimes. How will we deal with this? We'll get help. (We'll need it.) "We'll see hundreds of sites devoted to helping people sort through all these choices," says Philip Rosedale, vice president of core technology at Real Networks.

In other words, an infrastructure will spring up around this multiplicity of choices. (What did we do before *TV Guide,* or before local newspapers began printing television listings, or before reviewers told us what movies were worth seeing?) And consumers will do what they've always done: gravitate to the guides that they trust. "And that will be a dedicated business: to help you find what you want," points out Rosedale.

■ INTERACTIVITY GETS US WHAT WE WANT

Without question, the most profound change that the Internet will bring to radio is interactivity. Listeners will be able to request and immediately hear whatever they want, whenever they want, wherever they are—an amazing concept. But it is even more amazing when you consider how it plays out.

Here's how it works. Real Networks already offers every user of its service a customized *Daily Briefing*. You select the media sources that you want within each of the briefing categories (news, biz/tech, sports, entertainment, music, local information). For example, in the biz/tech category, you get to pick from ABS Stock Market News, C-NET Radio News, Daily Rocket Market Perspective, Electronic Industry News, Fox News—Business, Merrill Lynch World Business Report . . . and a whole lot more. You can select one of these—or all of them. And every day, when you log onto the Real Broadcast Network, simply click on your Daily Briefing, and it delivers—via audio—whatever you've requested. Of course, many services, including Yahoo! and Zip2, already offer this kind of customized on-line newspaper—this merely proves there's no reason why this kind of customizable service need be limited to text material.

➤ Interactivity Has the Potential to Make Advertisers Very Happy

This is where the advertisers start to drool, because in addition to specifying what you like, you are also sending out clear signals as to what you are likely to buy in terms of products or services. Already, web sites are displaying banner advertisements that are directly related to your actions. Try it. Type a rude word into Yahoo's search engine (not that we'd ever do such a thing), and you're suddenly presented with banner ads that are X-rated and/or erotic in nature. Not surprising, the same kind of customizable advertising already exists in the on-line radio tuners such as Imagine Radio, Spinner, and NetRadio. If you are listening to New Age music, your ads will be different from those of your spouse, who is listening to hip-hop. Your ads will even be different from the ads that someone else may be receiving on the same channel (because the advertiser knows *you*). This is extremely cost effective, and they've made the sale as easy as one click of a button. Be prepared to buy a lot more stuff. Check out Chapter 9 ["Brought to You by . . . (Ads)"] to find out why.

Not surprisingly, traditional radio broadcasters see broadcasting on the Internet as unsettlingly different from the way they've always done business. They do see how it opens up new revenue possibilities, and they also see how they can enhance their existing businesses with Web-based services for their communities. But, the way they capture large radio broadcast audiences to sell advertising space is entirely different today from the way audiences are aggregated on the Internet and advertising is used. So, it's just too different from today's business to see how it could work. It upsets the apple cart. "It's hogwash," says Terry Bratcher, when he hears arguments about how Internet Radio could threaten traditional radio. Bratcher, who has "done just about every job there is in radio," and is now director of new technologies at Business Development International, claims, "Radio is local, local, local. Joe's Diner in Louisville, Kentucky, isn't going to be interested in paying for a spot that's going to be heard, or clicked on, in New York, Palo Alto, or London."

Moreover, many traditional radio broadcasters say they already have all the entrepreneurial opportunities they could possibly want. Consolidation, alone, will continue to send earthquakes through the industry for many years to come. Mark Fratrik said, "in 10 years, the top 10 groups will control half of the business." The biggest fish are already eating disproportionately more than their share of the total industry revenue.

This is not to mention the challenges and opportunities brought about by Digital Audio Broadcast (DAB). DAB is radio broadcast via satellite with CD-quality audio. The first DAB services in the United States will be launched as subscription services in 1999.

■ IT'S AMAZING THAT IT FLIES AT ALL

Webcasters will be the first to admit that they have significant challenges in creating a business that rivals the $12 billion U.S. radio business. Namely, these challenges include widely deployed higher-bandwidth connections (at attractive consumer price points), eliminating network latency and compensating for lost data, not to mention radically changing the way advertising does business. They are confident, however, they can do it. They've accomplished near miracles in getting as far as they have, because even today's audio quality was considered implausible just a few years ago.

The Internet wasn't designed and created with broadcasting in mind—far from it. In fact, the more one knows about the Internet and its state today—as one peeks backstage at the man behind the curtain—the more amazing it is that broadcasting is even possible. It's a lot like those recent efforts to duplicate the original flight of the Wright brothers' *Flyer* at Kitty Hawk. To date, all efforts to successfully fly reconstructions of the original craft have failed completely. Maybe it shouldn't have worked back then.

Here's the problem. The network, created by the Department of Defense at the start of the Cold War, and which eventually evolved into the Internet, was designed for continuous reliable operation, even in the event that any of the network's components were not available due to a nuclear attack. So the Internet was designed as a loosely connected network of networks that doesn't depend on any one network node, or network path, being available. This is quite unlike the public, switched, telephone network (PSTN) design, in which for every telephone call we make, a connection is established (a durable path called a switched circuit) for the duration of the call. Because this design doesn't guarantee reliable operation impervious to unavailable network nodes, the Internet was designed differently.

All communication on the Internet happens via digital packets of information, ones and zeroes. To be transmitted over the Internet, all files, messages, and commands are first broken into portions of the message (called *packets*), that are sent on their way across the network. There's no durable connection established, so each of the packets makes its own way (finds its own adaptive path across the network) from the point of origin to its destination. Once all the packets reach their destination, they are reassembled into the original file (or message, or command). Of course, with this adaptive approach, there's actually no guarantee when, or even if, all the packets will reach the destination. It's a best-efforts approach. The design ensures that each packet will attempt to reach its destination as quickly as possible. It does not ensure this will happen quickly. And, therein lies a major problem for sending a live broadcast, audio or video, over the Internet. If some part of an audio broadcast takes even a few milliseconds longer to reach its receiver (the destination), it will sound unacceptably garbled. Oops.

■ IT'S ALL FOR REAL

Rob Glaser, CEO and president of Real Networks, and formerly a top techie at Microsoft, had a vision of how to achieve audio broadcasting over the Internet. Damn the torpedoes—full speed ahead. Able to finance the research and development himself, Rob and his team have accomplished what many observers thought unlikely, at best, only a few years ago: surprisingly excellent-quality audio broadcasting over the Internet. And, every new version of their software is clearly a significant improvement over what it replaced. If it wasn't for Real Networks, today's massive Internet radio deployment would have been significantly delayed. Sure, someone else would have eventually come along to play the role of market enabler. The honor goes to Real. They created the market by allowing content owners to easily and inexpensively deploy their content. When they had built a base of more than 20 million users, they had an irresistible target for content owners and advertisers.

Real Networks (originally called Progressive Networks) is currently the webcast technology leader. Rob Glaser is very cool, very savvy, and has built a promising company starting with what everyone agrees was almost unbearably poor technology. Thus far, Rob has had the considerable grace to dance Microsoft around the floor, as both supplier and competitor (friend and foe), and Real Networks is doing exceedingly well. But, because Microsoft now offers a similar technology for *free*, Real Networks will need a different business model. It's very hard to compete against "free," and there remain questions about the viability of Real's pricing for mass markets. Still, Real Networks is nothing if not agile and adept at leading the market with both technology and impressive business alliances. Real has done content deals with major broadcasters (CNN, Fox, NBC, and so on). Real has done a network deal with MCI, and this is the kind of deal we'll probably see more of. Real gets the award for making it all possible.

Peggy Miles gets to the heart of the matter: "I think they could change their licensing arrangement in 2 minutes. It's a race in a battle of giants: Real Networks with 85% market share today, and Microsoft. I keep coming back to Beta versus VHS. Better technology may not win out, but the marketing ability to push it in, may. It comes down to better marketing, not better technology."

■ BRAVE NEW WORLD

Yet, new Internet ventures, like Imagine Radio, continue to redefine the *business* of radio. Because the advertising is delivered over the Internet, there's a whole new relationship being formed between the broadcaster (Imagine), the advertisers (both local and national), and the audience (who can be anywhere in the world).

Perhaps most important, Imagine is completely free to experiment with new formats, styles, and performers at whim. Unlike traditional radio stations, which must create an identity in the community and stick to it by committing to a certain category or genre of broadcast (golden oldies, talk radio, country), Imagine is shaped by the ever-changing desires of its audience. The only caveat: "As long as we can build a loyal following—an audience that comes back frequently, and tells their friends," says Porteus. Thus, he says, "It doesn't matter which new formulas work or fail. Listeners will let us know by selecting what they will listen to, and what they won't." In turn, that gives advertisers an up-to-the-minute portrait of the interests (and buying habits) of the current audience. This is very powerful stuff for both the listeners and the advertisers who want to reach them.

"What's most fascinating about Internet radio," says Porteus, "is that it can grow in entirely different directions. It can become the place the mainstream radio audience goes, or it can become the place with all the eclectic alternative material that can never make it into lowest-common-denominator programming. Internet radio can do both."

Jacor and its subsidiary, Premiere Radio Networks, are playing it both ways—successfully. We've already seen (in Chapter 1) how Broadcast.com accomplished Wall Street's biggest IPO ever. They are masters of broadcast barter, and it doesn't hurt that they have Thomas Hicks as a major backer. Broadcast.com gets the award for aggregation (and making it all worthwhile).

Maybe it's because Premiere, as a syndicator, is already focused on regional and national ad sales, rather than on the very local ad sales of most radio stations. Steve Lehman makes it clear that the Internet benefits Premiere: "To deny the value or the existence of broadcast over the Internet is to bury your head in the sand and hope it will go away. Which will not happen. The reason it makes sense for a network radio is that instead of affiliating individual radio stations in cities throughout the U.S., we now have a global infrastructure that's available in either real time or on demand. And we have a new audience for the program that might not otherwise have access to the show. [Which is why most] of Premiere's shows are broadcast on the Internet: Dr. Laura, Jim Rome, Mike Reagan, and soon Rush . . . What we now have is an audience that was not available to us via radio."

The battle for broadcast hegemony is certainly not just limited to traditional and Internet broadcasters. The Internet opens the market to everyone and anyone, including other industries, whose traditional markets are also potentially open to disintermediation.

There is a polite saying that because of the Internet, it's foolish to be complacent about keeping your current market dominance. Which is why businesses as diverse as recorded music (producers and distributors as well as on-line and brick-and-mortar retailers), television, cable satellite networks and operators, and software and hardware technology companies all have a significant stake in the outcome. At its most basic level, this is a war for audience and ad revenues. We're your war correspondents, right at that battlefront. We'll cover the whole gory war in detail in Chapter 11 ("Family Feud").

Probably the most important challenge of all that radio broadcasters have to face is the recorded music business—if all the music in the world is going to be available on demand, on-line, via Internet webcast, for free (as subsidized by advertisers), why would anyone ever buy a record, CD, or cassette tape again? The $40 billion recorded music business, and the fundamental business relationship between radio and record makers, rides on the answer to that question.

The record industry is about to learn what television and radio broadcasters have long known—why it's smart to give it all away.

Chapter

It Ain't Groovy

"Thanks to the global reach of the Internet, people can now listen to and order music from around the globe on the web. Listening to music over the web can, in its way, almost be better than listening to a CD player. We as content providers can give the listener a richer experience, and a deeper understanding of the music, using eyes and ears."

—QUINCY JONES, musician, composer, producer

"In the future, there will be only two ways to get music: As a paying subscriber, or for free, accompanied by ads."

—JIM GRIFFIN, director of technology, Geffen Records

"It's the atom bomb you've created."

—Record Industry executives to MP3 patent holders

"David Robert Jones was born in Brixton on January 8, 1947. At age thirteen, inspired by the jazz of the West End, he picked up the saxophone and called up Ronnie Ross for lessons. Early bands that he played with, the Kon-Rads, the King Bees, the Manish Boys, and the Lower Third provided him with an introduction into the showy world of pop and mod, and . . ."[1]

Thus begins the on-line biography of one of the world's most successful rock stars, David Bowie. That David Bowie would have a web site for his fans to use to get the latest information on his recordings and live tours, to chat to each other, and, yes, simply to idolize him, is no surprise. Yahoo listed more than 40,000 such fan sites for recording music artists to be found on the World Wide Web as of October 1998.

BowieNet, however, is something different. After all, David Bowie does love to keep his fans on their toes. Every few years, he completely reinvents himself. Thus, David Jones became David Bowie, who morphed into Ziggy Stardust, who later became the Thin White Duke . . . you get the idea.

And, in a move that affects several entertainment industries, he has surprised the world of finance, too. In early 1997, Bowie raised $55 million by issuing a bond, backed by royalties from 25 of his best-selling albums. According to *Webnoize,* the entire issue was purchased by Prudential Insurance Company of America. "That deal was an early innovation in leveraging intellectual property and a first for a music artist. Most important, it set a successful precedent for a new financing venture that could become very common with music industry players. 'I've had meetings over the last six months with almost every Wall Street firm and now, they all get it,' says Charles A. Koppelman, chairman of CAK Universal Credit Corporation, a division of CAK Entertainment set up to provide such financing services. 'You know, what sounds radical today is going to be as commonplace as a home mortgage two years from now.' "[2] This means that financing will be available to successful artists who want to invest in building their own entertainment empires.

But it might surprise you most of all to learn that David Bowie is now operating a high-speed Internet Service. What's going on? Bowie set out to create, in his words, "The first community driven Internet site that focuses on music, film, literature, painting and more." Other Web pioneers might disagree (there are so many "firsts" claimed in cyberspace that it's a good idea to take such claims with a judicious dose of skepticism). Still, what Bowie also says about his intentions are quite interesting, making his personal Internet service sound more like performance art meets the psychedelic sixties than your typical Internet e-commerce venture. If you join him (and a couple million of his closest friends), Bowie tells visitors to his web site, "you can interact with all the members of our adventurous new project, knowing that this is an on-growing building, added to constantly, and that you will definitely be entertained (sometimes unwittingly)."[3]

BowieNet, as it's called, has everything you'd expect at a site intended as homage to the artist in question: a biography, a discography, film credits, albums for sale, music and movie videos for sale, memorabilia, paintings, samples of lots of his music, and perhaps even more merchandise than the typical fan web site. Our favorite was the BowieNet Contest: "the first of its kind Internet contest. Get plenty of rest before entering—this one will take you to the deepest corners of your creative mind."

What really distinguishes this site from most is the presence of the artist himself. Bowie doesn't just have a server send automatic replies to e-mails from adoring fans. He's there live every week. Using new video technology that allows each fan to have their own live camera view of Bowie. However you like to communicate—e-mail, telephone, or fax—he'll take your questions and reply on camera. There's nothing like it anywhere in the world. Oh sure, you can always find some celebrity showing up for an on-line chat session, but nowhere do fans have such regular access to their favorite star.

That's why everyone in the recorded music industry is taking notice. This isn't just a trophy piece for Bowie's ego. It embodies just about everything about how the future of the record industry is about to change beyond anyone's expectations. Here, we see an artist as a *brand* (nothing new about that). But, he is also acting as his own record label, broadcasting his own songs, controlling all aspects of promotion, and all aspects of sales and distribution direct to fans. And, not incidentally, he's reaping a much higher percentage of the net profit than if he'd gone through traditional recording, promotion, broadcasting, and distribution channels.

Many of these changes have already begun in earnest. Already, you can order recorded music on-line through any number of cyberstores (Amazon.com, CDnow, and N2K's Music Boulevard). The five major record groups (Universal, Sony, Warner, Bertelsmann, and CEMA) are all starting to test new waters—as retailers (pushing their recordings through direct on-line sales, as well as pay per play) and as broadcasters (using digital distribution and webcasting). And, traditional retailers like Tower Records are publicly scrambling to determine what they need to do to keep customers coming into their brick-and-mortar stores.

Jim Griffin, the former Geffen Records executive, says that in the digitally enabled future there will be only two ways to get music: "As a paying subscriber, or for free with ads." Sound familiar? That's right. Television and radio broadcasters already do exactly that, and they boast a combined annual domestic revenue of almost $50 billion. So, someday, it might just be possible for the recorded-music industry to figure out how to make this very old media business model work for them, too.

We've already seen why the Internet is such a promising new medium for radio broadcasters: it's global (not constrained by geographic boundaries), it offers unlimited shelf space (there will never be the need to reserve a specific place in cyberspace), and it's interactive (it responds to individual actions and desires). All of these advantages apply to the record business, too, but in a way that is much more threatening to the traditional way of doing business in New York, Los Angeles, Nashville, and Detroit. Think about it. The Internet is the most economical means of music distribution ever devised, which should be enough to send warning shocks throughout all the studios (and executive offices of recording labels) throughout the world. Here's some of what this means:

> Fans will have access to performances not otherwise available. There will be no need to buy a bootleg CD

to get that rare club appearance—just click on the icon.

➤ Fans will be able to *try and buy* music to see if they really want to purchase it. You don't like what you hear? Don't buy it. There is no need to ask for your money back. (Trying returning an open CD to a retail outlet and watch the clerks smirk.)

➤ Artists will have greater control over the entire process of recording, promoting, selling, and distributing recordings. (Whether this will result in better- or higher-quality recordings remains to be seen. Certainly, it means artists will retain more of the money generated by their creative efforts.)

➤ The nature of how music is packaged will change. Watch for the return of the single with bells and whistles on. Albums? Weren't they something your grandparents listened to?

➤ For true fans of a particular artist, a long-term relationship will emerge that results in discounts to new recordings, subscriptions to concerts, free tickets (a frequent listening program?), and other merchandise. In other words, the loyalty of individual fans will be rewarded, and you don't even have to hang out at the stage door.

David Bowie's web site already does this, and more. After all, he wants to be your Internet Service Provider (ISP), too. Who knows, but at this rate, it wouldn't be surprising if someday he'll want to be your long-distance telephone and cable TV provider, too—seriously.

■ TWENTY BILLION RECORDS, GIVE OR TAKE A FEW

To understand the fundamental shake-up that's already starting in recorded music, we need to take a quick tour of the past, to understand how the industry has traditionally operated. Not surprisingly, the record business is simply about selling records, a whole lot of records. So you can imagine the reception of technology that makes it unnecessary for anyone to buy music anymore, because it's readily available for free.

Hal Hall decided to be one hell of a collector. He wanted to own one of just about every record that had ever been made. In 1968, Hall was a young computer programmer just starting out at IBM, working in rustic upstate New York. A technologist by day, Hall's true passion was music—specifically, collecting it. Never mind the considerable cost or the difficulties of prospecting for rare, and sometimes dubious, material; Hal was on a quest to possess every recording in existence, and nothing would stop him.

Just five years after beginning this endeavor, Hall had amassed a library of almost 20,000 LPs. And, although today's total catalog of published music is close to the equivalent of 100,000 albums (because we no longer think in terms of records), 20,000 LPs is still an awful lot of music. If Hall had actually tried to listen to all the material in his collection, and if he kept his turntable running 10 hours a day, every day of the year, it would have taken him more than five years. That was back in 1973, so it doesn't count the thousands of new albums and CDs produced every year since then. To listen to all 100,000 albums of published music, just one time through, would take someone like Hall almost 30 years. What was terrible news for Hal Hall, and finally stopped his collecting days, was the birth of the CD and the eventual market death of the LP. But, more on that later.

➤ Picky, Picky

Unfortunately for record companies, people like Hall are rare. Unlike our undiscriminating consuming of television programming, the average U.S. household buys just 11 albums a year. Over the past 50 years, we have collected about 200 albums per household (which is just 1 percent the size of Hall's collection), an aggregate of about 20 billion records. Compare this with the 10 trillion hours of television we've watched, in aggregate, since the birth of that media, and you'll see we're a little pickier about our music choices, or at least what we'll pay for.

<h2>➤ Music to Their Ears</h2>

According to the Recording Industry Association of America (RIAA), the U.S. record industry's trade association, every year more than a billion units are sold, which adds up to more than $12 billion in annual domestic sales. But, that's less than one-third of the roughly $40 billion annual worldwide business. That's right, roughly 70 percent of the record business sales revenue is international.

Edgar Bronfman, Jr., president and chief executive officer of The Seagram Company Ltd., which became the world's largest record company with its 1998 acquisition of Polygram Records, knows that international distribution will be increasingly important. Because, according to Bronfman, "In many developing countries, half of the population is under the age of 15," he said. "They're becoming customers for the first time, and they will remain customers for many decades."[4] In other words, international sales are soon going to be a larger share of total industry revenue.

This global market, then, is at the heart of the music business. Harold Vogel's informative book, *Entertainment Industry Economics,* an essential reference for anyone interested in entertainment industries, explains that because the record industry "is the most easily personalized and accessible form of entertainment, it readily pervades every culture and every level of society.[5] As such, it may be considered the most fundamental of the entertainment businesses." So, unlike the radio broadcast business, which is "local, local, local," the record business is "global, global, global." This is dramatized by the fact that recordings of artists with a global following (U2, Phil Collins, Frank Sinatra, Celine Dion . . . feel free to add your favorite star to the list) account for a full two-thirds of total revenue.

■ THE NEXT BIG THING

Back in the early 1980s, the growth of the record business was slowing. But fortunately, by the end of that decade, technology once again "bailed the industry out of its funk," as Harold Vogel put it. As we mentioned before, what was terrible news for Hal Hall, and finally stopped his collecting days, was the birth of the CD and the eventual market death of the LP. This was terrific news, however, for the music industry, which desperately needed a boost. The CD was exactly the boost it needed, because now, all of us lucky consumers would be able to repurchase much of the same library we already owned in a new and improved format.

As we approach the twenty-first century, the growth of record sales seems to be slowing. And, the music industry could use a cool new technology to once again bail it out of a funk. The Internet could be just what the doctor ordered.

■ A RIVER RUNS THROUGH IT

Amazon.com has changed the business of selling books. Within just three years of starting business, it became one of the top three book retailers in the United States, which isn't at all bad for a company that doesn't have any actual

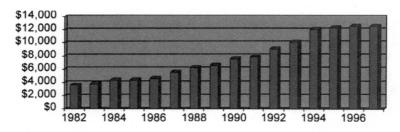

Figure 6.1 U.S. record sales revenue, 1982–1996.

Source: Veronis, Suhler, & Associates, 1997.

stores. Now, of course, it's making waves by trying to re-place Tower Records as the place you buy your latest CDs. So, watch out Blockbuster Video.

Just about everyone noticed this, not the least of which was Wall Street. When Amazon.com suddenly achieved that market share, it wasn't long before it also achieved a terrific market valuation ($4.79 billion), which it used to further expand its market position and to fund its invest-ment into new market opportunities like music sales, not to mention a surge of really annoying TV ads.

This was no surprise to the music business. Many record companies knew early on that the Web was, at the very least, a great new place to sell records. Yahoo.com, the most active web site in the world, lists more than 55,000 music-related sites, more than 1,500 of which are hosted by record labels themselves, who see this as a way to di-rectly connect with their most avid customers. After all, the record company doubles its profit margin on sales it makes directly to the consumer (as compared with sales via some other retail channel).

The six largest record groups, which together generate almost 90 percent of the industry's domestic revenue, are also well on their way to establishing a strong Web pres-ence. Sony Music (www.sonymusic.com), for instance, is doing what all the Big Five labels are doing on-line: mar-keting and sales. Take a quick look at what Sony Music had posted as of October 1998:

➤ Hundreds of audio and video clips you can preview, including recent hits (e.g., Mariah Carey, *Titanic*, Gloria Estefan, Des'ree, *Godzilla*)

➤ A list of all current material for sale, as well as an inventory of their enormous back catalog

➤ An on-line store to buy anything in Sony's catalog (e.g., music, movies, games)

➤ An on-line classical radio station (Sony Classical Radio)

➤ Tour information and advance ticket sales for Sony artists

➤ Links to Web pages for all their artists, reviews, bios

➤ Chat rooms for fans and artists to meet

➤ Contests, promotions, merchandise, and more

Although in 1997, all on-line sales accounted for far less than 1 percent of the recorded music business, some analysts have estimated that by 2002, as much as 15 percent of all revenue will come from Web sales. This is even more than the 12 percent of total sales that all record clubs (like Columbia House), in aggregate, contribute today. It's quite possible (there's no way of knowing) that most on-line sales may simply be extensions of these traditional record clubs (subscriptions sales moving on-line). Yet, even if this is the case, the trend is clear: on-line sales are already a significant segment of the total recorded music business, and that will only be more the case in coming years.

Amazingly, this phenomenal growth in on-line music sales happened at a time when only a small fraction of the world's record buyers had Internet access. By 1998, the Internet reached only 10 percent of worldwide music consumers. Not bad—and not surprisingly, record industry executives realized that this was just the beginning of a new kind of sales channel.

■ A RIVER RUNS OVER IT

Not surprisingly, we're about to see the beginning of a massive channel war as a result of this new distribution channel. As of early 1998, there were more than 1,000 record stores on the Web. This includes all the major brick-and-mortar record retailers (such as Blockbuster Entertainment, Tower Records, Transworld, and Wal-Mart Stores), and all the major on-line record retailers (such as

Amazon.com, CDnow, and N2K's Music Boulevard), not to mention the record companies themselves.

Of course, record companies usually sell only their own records on-line, but that is changing. Already, Warner Bros. has shown how a media company can creatively market and retail content from other media companies as well as its own. Interested? Check out its web site (www .warnerbros.com) and see how it is attempting to make itself a broad-based entertainment Web by offering content developed by other companies. "The new approach is a radical departure from traditional thinking in Web syndication," reported *Internet Week Online*. What is more typical: that media companies with valuable—and that means recognizable—content will try to license that content to other sites.

Instead, Warner Bros. is adopting what *Internet Week Online* calls a "studio-style model," in the sense that as an audience aggregator, it can use its high-traffic site to steer visitors to its smaller partners. Industry experts say this approach makes sense, because the separation of production and distribution has long been industry practice in the film and television businesses. Movie studios don't produce all the movies they distribute, and television networks don't produce most of the shows they broadcast (in fact, until recently, they were prohibited from doing so). So, a TV network like NBC will use its Thursday night lineup to attract a big prime-time audience, to which they promote less popular shows on other nights. "Warner Bros. doesn't produce all its own movies, and Warner Bros. does not produce all of its own TV shows," said Jim Moloshok, senior vice president for Warner Bros. Online. "This is just a way to extend that studio model online."

■ BIT BY BIT

But this on-line selling of CDs and tapes is just the first— you might even say baby—step toward a new kind of recording industry, one that no longer needs actual physical media to get its product out to consumers. The media, as used in this context, refer to the physical formats the recording studio uses to transfer the music from their premises to yours. The medium used to be predominantly record disks (or LPs, or albums, whatever term you prefer). Tapes (cartridge, or 8-track, or even reel-to-reel) have been other media choices over the years. But since 1983, the consumer's medium of choice has been the compact disk. Today, the CD accounts for the way that more than 80 percent of all recorded music is delivered to the consumer. As a digital recording medium, it's the first step in a truly remarkable journey toward the future of music distribution: pure digital.

What's the difference between this digital recording medium called CD, and a pure, digital method of distributing music? Everything in the world. It may not seem like much of a difference at first, but for the record industry, it is. To the consumer, today's digital distribution of music looks like downloading a file from the Internet onto their PC's hard drive.

Today, all you need is a decent PC and an Internet connection to download CD-quality music. Yes, at this point, your hard drive needs to be big enough to be able to store the music in digital form once it's downloaded. But some time in the not-too-distant future, you won't even need that. It will then seem more like a radio to consumers, except that as you do with your CD player today, you'll play whatever you want, whenever you want. And there won't be all those disks and jewel cases.

What's the advantage of digital distribution? For record makers, it's one of cost. Edgar Bronfman, Jr., pointed to the significant value of digital distribution for record makers when he told an industry conference, "we are on the threshold of eliminating [significant] costs."

That was an understatement. Digital distribution is less expensive in a variety of ways. First, there's no need to forecast sales of a particular recording, so record companies are much less apt to produce costly overruns, which result in both inventory overstocks and returns of unsold product from retailers. Secondly, you've eliminated all the raw materials and associated services that go into transforming the music onto the media—the pressing of the CD, for example. There's no media to ship or break, so you've reduced shipping and breakage costs.

Interestingly enough, not having to manufacture the physical media itself is not where the savings are. As Albhy Galuten, vice president of technology at Universal Music Group, told a recent industry gathering, "the cost of manufacturing a CD is so low—10 cents or so—there's no real savings to be had there."[6] He agreed when Mike Farrace, vice president of Tower Records Online, added that it was the shipping, or, "the costs of shipping the CDs, back and forth between manufacturers, warehouses, distributors," that added up to significant dollar amounts. So, eliminating all associated shipping costs could make a substantive difference, indeed.

But, in fact, the real potential savings to digital distribution will come in surprising ways—specifically, by changing the very nature of how the recorded music business operates. Hal Vogel points right to the problem: "Success in distribution depends on the size of the capital commitment and on the ability to quickly sense where and how new music is selling," he writes. "To this end, distributors employ large staffs of sales and promotion people and rely extensively on outside intelligence-gathering sources." To paraphrase Vogel, if music is distributed digitally, the labels won't have to be as smart about predicting what's going to sell. They don't have to guess at future trends and tastes of consumers. They don't have to worry about how many CDs to press, and where to ship them. They simply make the music available, digitally, and let the customers vote by downloading whatever they want.

This is the heart of where the potential savings lie. True, promotion and marketing activities designed to sell existing and rising stars and their new recordings will still be necessary and significant, but major expenses required to prepare for a potential hit are eliminated. Once the music has been produced, there's no incremental cost to getting as much product as the consumers demand out the door (or modem, as the case may be). So—no surprise— the six major record companies who collectively control over 85 percent of worldwide sales of recorded music are looking closely at digital distribution, which promises so handsomely to inflate profit margins.

Still, nothing is ever simple, and digital distribution poses three extremely challenging problems, as well as opportunities, for record makers:

1. It makes piracy a lot easier. (What's to prevent people from posting digital music free on the Web for the whole world to access?)
2. It upsets the industry food chain by disrupting long-term business relationships. (Artists like Bowie become labels, and labels become retailers and broadcasters.)
3. It can even eliminate the necessity for record labels entirely. (After all, why shouldn't other artists do what Bowie has done, and simply become their own label—and reap the subsequent profit?)

■ "TO EVERY MAN IS GIVEN THE KEY TO THE GATES OF HEAVEN. THE SAME KEY OPENS THE GATES OF HELL."[7]

The first problem is that the very technology that permits the extremely low-cost distribution of record-quality audio is widely available to anyone who wants to use it, not just to the record labels themselves.[8] That means that (inevitably) several someones are going to overstep the legal limits and distribute material they don't have the right to distribute. This is already happening, of course, on the Internet where it is called *sharing;* never mind that in the real (as opposed to virtual) world it is called *theft.* Remember that the Internet is one of the first truly populist movements to come along in decades, and the fact that existing organizations' power and influence can be subverted is precisely to the point for many of its leading citizens.

That difference is confused by the bewildering array of copyright laws and licensing agreements that crisscross the globe. Although ignorance of the law is never an excuse, ignorance of what's permissible is nevertheless widespread. Some of the theft is committed accidentally and unknowingly, some quite deliberately, and publishers worldwide are going to do whatever it takes to protect their basic assets—their entire businesses are at stake.

So, in 1998, the RIAA launched a campaign with colleges and universities to educate students about the importance of respecting copyrighted sound recordings in cyberspace, and it sued music archive sites that were illegally distributing full-length songs for download. "When these organizations sue Mom and Pop stores for playing music, and sue the Girl Scouts for singing around a campfire, you know you've got trouble," wrote radio broadcaster Rick Wood in an Internet newsgroup for webcasters.

➤ This Is the Atom Bomb

Already, even before the wide availability of consumer broadband access, digital delivery of record-quality music had begun. One of the earliest technologies to make this possible is MP3 (short for MPEG-1 Layer-3 Audio). Although this technology design had been defined over a decade before, in 1998 its usage began to grow geometrically.

This book is making a deliberate attempt to explain the interactive revolution without resorting to in-depth discussions of technology, but MP3 is truly significant and worth introducing. MP3 is a combination of software and hardware that, at the distribution source, enables the compression and encoding of audio for efficient network transmission, and then the decoding and decompression into high-quality, almost-CD-quality audio at the receiving end. In short, when you play an MP3 file, you get something that sounds almost like the original CD it was copied from. In fact, the resulting quality is so good and the cost of using MP3 is so low that record companies are justifiably concerned that it enables mass piracy and bootlegging of their records—their business. So much so, that at a meeting with the holder of the relevant MP3 patents, record company executives said of MP3, "this is the atom bomb."

To use MP3, you need an MP3 player (just like you need a CD player to play a CD). As of 1998, more than 6 million MP3 players have been distributed worldwide, and the often illegal exchange of records has skyrocketed (copies of albums sent as files on the Internet)—some following immediately after initial release, and some even before they are officially released. More than 500,000 songs have been encoded and distributed using MP3.

If you had been managing the worldwide record business, you'd be quite concerned, too. Even a 13-year-old (or even possibly younger, given the age at which kids are being introduced to computers these days) can encode and then distribute record-quality material throughout the world—possibly for free, possibly as barter, possibly for revenue—but for whatever reason(s), that student has the ability to completely undermine your entire business. At least, that's the fear, and some of the reality, too.

There are some in the industry, however, who think that this exchange actually increases sales and certainly does no harm. They argue that the vast majority of the exchange occurs between fans of these artists, who will (eventually) want to own copies of all the performances anyway, and that this exchange of material between fans actually further promotes record sales of those albums. The argument is that the on-line exchange of files is just for convenient access for die-hard fans, until they have the chance to buy it. Of course, the music industry doesn't see it that way; they see it as theft. The record industry itself distributes free promotional copies to stimulate sales, but under tightly controlled circumstances.

It may be somewhat ironic that the very unlimited nature of the Internet, as a key enabler for change and new opportunities, also creates some of the most difficult challenges. Many of these challenges, however, would exist even if there were no Internet, because the speed of technological innovation is rapidly outpacing the laws that govern these matters.

There's good reason to believe that the potential financial benefit is enough incentive to overcome all the technical, legal, and business issues, but it all comes down to this: none of the revolutionary changes we're talking about will happen until rock-solid copyright protection mechanisms are in place. There's simply too much at stake to risk proceeding otherwise. Later on, we'll see how technology is possibly coming to the rescue again.

■ OLD FRIENDS, NEW ENEMIES?

The second problem that rears its head in the face of digital distribution is that the very stable business relationships that have evolved over time between the major labels, independent labels, producers, retailers, artists, and radio broadcasters are all about to be undermined by the new technology.

➤ Labels As Retailers

For starters, record companies themselves have to be just a bit careful about how they approach consumers with their newly digitized wares. After all, traditional music retailers, the brick-and-mortar folk, generate nearly 90 percent of the record industry's $40 billion worldwide revenue, and it's never smart to bite the hand that feeds you—at least, not until you can comfortably feed yourself.

So, until such time as the record manufacturers are generating at least two-thirds of their worldwide revenue through their own direct sales (both through on-line sales and record clubs), they will need to continue to work co-operatively with their retailers. Even then, they might need to retain a viable relationship. After all, there will always be people who want to wander into a physical place, rub elbows with other music lovers, and enjoy the social experience of retail shopping.

Understandably, the record companies are somewhat reticent to talk about these issues publicly, and they are loathe to offend their retail partners. But, it makes no sense that the only music industry players not selling music on-line would be the labels. So they are.

Log onto www.SonyMusic.com, and you'll see thousands of albums for sale, from Fred Astaire to Pinchas Zuckerman. Or, check out www.BMG.com, and you'll see the BMG Music Club (12 CDs for the price of 1—join now).

You can be sure that with 88 percent of all record sales (that's $35 billion worldwide), the record labels are still "best pals" with their brick-and-mortar retailers. But, as comfy as things are today between the labels and retailers, the obvious question is how long will it remain that way? You may remember a similar situation in the early days of PC sales, when you couldn't buy direct from IBM or Compaq, because they were afraid to upset the distribution channel. Just look at them now.

On-line sales lead directly to digital distribution of samples. What better means is there to evaluate the music before purchase? Just go to www.atlantic-records.com and listen to samples from the latest Tori Amos album, or watch clips from the latest Hootie and the Blowfish video.

It's a slippery slope, and there's no turning back once this trend really gets under way. So, with the sole exception of the potentially showstopping issue of copyright protection, these changes in the recorded music food chain are pretty inevitable. "The digital delivery of intellectual property, including art, is the most important technological development that could possibly happen in our lifetime," says Jim Griffin, director of technology for Geffen Records. Why? Because what the printing press did for freedom of expression, digital music distribution is going to do for the freedom of artistic expression. "It will lead to a renaissance of expression, and will lead us to things we were never able to do before," says Griffin.

➤ Labels As Broadcasters

Radio broadcasting and the recorded music business have had a deep, enduring marriage. Each provides the basis for the other's business model. They depend on each other.

How does that work? As the basis for more than 80 percent of advertising revenues, recorded music provides, by far, the dominant content for traditional radio broadcasts. In turn, radio provides the most efficient mechanism to introduce and promote the newest recordings, as well as remind the listening public of the items in music makers' back catalogs. This is not to mention, of course, that radio broadcasting generates roughly $1 billion in performance royalties for the record business—a nice chunk of change by any measure.

But, as cozy as things currently are between radio and recorded music, the Internet is threatening to change that. It's going to cause both industries to reevaluate their relationship with each other. Will this lead to a deeper commitment—or to Splitsville?

It's inevitable that the means of digital distribution will increasingly blur the distinctions between distribution and broadcast. Here's why: To start with, the technology of digital distribution is the same technology for broadcasting over the Internet. As we saw, streaming audio broadcasts over the Internet are nothing more than digital audio files that are downloaded in such a way that they can be played while the download proceeds, without hav-

ing to wait for the download to finish. So, there's no difference between real-time, play-as-you-download and broadcast. Distribution is broadcast.

Once the record companies started offering music samples live from their web sites, they became broadcasters. Not
in the important sense, mind you, that their business model
is anything at all like a broadcaster's business model (aggregate a big enough audience to profit from advertising
sales). Think about it, and we'll come back to this question later on. Technologically, there's no difference between sending digital music samples to an audience and
broadcasting those samples to the same audience. Distribution is broadcast.

Now, there are significant differences that matter
here, but the central point remains that, slowly but
surely, record companies are starting to be broadcasters.
Some of the differences that matter most are audio quality (which depends on network bandwidth and capacity),
cost (which depends on lots of things), and copyright
protection (which isn't even possible without the right
technology).

➤ What Technology Giveth, Technology Taketh Away

Fortunately, technology can often effectively address the
issues that it creates. Several companies (a2b music, Liquid Audio, and others) have already introduced products
that enable an even higher quality of audio, with improved compression for distribution, and that prevent
piracy and copyright infringement.

It's not news, of course, that technology companies
have to compete to survive. When someone comes up with
the latest hot invention, there are bound to be several competitors who each have entirely different—and almost always incompatible—ways of bringing those products and
services to market. Although this can be a bit inconvenient for anyone who buys any of the ones that eventually

lose (e.g., Betamax, 8-track tape, etc.), that's not currently the case with technology for the digital distribution of music.

➤ Go with the Flow

Liquid Audio, which was founded by veterans of the music industry and professional recording engineers in 1996, focuses exclusively on the needs of the music industry. As music professionals, the founders' focus was professional audio quality, and secure technology for network delivery of music. Their products allow music companies and artists to prepare and publish CD-quality music for secure distribution via the Internet, as well as provide all the Web server technology required for electronic commerce. As a result, Liquid Audio has managed to forge strategic alliances throughout the industry with leading players, such as ASCAP, *Billboard* magazine, BMG, and N2K's Music Boulevard.

The Liquid Audio Player (a piece of software) is free for anyone to download and use. Anyone who wants to use their Web server and encoding technology pays to license the Liquid Audio tools. And, the licensees are free to choose any business model that suits them, because the Liquid Audio technology does not dictate which business demo they have to use. Record companies are free to use free samples, try-and-buy, pay-per-play, subscription, and even the possible eventual winner—that old standby for radio and television—advertising.

➤ The Quickest Way from A to B

Veterans of the music industry and AT&T Labs founded a2b music, and so whimsically named it because a digital network is now the fastest way to get any sort of digital material from Point A to Point B. Using AT&T Labs' compression and security technologies, a2b music was the first music delivery system to combine physical and on-line retail options for the music industry. For example, Tower Records customers who purchase albums at either the company's stores or on-line will be able to download exclusive songs not available elsewhere.

a2b's policy management technology allows labels to enforce whatever terms of use they desire for their content. For example, unlike other current technologies for digital distribution, a2b allows music companies to easily change their licensing policy without having to alter the original music file. This policy management tool is a uniquely valuable technology for record companies, and it had been used in promotions by several of the major record companies, such as Atlantic Records, RCA/BMG, Tower Records, and others. Tower Records Vice President Mike Farrace says that policy management "provides unique ways for retailers to market music to a global audience."

a2b music and Liquid Audio are competitors with competing (and incompatible) technologies; that is, a music file encoded with either technology won't play on the other's player. But, because the end-consumer audio players are free (at least all the software players), it costs nothing for the consumer to try the different solutions—a little inconvenient, perhaps, but not costly. So, these products (and any others that enter this market) are likely to coexist for a long time.

■ ARTISTS AS LABELS

The third problem, and possibly the most corrosive problem of all, facing widespread digital distribution of music is the already volatile relationship that many artists have with the labels who sell their music. When unknown artists are discovered by a record company's fleet of scouts, the artist has little or no bargaining power in contract negotiations. "They can either sign the contract they're offered, or try to find another publisher. That's the way it is," says David Kessel, now chairman of IUMA, who has spent 25 years in the business. "In the 1950s and 60s, now famous artists such as Bo Diddley and Chuck Berry, even had to accept horrible, truly usurious, terms. The labels added songwriting credits for other people who had no involvement whatsoever with the writing. The real R&B writers happen to be black, and the song-writing cocredits went to white people who did nothing to be credited. But it was either that, or find someone else to publish your album."

Of course, if a music artist or act starts generating significant sales, then the balance of power changes. Here is where digital distribution will significantly change existing relationships, because digital technology frees the artist to do any part of the production, marketing, and distribution process with anyone they choose. They no longer have to rely on the label to do it all, from soup to nuts.

For example, labels subtract from 10 to 15 percent for breakage in shipping, regardless of the actual breakage that may (or may not) occur. This is usually much more than actual losses, but because it's deducted as an expense from royalties, it's a net profit for the labels (in effect, paid by the artist to the label). There isn't any breakage with digital distribution, because there's nothing to break. So, the labels won't be able to deduct such nonexistent costs.

Every industry has its open, dirty little secrets, and the record business has its share. As Albhy Galuten said, "everything is a negotiation." This is all going to change, as digital distribution empowers artists—even unknown artists—with alternative means to produce, promote, sell, and ship their songs. Anybody can now be a publisher.

■ EVERYBODY'S DOING IT

Still, despite all of the risks inherent in on-line sales and digital distribution, every major company in the industry is actively engaged in exploring these areas. After all, it's even riskier to be left behind by your competition. This is why all six major record makers, all the top record retailers, and just about every major record label, are already operating web sites for the purpose of on-line sales and marketing. And, this is why several megastar artists, such as Willie Nelson, Todd Rundgren, and David Bowie, have started to leverage their star status into their own on-line operations and sales.

Naturally, and quite sensibly, the record companies operate their sites with as little risk taking as possible. The vast majority of the music in their catalogs is not yet available on-line, even for sampling. Mostly, what you can find on-line today is just music samples, or sales teasers (like one cut from an album for fans to see if they like the material enough to buy it or not). There are even a small number of complete albums available for download from major artists.

The distribution channel has already begun to reshape itself, like a river that has overflowed its banks and created itself a new course. It still runs down to the sea (the consumer mass market), but it gets there via an entirely new path.

■ IT'S GROOVY THAT IT AIN'T GROOVY

That's nothing compared with the biggest changes of all that may be coming. We've been talking about eliminating media in distribution. That is, because the music is in digital form, and moves from the recording studio to you via a network, there's no physical container that must be passed through a distribution channel. There is no CD; therefore, there is no need for you to physically visit Tower Records (or have Amazon.com ship you a package via UPS).

But, one thing remains the same: you still possess, at the end, a physical copy of the music. It resides on your PC hard drive, or on a CD that you've pressed yourself (yes, you will start doing this at home). You've still paid a price to own an actual physical copy of the music itself. In that sense, nothing has changed—yet.

Eventually, even the need to physically possess a copy of a piece of music you love will go away. How is that? Think of it as radio on demand or, as it is being described in musical circles, "the ultimate jukebox." Such an ultimate jukebox would have literally every song ever recorded; you'd be able to play whatever you want, whenever you want, wherever you are.

"The distribution of intellectual property will eventually atrophy and disappear," says Jim Griffin, former director of technology for Geffen Records. "It will not be downloaded; it will not be distributed." It will, in short, be broadcast. "If we can have all the music we want, wherever we are, and whenever we want it, in a future of ubiquitous connectivity, why would we carry it around with us?" Griffin asks. The answer is clear: we wouldn't.

"The device we know of as a CD player will eventually be replaced by a cabinet with a hard drive connected to a broadcast network," writes J. William Gurley, a general partner with Hummer Winblad Venture Partners. "[It] will have unlimited and immediate access to songs and have a virtually unlimited number of features . . ."[9] In short, asks Gurley, why bother to maintain a host of troublesome mechanical devices and parts that are superfluous in the age of digital transmission on demand? "The only reason to have physical copies of content is because we're insecure about the efficiency and availability of the system that could deliver it to us," points out Griffin. Once we feel secure in the new digital world—and confident that our favorite recording of "Stairway to Heaven" will be available to us whenever we need it—our emotional need for a CD or tape to be sitting on our living room shelf will disappear.

The way this would work is that a music system of the future would consist of a player, with new kinds of controls for selecting music, a network connection, and an on-line music service.

The Player. We'd all still have devices that would play the music, and the controls might even look a lot like our familiar CD player buttons (play, stop, pause, fast forward, and so on). Also, it might have controls like the preset buttons on our radios. These devices will certainly come in many shapes and sizes and some will be portable.

The Selecto-Matic. In place of all that dusty stuff that's filling our shelves (stacks of CDs, tapes, and LPs), we'd have a few more device controls for selecting the music. Possibly not unlike the menu systems we use today to select material on an Internet web site. Click enough times (or talk to it, if it has voice recognition) and you finally get to the music you want to hear. With imaginative new ways to select the material—not just by artist, song name, or genre—the devices would learn what we liked to hear, and would be able to offer us more of that kind of material. This technology exists today. Tuners from Spinner.com and Imagine Radio are good examples.

What do these components add up to? They compose the ultimate jukebox. A network connection to a music service is potentially like the perfect, ultimate jukebox. It would have everything that has ever been recorded, would play whatever was requested instantaneously with CD-quality audio (or better), would be available anywhere on the planet, and of course, would be totally free to use. There would be no media, no grooves, but all the music in the world. Hal Hall would approve.

■ AN EPIC STORY

The grand finale, the pièce de résistance, may be the transformation of the record business into the broadcaster model, in which advertising pays for everything, and you the consumer get it for free—well, at least without paying dollars. (As we've observed before, there's no such thing as a free lunch. So, you're paying somehow—probably by being fed a steady stream of advertisements.)

■ CENTS AND SENSIBILITY

All these changing roles have opened the possibility that someday you may not have to pay for records any more. If this ever happens, it will be nothing less than turning the music industry's business model on its head. Nevertheless, it could possibly work out exceedingly well for everyone. For now, we'll introduce why this could possibly eventually happen, and then later on, we'll talk about the enabling factors, consequences, timing, and how this would coexist with traditional business approaches for decades.

Of course, it's a somewhat ironic notion that the best way to earn colossal profits is to give away all your content absolutely for free. But this is not as profoundly stupid as it may appear on first glance. After all, television and radio broadcasters do exactly that, and collectively they have annual domestic advertising revenues of almost $70 billion.

So, if records are free, how are record companies going to thrive? Like broadcasters and retailers, when offering free content, there are potential revenue sources from advertising, subscriptions, and sales. Music companies are already, to varying degrees, seriously considering this prospect.

Here's the reason it's all possible: music is a bargain. It's the least costly of all the media we pay for. The average record buyer buys $60 of music every year, and listens to those paid-for albums an average of 289 hours. This means that the cost per hour is just 60 cents; the cost per minute is less than $1/3$ of a cent. This is just a fraction of the cost of a local phone call; it's less than the cost of a long-distance phone call; it's less than the cost of a cellular phone call;

and it's less than the cost of watching a pay-per-view movie on TV.

So what? So, because the cost to play music is so low, it can be combined with some other service, and be offered for free. In Chapter 10 ["Brought to You by . . . (Networks)"], we'll see that's exactly what might happen when phone companies start to offer consumer broadband services. When AT&T bought TCI, the chances of this eventually happening soared.

Don't expect this to happen overnight, however. Record company executives aren't going to wake up one morning and want to start giving away what amounts to a $40 billion business. It's going to take more than just a compelling idea—even if it's totally cool, technically speaking. It's going to happen if, and only if, three major forces all come into place:

1. The relevant technologies must exist, be widely deployed, easy to use, and priced to make sense for the average consumer.
2. The record companies need sensible business models (and the right alliances) that address the needs of everyone in the food chain (artists, manufacturers, retailers, distributors, and consumers).
3. There need to be compelling reasons for changing from the pay-to-own (or pay-per-listen) and the advertiser-supported broadcaster revenue model.

Because these same issues affect all entertainment industries entering the Digital Age, we'll spend three chapters discussing them:

Chapter 9 ["Brought to You by . . . (Ads)"]. About money and profit: who pays, how much, and why. The profit motive is the universal solvent here, and it is one of the most important factors in breaking institutional barriers and reshaping oligopolies. Slowly and conservatively, as befits a rather stable oligopoly with a very profitable cash cow, they are starting to deploy and test these new technologies and business approaches.

Chapter 10 ["Brought to You by . . . (Networks)"]. About the enabling technology that remains to be accomplished—bandwidth and network capacity for mass-market, quality, cost-effective solutions; new user interfaces for new devices; and when we can expect to see these technologies deployed. Today, there's still a very long way to go, but significant technological progress is being made. Overall, it looks as if all the right technologies will become available, and with attractive price points.

Chapter 11 ("Family Feud"). About how entertainment industries are all growing into each others' territories, with the disintermediation and remediation that will reshape these markets. It's about broken marriages, leading to new partnerships, new alliances, and new forms of entertainment.

Before we get to those discussions, however, we're going to take a closer look at one more entertainment medium: television. After all, if it's a good and profitable idea to give away your content, why are television broadcasters currently looking at the money-making opportunities in digital TV as dismally small? And, why are television broadcasters looking at this technology, although long anticipated, as something they now wish they hadn't wished for?

Why interactivity, more than high-definition video, is key to the success of digital TV.

Chapter

Tube or Not Tube

That is the question.
Whether 'tis no blur in the mind.

*"The interesting thing about the interactive forms of entertainment is
we only need to call it interactive now because this is the first century
in which we've had non-interactive forms of entertainment: radio,
TV, movies and so on. All non-interactive."*

—DOUGLAS ADAMS, author, producer, computer game developer

*"Play is inherently interactive. You can't play with other people with-
out being interactive. But all other forms of entertainment are not interactive. And never will be."*

—RICHARD HART, Emmy award–winning producer and on-air host of
C-Net Central

Just for a moment, try to think of something that's *not* on
the Internet—something really, really big. Hard, isn't it?
The Internet has just about everything. As we've seen in
earlier chapters, everything from island music from the
Bahamas to complete transcripts of Congressional sub-
committees can be found there. But there *is* something
largely still missing and—interestingly enough—it's the
medium we're most dependent upon for amusement.
That's right, video, or rather, that mixture of video and
audio delivered to our homes that we call *television*.

We like television a lot, and the statistics, as you prob-ably know, are dismal. On average, we each spend more than 1,500 hours a year watching TV. That's more than four hours a day per person. But slowly, and surely, we're increasing the time we spend surfing the Web, largely at the expense of our TV viewing.

Still, the vast majority of Web surfing we do is done without the key attributes of this fundamental entertain-ment media we've come to be so dependent upon. We'd consider it very odd, and not very entertaining, to turn on a television set and see only static text, some fixed images, or perhaps some primitive animation. Yet, that's what we're used to seeing when we surf the Net.

True, the Internet is starting to be a less silent universe, thanks to pioneers in Internet radio and recorded music venues, but video is largely missing in action. There are several reasons for this, not the least of which is the lim-ited network bandwidth available to the average consumer, as well as the absence of a decent broadcast revenue model. We're already seeing this change, as evidenced by the popularity of several web sites and events:

➤ Live and on-demand video news from CNN, Bloomberg Television, and Fox. You could have watched the infamous grand jury testimony of Pres-ident Clinton, or the approach of Hurricane Georges from a Web camera in Key West.

➤ A growing array of wildly eclectic home videos: Jen-niCam (a woman whose video camera broadcasts everything that goes on in her bedroom), a live childbirth (seen by more than a million people), and the false promise (or was it a threat?) of a cou-ple having their first sexual encounter broadcast live on the Internet.

➤ Reruns of some of your favorite TV episodes—check out AENTV.com.

➤ An increasing number of professionally produced, made-for-Internet videos that attempt to explore the borders of this new media form. For example, *Monster Home* (a B horror movie meets quiz show meets Yahoo), marries elements of film, computer games, and Internet surfing in a mock horror movie that you can only view via the Web (www.monster-home.com).

➤ Celebrity appearances on the Web that allow wired viewers to both see and hear such contemporary idols as Don Imus, Rush Limbaugh, and Willie Nelson, and to participate as if they were in the studio audience by sending in their questions via e-mail and fax.

In just a few years, video should be commonplace for the average Web surfer. What this has to do with what we currently categorize as broadcast TV, and why the Internet might have a major role in the future of television, are the subjects of this chapter.

Yes, perhaps not surprisingly the digital video experience of the future will be both *entirely similar* and *entirely different* to what we've long been used to. In other words, what do you get when you cross television with the Internet? You get something completely different, and that difference has to do with interactivity.

In earlier chapters, we've talked about how various degrees of interactivity will affect other entertainment media, and the change couldn't be more profound for television. Television broadcasters have always had one goal in mind: to have as many viewers as possible, watching for as long as possible. Their dream is a populace that does nothing but watch television—passive in everything, except to turn on their channel whenever we're not watching their network(s). Interactivity is exactly the opposite of this passive viewing: they will now want us to do something. For an interactive TV venture to succeed—and although there have been many trials, none has succeeded thus far—it must make us, the viewers, want to do something in a way that somehow increases its revenue. How—and if—existing TV players decide to incorporate various modes of interactivity into their offerings could change the future of the media forever.

■ AND SOMETHING COMPLETELY SIMILAR

What's not going to change is human nature. We're still going to want to be entertained. We're still going to want to see our favorite actors, storytellers, and athletes perform for our amusement. We may or may not want to exert ourselves while being entertained. (After all, there's a reason we're in front of the television and not at the bowling alley.) In many ways, we'll continue as we have been doing for the last 100 years, passive recipients of whatever the entertainers choose (or are able) to deliver to us.

Yet, visionaries like Disney's Michael Eisner, who don't think that traditional passive forms of watching television and movies will ever go away, also passionately believe in the brave new world of interactivity. Speaking at the 1998 Society of Business Editors and Writers Annual Conference, Eisner said:

> I don't think passive television is going to disappear anymore than movies disappeared when television came in or radio disappeared when movies came in. I think the passive meaning of being entertained—with comedy shows, and dramas, and football shows, and all the rest—will all stay the way it is.

> But there'll be—particularly with kids, and they'll lead the way I believe—"interactivity." A different form of television which will be a combination of television and the interactive world you're starting to see on the Internet. A completely new medium. It is as much a revolution to television as television was to motion pictures, and as much as motion pictures were to radio. I think the Internet, and this idea of being connected to everybody else in the world is, really, to

*me, the excitement of going into the next century. It
really is as much a leap as what television is. [Which
is why] we're investing as if it's going to be.*

In short, Eisner realizes that the largely passive medium of
viewing the mixture of images and sound that we call television is a very effective, very lucrative, and very big business.

We can witness, in the comfort of our living rooms, the
graphic horror of the Zapruder videotape; the tragic explosion of the space shuttle *Challenger;* the grace of Martin
Luther King as he tells us, "I have a dream." Television is
compelling—the emotional angst exhibited when *Seinfeld*
came to an end proves that, if nothing else. But, perhaps
more important, it's easy to access. It comes directly to us,
largely without technical hassles, and is organized in a
way, using channels, schedules, and time slots, that we're
comfortable with.

Television is powerful, and it's easily accessible. That's
why it's such good business. And, that is why certain
things will never change.

■ YOU AIN'T SEEN NUTHIN' YET

Don't get too comfortable on your couch, because the possibilities of what this media we now call television can do
are about to explode. In fact, the coming changes are so
fundamental, that we might need to call it something
other than *television* (derived from Latin and meaning *distance viewing*). It will no longer be just about passive viewing; it will be interactive and participatory, and will
involve all the other media (text, graphics, audio, and animation). Also, the various forms that interactivity can
take will begin to meld into television, regardless of how
we receive the programming—whether through traditional broadcast, satellite, cable, or Internet.

In the United States, we receive the major network
television broadcasts in a number of ways. A full 67 per-

cent of households receive them via cable services (such as Time Warner and TCI), 10 percent receive them via satellite services (such as DirecTV and EchoStar), and the rest of us use good old TV antennas. In the not-too-distant future, we'll also have other ways to receive television as well: via telephone, Internet, and wireless services (all of which we'll cover in Chapter 10 ["Brought to You by . . . (Networks)"]. We'll shortly see why television via the Internet is a harbinger of what's to come; still, however we receive television, it's going to be a new combination of passive viewing and interactivity. It's going to be different.

For starters, the concept of program schedules will seem archaic. We won't have to watch *ER* after *Seinfeld*. We'll stop thinking of Sunday night as the night we must watch or tape *Sixty Minutes*. Instead, we'll watch television like we read the morning newspaper: in whatever order makes sense to us. We don't have to read the newspaper in strictly sequential-page order. We can read the front page headlines first, then the local weather, then the technology news, and finish up with the local weather. The same will go for watching television: we'll watch what we want in the order that makes sense to us—that day, right now, or tomorrow. Bookstores are often organized by topic, and someday so will the viewing options that TV services offer.

On-line guides to TV content, such as *UltimateTV, OnNow,* and *AENTV,* are already starting to morph from the old-style matrix (programs by channel at a certain time) into content categories.

Another big difference will be the greatly expanded list of options of *what* to watch. It will be more than just sitcoms, soaps, talk shows, and news; rather, it will be a smorgasbord of offerings, and they won't fit into today's cookie cutter shapes. For example, they won't all have to fit into 30-minute slots, and so there'll be pieces of 5, 7, and 13 minutes. For instance, one television special, *Casino,* which was produced for ABC Television, was later made available on the Internet as a sequence of four-minute segments—without commercials!

Possibly, most important, programs won't necessarily have the same lowest-common-denominator themes as prime-time television currently has. Commenting on whether diversity of choice leads to the pursuit of excellence, George Gilder, futurist author and professor at Harvard University, says, "Choice is crucial to the advance of civilization and culture. The book market thrives on diversity of offerings, and represents a morally superior environment to movies or television. The book market is epitomized by the pursuit of excellence. Broadcast networks pursue the lowest common denominator, and have a bias towards prurient interest, morbid fears, and anxieties. Choice leads towards the pursuit of excellence. The Internet is going to emerge as a gigantic book market, that will transform and uplift."[1]

To everyone who points to the current woeful lack of quality offerings, despite the expected arrival of 500-channel cable or satellite offerings, the cable TV business has just pulled ahead of the broadcast TV networks in both combined viewership and revenue. Aggregation has worked very well for the cable networks.

"The blessing and curse of the Internet is that there are so many choices," points out Richard Hart. "5,000 channels isn't necessarily better than 50 channels. In many ways it's worse. So we have to turn to someone we can rely on to help us sort through all this. There has to be an intermediary to help people wade through this, and it won't be automated software. Computers will never customize the web for me. It has to be people doing this."

It just isn't a good assumption that if you like one program in a genre, you'll like another. Some people don't even like all of the spin-offs from the same program. Just because you like *Star Trek: The Next Generation* doesn't mean that you'll like any of the other *Star Trek* spin-offs, let alone different sci-fi programs such as *Earth-2* and *Babylon/5*. Computers just don't do a good job at such subjective comparisons and linkages, which is why Amazon.com and reel.com have an expert staff of people who make editorial decisions for related book and movie suggestions.

In short, other people will soon step in and *help* us to make our television viewing decisions. This is something network programmers have always done, of course, but in their case, we're not allowed to see what they don't like. Now we'll be able to take or leave the advice of people who will help us sort through the chaos.

We'll gravitate to the people who steer us most closely to what we like: Studs Terkel, Terry Gross, Jim Svejda, and Siskel and Ebert. And what this means, when there are thousands of channels from around the world to tune into, and new guides (rather than gatekeepers) to help consumers choose the best products, is that today's network heavyweight broadcasters will continue to see erosion of their power base. After all, their captive audience, which is what advertisers pay for, will no longer be quite so captive. Gary Arlen says, "It marks the beginning of a fundamental shift, akin to the move from newspapers to radio, movies and newsreels three generations ago."

■ IT'S BEEN A LONG TIME COMING

Interactive television has been "in the works" for some time, of course; though, "in the never works" might be a more accurate description. Mostly, it's a story of overblown expectations and expensive failures (though that's common to the ongoing march of technological progress, and therefore, not all bad). Here are a few of the most publicized flops:

> ➤ Time Warner's Full Service Network (FSN), launched in 1994, flopped by 1997. FSN offered movies on demand, a customized news service, video games, a guide to local businesses (in Orlando, Florida), interactive shopping, and a lot more.

> ➤ Tele-TV, arguably the biggest flop of all, was a consortium of telephone companies, managed by top

network TV executives. Announced in 1994, it terminated just two years later, having spent (wasted) nearly $400 million. All they ever tested in deployment trials was movies on demand. Media technology analyst Rob Glidden says this was "the telcos rattling their sabers to scare the cable companies away from entering the telephone business."

➤ The "Deal of the Century" between Bell Atlantic and TCI was announced in 1993. Although it was intended to provide a lot more than just interactive TV services, it was halted just 18 months later, having accomplished nothing at all.

The common cause of these failures was the "absence of a common deployment environment for products," says Rick Ducey, the NAB's VP of technology. "Since there was no common deployment environment for products, each new provider had to come up with a custom solution for yet another thing to hook into the TV set. And the user interfaces were clunky, and techno-geeky."

It hasn't all been bad news, of course, and Glidden says that OpenTV, a partnership between Sun Microsystems, SGS Thomson, and Television Par Satellite (TPS), is actually an excellent proof of concept. OpenTV provides technology for digital TV broadcasters. OpenTV has grown its subscriber base in Europe to more than 1 million households, and it's making inroads on other continents. Using satellite network technology, it's a successful business, and it proves the value of interactivity.

■ A GOVERNMENT MANDATE

Over time, the term "interactive," when used with television, became synonymous with "digital." By the mid-1990s, it became clear that the largely analog world of television needed a firm push before it would venture into the brave new world of digital media. When your analog TV (where you can change channels, volume, and not a lot else) is replaced by digital TV, your TV will be able to do just about anything your desktop PC does.

The FCC, which sets the standards for broadcast television, has decided that the time has come for digital TV. With the help of the U.S. Congress, it has placed broadcasters under quite a bit of pressure to deploy digital TV (DTV) broadcasting, with mandates for both regulatory and broadcasting rollout. And, FCC mandates are always taken seriously by broadcasters, because the FCC can withdraw their broadcast licenses at will.

Why is the FCC in such haste to implement DTV? According to Ducey, "it's a government imperative to (a) get spectrum back for auction now allocated to analog television; (b) to stimulate the domestic microelectronics industry; and to (c) provide a better service for the American public."[2] So, in 1997, the FCC set an ambitious schedule in place for DTV deployment. Knowing it would take some time before consumers would replace their current TV equipment with digital TV receivers (or install converters that could convert digital signals), the FCC assumed traditional analog broadcasts would continue before digital TV was widely accepted. It therefore made TV stations an offer they couldn't refuse: in exchange for agreeing to a breathtakingly rapid DTV deployment rollout, existing television stations were given free licenses for broadcasting digital content for a separate channel for each analog channel they operated.

Breathtaking may be an understatement. By the end of 1998, TV broadcasters had committed to start digital program transmissions in the 10 largest markets (New York, Los Angeles, and so on). By May 1999, 30 percent of all stations promise to be transmitting digitally; by December 1999, a full 50 percent of all stations will be providing DTV programming; and by May 2002, 100 percent of the TV commercial stations in the United States will be transmitting digitally. This is much faster than most industries have ever been able to rework an existing infra-structure.

More than anything, the problems inherent in actually deploying DTV are economic rather than technical. The biggest initial hurdle is the total lack of capable, affordable receivers (no one has a digital TV). There are also difficulties obtaining local government approval for setting up new TV towers, and there is considerable expense upgrading to the necessary digital equipment. But, in the end, the biggest question of all has to do with business models: how to provide offsetting revenues for what is now an all-expenses proposition. Or, as Rick Ducey says, "the real question is will anyone come to the DTV party?"

In short, the transition to digital television is fraught with difficult and largely unanswered questions; there are unresolved technical standards issues; there are conflicts with cable operators over carriage, which is how the cable industry refers to carrying network TV broadcasts; there is a dearth of digital content (because there's no audience to watch it, and no digital TVs to watch it on). And, questions about the DTV business model abound. Does anyone have one?

No network knows with any certainty what's going to make sense in a couple of years. What they do know is that their business today is 100 percent dependent on advertising, and that is always subject to prevailing economic conditions—the general economy plays a major role in advertiser and consumer spending. Ducey says, "One thing's clear, business models must address new revenue streams while not overdoing expenses. It's a tough balance to reach while developing new markets."

As we'll see later, interactivity will bring the most dramatic changes of all for advertisers, with entirely new kinds of relationships with consumers, and new ways of doing business. Chapter 9 ["Brought to You by . . . (Ads)"], is about how the ad business will change for all media, and how it will thereby force changes in the way all media do business.

■ GODZILLA GENTLY PLACES A TOE IN THE OCEAN

The entertainment business in the late twentieth century will, in retrospect, be seen as a cannibalistic scramble of mergers and acquisitions. The large entertainment conglomerates largely got that way by conglomerating, like giant sticky balls of taffy, getting larger and larger as they collided: Time meets Warner (publishing meets movies and cable), Time Warner meets Turner (to add more cable); Capital Cities meets ABC (group TV station owner takes over the network), Disney meets Cap Cities; Seagram's meets Universal/MCA, and so on. The 1980s and 1990s were rampant with merger mania.

"As it happens in many other industries, the cost of capital and the amount of it required for operations becomes a formidable barrier to entry," Hal Vogel observes. "Most entertainment industry segments thus came to be ruled by large companies with relatively easy access to large pools of capital."[3] Rob Glidden adds, "there are significant competitive advantages to vertical integration." That's why it's so interesting to see how, in addition to their forced march into broadcast digital television, some major broadcasters are stepping rather gingerly and cautiously into the brave new world of Internet broadcasting.

■ SOME MORE QUICKLY THAN OTHERS

Like it or not, it's already begun to happen on the Internet. Just as we saw in radio broadcast and recorded music industries, there's nothing to stop literally anyone from being an Internet broadcaster. There are no government agencies to get approvals from, or assigned broadcast spectrum. There are no legal limits on how many channels you can own in the market, or in the entire nation. Just use some very inexpensive, off-the-shelf software and hardware, and you're ready to broadcast (assuming you have something to broadcast).

The same caveats we described in Chapter 5 ["Stop Making (Radio) Waves"] about the quality of audio that one can expect to receive over narrowband connections apply even greater to video. Over low-bandwidth connections, you should expect to see melted heads in tiny windows with barely acceptable audio quality.

Naturally, all TV broadcasters currently have some sort of presence on the Web. As in just about any other business in any other industry, they can't afford to be left out. There's quite a difference, however, in just how deeply they're embracing the Internet—and in their vision of how it will affect the future of television broadcasts.

Disney, NBC, and Time Warner Turner have deeply committed themselves to the Internet as a future broadcast medium. CBS, Fox, and UPN have somewhat more tenuously dipped their toes in this possible future mass medium. Here's a snapshot of what these major networks are doing on the Web.

➤ Disney, along with its ABC and ESPN subsidiaries, has begun to invest heavily in the Internet. It owns such popular sites as ABC.com, ESPN's SportsZone, and its own Disney Blast, all of which are high-traffic sites (drawing millions of unique visitors every day, and always in the top 20 most popular web sites). Collectively, all of Disney's sites are the third or fourth most popular sites on the entire Web. In 1997, Disney launched Disney Blast, its Web portal for kids, which has games, comics, and live events for its subscribers. Disney Blast is one of the few profitable content subscription services on the Web.

Disney uses every opportunity to cross-promote all of its news, sports, and entertainment properties across a broad range of potential audiences. For example, ABC's "One Saturday Morning" site mentions ABC just once, but mentions Disney a dozen times, and could easily be confused for Disney's kid portal. And their ESPN SportsZone site has links to their ABC News site, which has links to their Disney site, and other entertainment sites they own. "Our goal is to link all of our sites, very deeply," says David Geller, director of engineering at Starwave (a company that Disney acquired to produce and operate all of its web operations).

➤ NBC is investing heavily in the Internet, too. Its MSNBC cable and Internet partnership with Microsoft has been steadily garnering a growing and loyal audience on both traditional broadcast channels as well as on the Internet (www.msnbc.com), and it hasn't exactly set the world on fire. Despite ferocious promotion from both of its parents, Microsoft and General Electric's NBC. It's worth noting that Microsoft and GE have the two highest market valuations of publicly traded companies in the United States (roughly $200 billion each). So, it's not as if they lack the resources to promote anything they want.

But when NBC purchased a significant equity stake in, and placed its own executives in key management positions at, a rather unknown Internet operation in San Francisco, they signaled exactly where they really wanted to go today. The San Francisco–based start-up is C-Net, and it is one of the most accomplished, if not most profitable, of on-line news services. It's located in a building (not far from San Francisco's Colt Tower) that was once a sugar factory, and was home to TV's Quinn-Martin Productions (whose popular series included *The Fugitive* and *The Streets of San Francisco*). C-Net has been leading a revolution in how we can use the Internet to get our news. C-Net, seeing the opportunity to grow into a portal as successful as Yahoo!, created Snap!, which is one of NBC's most important Internet investments, because it's going to be a place where broadcast meets the Internet.

Richard Hart is an Emmy award–winning producer (*The Next Step*), veteran broadcaster, and C-Net founder. Here's how he described Snap!: "What distinguished Snap! from the beginning, was something that would be customized for you by people. A staff who peruse everything you're interested in, and make a human editorial decision about what to show you." This is exactly the same as Stuart Skorman's goal at reel.com—to customize their content for you, but preserve the human touch that makes all the difference.

➤ Time Warner Turner (TWT) has been investing heavily in the interactive future of television since the late 1980s, and despite its failed Full Service Network trial, it owns CNN—and its group of related sites where broadcast has successfully met the Internet. CNN's family of sites—CNN.com (news), CNNSI.com (sports), CNNfn.com (financials)—are all among the most popular web sites (collectively, they're always among the top 10 most popular web sites), not to mention Time Warner's Pathfinder site, which hosts content from the rest of Time Warner's enormous publishing empire (such as its magazines like *Time, People, Money, Fortune*).

It's not that CBS, News Corp's Fox, and Viacom's UPN have been ignoring the Internet. They're not. Each one has a web site; they do a good job of covering news, sports, local weather, financial matters, and links for their on-air programming. Their investment strategies, however, seem quite tame in comparison to Disney, NBC, and Time Warner Turner.

Gary Arlen, president of Arlen Communications, and an oft-quoted media analyst, compares the networks this way: "NBC has established itself as a leader, not only because of its MSNBC relationship and recent Snap investment, but also its experiments with Intel's Intercast, its work on Interactive Neighborhoods. Disney now gets it (Infoseek, Starwave acquisitions) and ABC.com is a real factor. CBS would like this to go away."

Arlen reflects on the entertainment conglomerates that see the importance of the Internet: "Some get it more than others. Sony gets a lot of it. Time Warner thinks it does, and some units get it. Universal was clueless, but Diller may enlighten it."

Rupert Murdoch, chairman of News Corp, has repeatedly made his views known that he sees the future as news, entertainment, and sports—delivered by *his* satellites. "News Corp has focused on satellite delivery to establish itself as an independent player, not dependent on entrenched network providers such as cable and telco," says Peter Krasilovsky, senior analyst at Arlen Communications. "In the end this allows News Corp to be a stand alone provider of services, though they do deals with other industries, so they can be in the driver's seat."

Although CBS has made several successful ventures into the Internet with CBS Sportsline (a leading Internet media company that provides sports-related news, programming, and merchandise to sports fans worldwide) and CBS Marketwatch (its full-service financial investment site), it has not yet begun Internet video broadcast. Richard Hart, who spent the first 10 years of his career at CBS's San Francisco affiliate KPIX, says, "CBS blew it long ago. It has missed every opportunity to get into new media. It didn't even invest in cable."

Why all the concern about choosing a platform—the Internet, satellite, traditional broadcast—for digital television? Predicting the future of interactive television, and trying to invest up front in the appropriate platform, is a very risky business, as we've seen with a brief review of expensive false starts and failed attempts.

■ A NEW KIND OF TELEVISION

There's just too much at stake to ignore: the major TV broadcasters own the mass-market audience that all other entertainment media envy. Collectively, U.S. citizens watch 300 billion hours of TV a year. Advertisers simply have no better, more economical, way to reach that mass market. What's at stake is their $40 billion a year in advertising spending. Chapter 10 ["Brought to You by . . . (Networks)"] is all about how these alternative delivery systems will compete.

It's this simple, if the networks don't provide this new kind of interactive television, someone else will. There has always been a very small number of outlets for television producers to air their creative wares: the four commercial networks, PBS, cable, and satellite TV. No matter how digital interactive television gets delivered (to your TV via cable or satellite, or to your PC via the Web), that's no longer going to be a limiting factor.

We've seen how the record industry has a multitude of independent labels, and the book publishing industry has the small press, to create and test new kinds of material. The television world is about to experience the same sort of Renaissance, creatively. It will eventually have an emerging class of new and powerful independent producers that are able to reach their audience directly, without all of the many limitations (regulatory, artistic, and commercial).

Experimentation has already begun. An entirely new class of video experience is being invented for the Internet-viewing audience. What's learned here will be the basis for what the major broadcasters decide to do, however television is distributed, and whether they'll succeed.

➤ In 1998, six Japanese war criminals came forth to publicly atone for war crimes they had committed in China more than 50 years ago during World War II. Because U.S. laws prohibit granting visas to convicted war criminals, the opportunity arose to use television and the Web as a means to broadcast the event to the world. These men offered their statements via live video feed and answered questions from a panel of U.S. academics—far too little, too late, some would say, but certainly a hint of the powerful possibilities of how digital connections in the modern world can play out.

➤ Alternative Entertainment TV (www.aentv.com) already offers a wide range of video programs on the Internet: comedy, drama, sports, historical events, business, TV classics, specials, and more. Click on aentv.com and you can watch a live comedy webcast from the Improv, in Los Angeles. Or, you can watch an entire show (complete with the original ads) of *Abbott and Costello, Milton Berle, Topper, The $64,000 Question, The Cisco Kid,* or *This Is Your Life*).

➤ Tune into Rick Siegel's OnlineTV site, where you can watch live, and on demand, concerts from some of New York's hottest dance clubs, as well as music videos from across a wide range of genres. Siegel is happily ensconced in his plush new offices on Manhattan's Upper East Side ("a result of a very lucrative deal"), although he spends a lot of time in the dance clubs from which his company broadcasts ("the things I do for Rock and Roll," he says, gleefully). Rick claims to have been in the entertainment business since he was three years old, adding that he's now "four and a half." (Some of his fellow webcasters might not dispute this.) OnlineTV broadcasts live from some of the most popular dance clubs in New York City, and it also hosts new talent.

Advertisers seem to like the mix and audience, and OnlineTV has regular ads for large companies such as Budweiser and Seagrams. MTV won't lose any sleep over this, but if OnlineTV (or someone like them) grows its audience, they can eventually become a genuine competitor. If they don't, someone else will sure try.

■ OUR PROGRAMMING CAN GENERATE MORE MONEY THAN YOUR SLUDGE CAN

Now, it's one thing to have a wide range of cool content available, but it's quite another thing to make this a profitable business. Business models need to be revised to match these new broadcast opportunities, and this will send shock waves throughout the television industry, just as it's doing in radio and recorded music. Let's start by examining the relationship between the TV network and its local affiliate stations.

Peter Dougherty is president of Digital Bitcasting Corp. (DBC), which provides software solutions for companies that want to broadcast live video events via the Internet. Their impressive list of prominent customers includes Playboy, Boeing, and NorTel. Playboy broadcasts video content to its subscribers, and companies like Boeing and Nortel use the DBC technology for intracompany broadcasts and customer support.

Dougherty grew up in the television industry. His father was general manager of a local TV station in Boston. Later on, he took over as president of the broadcast division of Capital Cities Communications for 18 years, continuing on after Cap Cities purchased the ABC Television Network. Dougherty himself has 14 years' experience in sales and management at Fox and ABC.

Local TV network affiliates are very similar to local radio stations, argues Dougherty, in that local "brand awareness" is key—especially for news. After all, 45 percent of television advertising is from local businesses, and most of that is dependent on the local news broadcast. "The question is," he asks, "when you go to the web, how does that business model translate?"

Before the advent of Internet broadcasting, television stations have had little choice but to pick a powerful network partner, and the locals aren't always happy with the deal the networks have offered them. "The problems between the networks and their affiliates is the way they try to aggregate the affiliates content. They do it with the stupid network mentality of let's force our content and branding on them, and for just 20% of the ad revenue, the affiliates run away from them. So the locals are ripe for another aggregator who will offer them their own true brand, unless the network has some kind of economic pull on them."

Dougherty goes on to explain that that's okay when the ratings are high, but "when the networks screw up their programming like ABC or CBS, the only strength they (the local stations) have is news." The reason is that when prime-time lineup isn't helping the stations much, 4:00 P.M. through 7:00 P.M. is where the majority of their programming revenue comes from (with local spots). "They might say thanks for saving our ass with NFC programming, but when it comes to 11:30pm every weekday evening, we're going to preempt your programming because our local programming can generate a lot more money for us than your sludge is."

So, the local stations want a better deal from their network partner, and are ripe for better opportunities—namely, deals in which they can improve their *local* brand. The Internet is creating the kinds of opportunities they want, such as new audience aggregators like Broadcast.com.

For their part, the networks would just as soon have a less expensive way to distribute their programming than local stations. Someday, though few would admit this, they'd like to be their own distributor. Satellite would be nice; so, too, would be the Internet—as soon as there are enough people with the right kind of access bandwidth.

■ I LIKE AGGREGATORS SO MUCH, I BECAME ONE

Dougherty thinks that local TV stations will eagerly partner with aggregators like Broadcast.com. AENTV's Drew Cummings thinks the same: "The Internet is a new medium, and there is no reason we can't learn from the evolving business models of other media and adapt and modify them to fit our own needs. Joining together to finance the production of new streaming media content is the future."

It's not just that people are impressed with Broadcast.com's IPO results. Aggregation and syndication have long been staples of the broadcast business. It's hard to become an aggregator and syndicator for the simple reason that it takes a broad audience. Until you have enough of an audience, you don't have enough of an income to cover your costs, and that takes time and a lot of money.

Drew Cummings had an idea to short-circuit that problem, which involves appropriating the basic television syndication model. A group of stations come together and fund production of a television series. They then air that program on their own stations, and they also get a share in the profits if that program is sold to stations not involved in the original agreement.

Therefore, his idea is to simply use that business model on the Internet. "Just apply this business model to the production of original video content on the Internet with a number of high traffic–high profile web-sites that do not compete," says Cummings. In other words, if a few high-traffic Internet video sites get together, they can pull together a large enough aggregate audience to sell enough ads to cover their costs—and then some. The coproduction partners would each have substantial existing traffic, and the aggregate of the traffic and the ad inventory could make this a profitable venture almost from inception.

➤ Or Both (Thanks to Deion Sanders)

Noel Moore, a veteran Canadian broadcaster, believes the right financial model for a commercial project of this sort would be a combined webcast-cablecast production. Essentially, the people funding the production would hedge their bets by funding the webcast through sales of the pro-

gram to cable television. After all, cable currently has
48,000 leased access channels just screaming for content.

"Each cable system in the U.S. has four channels available for leased access. They can sell ads on each of these.
Local programs sell," says Moore. Next question: how do
you get local content in a network program? Simple—use
the Internet. "Most of the cable systems are online. You
make a profit sharing deal online—then allow holes in the
lineup to insert local content—produced locally," says
Moore. What's in it for the cable companies? A free program, plus 60 percent of the advertising revenue from
local advertisers. "All you need is a critical mass of content
and audience," says Moore.

➤ Portalopoly

Better profit margins certainly aren't the only reasons
that television producers are interested in the Internet. If
the end game for winning the battle of the eyeballs is to become a *portal* (one of the most popular sites) on the Internet, then content creators have just as much chance as
anyone to win that role, as much chance as today's major
broadcasters, which is why *they* want to be portals, too.

If Camille Alcasid, director of new technologies at *UltimateTV* (www.ultimatetv.com) has her way, then she's
going to be that portal. UltimateTV is determined to be the
premiere on-line guide to everything about TV. (Notice, we
didn't call it *TV Guide,* but that's the idea.) Not only can
you check out the TV listings for your area (and cable and
satellite), you can actually watch previews of the shows. In
1998, UltimateTV, in collaboration with Rysher Entertainment, actually broadcasted the first episode of a new TV
program on the Internet—before its broadcast premiere on
regular television. The show was the first episode of *High-
lander: The Raven,* and "this was a historical first for both
TV and the Internet, as a television series had never before
been sneaked to an online audience prior to its TV debut."[4]

Naturally, UltimateTV will have competition, including *TV Guide* itself, the broadcast networks, and all the

other megaentertainment sites who would like everyone to come first through *their* front door on the way to wherever you're headed. Think of the potential ad revenues. NBC did, and invested in Snap!, which is essentially the same strategy that audience aggregators like Broadcast.com are using. Bring enough return visitors to your site, through whatever means, and you'll generate significant ad revenue (direct and bartered). For all the amusements that television broadcasters have in store for us in the interactive world, the real issue for them is (increasingly) finding new ways to generate revenue.

Think about it: the average person already watches five hours of TV a day. There's not a lot of time left to watch more. Then, you've got other entertainment media—from traditional radio, movies, and books, to the Internet—competing for the attention of consumers, and many more television channels to choose from when the TV is on. All of this signals the likely fact that television advertising revenue won't be growing significantly, which means that TV broadcasters will have to find another, different, way to massively grow their revenues.

Although advertising will surely remain the steadfast core of TV revenue for decades to come, broadcasters will soon be adding the only other way there is to make money with broadcasting—they'll try to sell us something—anything—everything. Dr. Joseph Kearney, vice president at A.T. Kearney, says there are only three ways to make money: "advertising, subscription, and transactions."

This is exactly where interactivity comes in to the equation. We've already seen how radio broadcasters and record distributors are using the interactive elements of the Internet to target and sell products and services on the Web. Television broadcasters don't want to be left behind in the race to empty our pocketbooks. Interactive TV, like it or not, is their best shot at selling us something. Click here. Buy now. Don't delay. While supplies last. Only available on TV.

What's new, you say? That's the way it's always been: endless advertisements that urge us to buy. Yes, we've always

had advertising, but this time it's the broadcasters themselves who want to sell us something. They want to become
our shopping mall; Hence, the Home Shopping Network,
QVC (which, they say, stands for Quality, Value, and Convenience[5]), WowGlobal, and all the rest that will surely follow.

When you're watching a baseball game, you'll be able
to buy T-shirts, team jackets, mugs, fan memorabilia, and
tickets to upcoming games. Click here to select your seat
with Ticketmaster. Again, NBC, Disney, and Time Warner
are leading the way.

For example, according to a report in *Webnoize,* NBC
has invested heavily in a new company called Intertainer.[6]
Intertainer is an interactive broadband entertainment service that has content agreements with creators and distributors of movies, music, and other programming
(including BarnesandNoble.com, Disney's Buena Vista Internet Group, Public Broadcasting Service, Sony Pictures
Entertainment, and Time Warner). To be launched late in
1998, it would be the first on-demand service to offer network programming (and e-commerce) to consumers. Intertainer's other investors include Intel Corporation, Sony
Corporation, and US West.

The convergence of television, e-commerce, and the
Internet is by no means limited to the TV networks. Here
are some notable examples of what's happening:

➤ Broadcast.com and National Media Corporation
launched a 24-hour-a-day Internet shopping channel. It is the first 24-hour-a-day live and on-demand
streaming video shopping channel on the Internet,
offering "Live on Tape" programming on five
themed video channels (health and fitness, beauty
and cosmetics, housewares, automotive, and motiva-
tional). National Media is the world's largest publicly held direct-response television company, and
Broadcast.com is the leading aggregator and broadcaster on the Web.

➤ Children's Television Workshop, founded in 1968
and best known as the creators of *Sesame Street,* pro-

vides programming that extends far beyond the loveable furry monsters of *Sesame Street*. CTW and Nickelodeon launched NOGGIN, an educational cable network for children, and CTW television titles include *The New Ghostwriter Mysteries, 3-2-1 Contact, Square One TV, Kid City, Encyclopedia,* and *The Electric Company.* CTW is launching a kids' portal, where kids can tickle Elmo to their hearts' content, because e-commerce is an integral part of the site.

➤ MGM, United Artists Pictures, together with Moda-CAD's Fashion Site, will allow consumers to pick out outfits worn by actors and model them on virtual mannequins tailored to their own sizes, and then buy them. Hey, I look really good in this Star Trooper outfit, don't I?

■ TUBE OR NOT TUBE—THAT IS THE QUESTION

It all comes down to this: whether people will mostly want a noninteractive, couch potato experience (it's easy, convenient, and lulling), sitting before the boob tube; or whether they'll lean forward, remote control device in hand (obviously, more sophisticated than today's remote control), and engage themselves, at least enough to click and buy. In the end, even if interactivity fails to change the nature of the entertainment itself, as long as it lures us into buying things—lots of things—then, it will succeed. Tune in next time for the exciting conclusion. This story is "Tube continued. . . ."

Computer games are emerging
from their largely adolescent
male ghetto. Will this long-
heralded entertainment
wunderkind finally come
into its own?

Chapter

Computer Games for the Rest of Us

"I recently learned something quite interesting about video games. Many young people have developed incredible hand, eye, and brain coordination in playing these games. The air force believes these kids will be our outstanding pilots should they fly our jets."

—RONALD REAGAN, from a statement made August 8, 1983

"The very idea of 'computer games' has been long rooted in the perception that they are for kids. Adolescent boys, to be specific. Many people are simply not aware that there is now computer game fare for people of all ages, sexes, and interests."

—CHRIS HOLDEN, president, Kesmai, an on-line game company

"For computer games to break out to a level of mass market acceptance, there's a need to think of computer entertainment, not games. Games produce a very specific image, and contain connotation of being for the hobbyist or niche enthusiast."

—JOHN BAKER, senior vice president of corporate development, Activision.

"I design games that I want to play. I'm not interested in designing a Deer Hunter, or a Barbie. Those are non-games for people who think they want to play games. The good thing is, the more people who get started, even if it's with something like Deer Hunter, might eventually move on and start playing real games."

—JOHN ROMERO, chairman, Ion Storm, creator of Doom and Quake

Beginning in 1993, people who thought they knew the computer game industry were blindsided by a sequence of unlikely blockbuster hits. That's when an odd, nongame-like game called Myst hit the streets. More like a beautiful, moody, and slow-moving art film (accompanied by a breathtaking soundtrack) than a traditional computer game, Myst nevertheless shot to the top of the computer game charts. Myst remains the best-selling computer game of all time, having sold more than 3.5 million copies at the time this book went to press. It remains on PC Data's (a market research firm based in Reston, Virginia) best-selling list more than five years after being released—something unheard of in the fickle and fast-paced computer games business.

Three years after Myst made its stunning debut, in the fall of 1996, veteran toy manufacturer Mattel released another digital oddity (for the times) that went on to baffle conventional wisdom. Barbie Fashion Designer was a $39.99 CD-ROM that allowed teenage girls to design and print out clothes intended for their Barbie dolls. Largely ignored (when it wasn't being ridiculed) by the gaming establishment, Barbie soared to the top of the Christmas charts in 1996, outselling such blockbuster smash titles as Quake and, yes, even Myst, and proving to an astonished world that—gasp—girls *would* play computer games.

In 1998, there was Deer Hunter. Yes, it's exactly what it sounds like. You install it on your PC, and up come some fairly simple woodsy graphics that allow you to aim a gun at . . . what else? Deer. You try to kill the deer that leap across your screen. That's about as complicated as it gets. Made for just $100,000 (and keep in mind that the average computer game in 1998 cost $1.5 million), as of press time, Deer Hunter had sold more than 1 million copies, and had been a fixture in PC Data's list of the top five best-selling games for six months. Thus far, it has managed to beat to a humiliating pulp such revered titles as Quake II, Diable, and, yes, Myst, which however still remains a steady seller (along with its successor, Riven). Go figure.

You decide: what do these three titles have in common? Wandering around an eerie fantasy world and solving complex puzzles? Designing Barbie clothes? Killing deer? On the surface, not much. But in another sense, everything.

By mid-1998, it was clear that something extraordinary was happening. Computer games were finally reaching audiences that had previously been thought largely unreachable: adult women, girls, and American heartland types.

Myst was a surprise because it lacked what it was assumed every best-selling computer game had to have: riveting gameplay. (Gameplay is a difficult term to describe to the layperson. To avid gamers, it is a mixture of the need to focus your attention on what's happening in a physical sense—usually so you don't get killed too quickly—and the feeling when you stop playing that you've been somewhere outside of the real world. "Where *was* I?")

Myst was also difficult because it didn't fit into any particular category. You weren't out to kill everything that moved. Although you certainly were given puzzles to solve as you continued on a quest of sorts (both features a staple of role-playing games), Myst depended more on atmosphere and mood than on typical clue solving to keep the player interested. You'll gather by this that games, like movies, tended to fall into easily recognizable genres: shooters, simulators, puzzles, or role-playing games. Myst was none of those things; rather, it was an odd conglomerate containing features from all of them.

What Barbie proved, without a doubt, was that a niche formerly considered a no-man's-land for game revenue—adolescent girls—was, in fact, highly fertile soil just waiting for the right seedlings. The market has since been quick to jump on the money-making possibilities; between 1996 and 1997 alone, sales of girl games doubled from $26 million to $57 million, according to PC Data. "Two years ago, when I took over this company, the question was, 'Why would you want to produce games for girls?'" Jan Claesson, CEO of Her Interactive, a girls-only game software company, recalls. "A year ago, that question had become, 'So, *how* do you produce games for girls?' "

Finally, Deer Hunter appeared on the computer games shelves at Wal-Mart, and the rest is history.

Let's be clear that there is a key difference between Myst and the other two titles. Myst was (and is) revered by hard-core gamers as a stunning technical and creative achievement. Despite its unconventional content and approach, even the most skeptical Doom fanatics admired its stunning graphics, evocative music, and the immersive and compelling universe created by the designers at Cyan Inc. Hard-core gamers might not have seen Myst coming, or predicted that a game of this type would have such broad appeal, but they certainly admired it and respected its designers' creative and technical talents.

But, almost without exception, ask a hard-core gamer what he (and it was usually a he) thought of Barbie and Deerhunter, palpable scorn and disbelief will drip from his voice. "I didn't get it, and I still don't get it," flatly says Jonathan Simpson-Bint, president of the games division at Imagine Media, Inc., a publisher of magazines that cover the computer-gaming and Internet markets. John Romero, the creator of fantastically gruesome (and successful) shooters Doom and Quake, who has risen to the status of almost deity within the computer game world, just shrugs. Not only does he not get it, but "I'm not all that interested in figuring it out," he says. "I wouldn't want to design a game like that, even if it did go on to sell millions of copies."

■ AVOIDING THE "G" WORD

Others in the industry are less . . . purist. They see an opportunity—a big one. Activision, one of the larger game publishers, is making a concerted effort to broaden the demographics of people willing to shell out $20 to $50 for a computer game. It's distributing games from Girl Games

Inc., a small design firm devoted to creating digital entertainment for girls. It's having decent success with children's titles like Muppet Treasure Island, and is even breaking into computerized versions of traditional board games, like mah-jongg.

John Baker, senior vice president of corporate development for Activision, believes a shift in focus is necessary for survival in the future games market. "We can't be thinking about creating computer games anymore, but about designing computer-enabled *entertainment* that will appeal to a broad audience," he says. Games like Barbie or Deerhunter are almost purely "experiential," points out Baker. By this, he means, "the point of these, and other similar titles, is simply to provide an experience *that also happens to be entertaining.*" If the computer games industry hopes to finally break through to the mass market—the way television, radio, and film offerings already do—this broader notion of what a game can be is essential, insist Baker and others.

One of the key ingredients for mass-market success includes greater accessibility. Even to boot up a copy of the best-selling game Diablo requires a certain familiarity with gaming conventions, or assumptions (how to move about the screen, how to shoot, etc.). So, at the very least, computer games companies need to focus on creating products that "possess deep and lasting play appeal, but which are also easy to use and easy to learn," says Chris Holden, president of on-line games venture Kesmai. This is not a trivial thing. To lead a new player into a world, and help them to gradually understand rules and conventions without boring more advanced players is a matter of craft—even art—not bits and bytes.

And, "it's a bit of a mystery, always, as to what sells and what doesn't," says Stephen Clarke-Wilson, the former vice president of worldwide product development for Virgin Interactive Entertainment. Clarke-Wilson has an impressive list of hits that he produced during his tenure at Virgin; he points to Seventh Guest, one of these titles, as a prime example of well-designed *accessibility*. "The creator of Seventh Guest was very clear: he wanted to make it as easy to play as channel surfing on television," says Clarke-Wilson, who now runs his own production company, Above the Garage Productions. "This was very smart. Because the true competition for a computer game is not necessarily other computer games, but the lure of the couch, and the remote control. And that's a tough thing to compete against."

Previously, the computer game industry had been a niche, but a very fertile niche. According to a 1998 survey by *Computer Gaming World,* out of the 41 million households that currently own PCs, a full 78 percent have games installed. "Core gamers," as defined by *Computer Gaming World,* comprise only 14 percent of the total population of game-playing PC owners, yet they buy 54 percent of revenues. That's $810 million of the roughly $1.4 billion PC games—not a bad business for such narrow penetration. By 2001, the entertainment software market is predicted to grow to $8 billion, according to IDC/Link Research. (It was approximately $5.6 billion at the end of 1998.) Again, not bad for a niche.

"I always say, never underestimate the power of a niche," says Celia Pearce, a new media and interactive entertainment developer and consultant who heads her own firm, the Momentum Media Group, and has spoken out (and written) against the narrow vision of most computer game designers, which has resulted in titles so focused on violence and sex.

The installed base of computer owners continues to change rapidly. By the end of 1998, a full 45 percent of U.S. homes owned PCs, according to a study by the Interactive Digital Software Association. As PC owners changed from rabid technophiles to ordinary Joes and Janes, tastes in related products were certain to follow.

"Beginning in 1998, we saw the emergence of what we called 'the Wal-Mart customer,' " says Bing Gordon, executive vice president of marketing for Electronic Arts, currently the largest game publisher in the world, referring to what in the industry had become known as the "Deer Hunter Phenomenon." It was the beginning of a new era, and gamers themselves were commenting on it. "We're finally on the verge of a breakthrough," says Kesmai's Holden.

■ CHOOSE YOUR PLATFORM

Before you can completely understand the changes underway, it's also important to know that the game industry has traditionally been segmented by hardware platform, and why this is likely to continue for some time. That is, when you go into Wal-Mart or Toys "R" Us to buy a new game, you're not only making a choice of title, you're forced to choose based on which game console it can run on. And, not all titles run on all platforms. In fact, it's often been the point that you can only play certain titles on certain platforms. If this sounds familiar, yes, it's the case of competing technology standards; it's the old Beta-versus-VHS format issue all over again. You want a *Sesame Street* game? One based on popular movies like *A Bug's Life* or *Rug Rats?* You need to buy a Sony Playstation. How about NFL F\Blitz? John Madden Football? You need to have a Nintendo 64.

By the mid-1990s, the three big console makers that emerged from the melee of the 1980s included Sony Corp., with its Playstation; Sega Enterprise, with its Saturn; and Nintendo, with its Nintendo 64. There's a constant battle for market share among these big three console makers, and it's a highly cyclical business. At any given time, one of these manufacturers has just brought out (or is about to bring out) its latest model, which vastly surpasses existing consoles (including the machine it replaces) in terms of processor speed, power, connectivity, graphics, audio quality—you name it.

As of the end of 1998, here was the score:

Sony PlayStation (introduced 1994): 11.5 million units sold

Nintendo 64 (introduced 1996): 7 million units sold

Sega Saturn (introduced 1994): 1.5 million units sold

Although the Sony Playstation seemed clearly the market leader at the end of 1998, Sega was about to bring out its much-hyped Dreamcast platform (the successor to its failed Sega Saturn), which would surpass the Playstation technically in all sorts of ways. But would it entice enough developers to write games for it to push Sony off the winner's box? Industry pundits were devoting miles of ink to speculation. By the time this book is released, the results will be known. But whoever wins this particular battle of the box, be warned this is a *highly* volatile market. "Nintendo at the Top of its Game," trumpeted *BusinessWeek* in the summer of 1997; but just four months later—by Christmas 1997—it was clear that Sony, with its PlayStation, was edging ahead. A year later, the gap was several million units wide.

Predicting what may or may not happen with Sega's Dreamcast is probably a waste of time. What's important is that at the time this book went to press, Dreamcast was being called Sega's final chance. (Of the 20 million game consoles in the United Sates, Sega accounted for just 1.5 million of them by late 1998.) So Sega is taking Dreamcast very seriously, with a planned $100 million promotional blitz upon rollout in the United States that would hype Dreamcast's faster procesor, more powerful graphics and audio capabilities, plus the fact that it will run on a version of the ubiquitous Microsoft operating system, and contain a built-in Internet connection (features Sega hopes will tempt PC developers over to the console platform).

The volatility caused by console wars affects the computer games industry in two significant ways: developers are always worrying about which game platform they should be making a game for, and consumers are wondering what platform to invest in if they want access to the best future titles.

The emergence of the PC as a viable game platform has complicated the matter. At first dismissed because of high cost ($2,000 and up compared with consoles, which were already selling for under $200), as well as poor graphics and sound capability, the PC has rapidly become a legitimate game platform choice—so much so that in the early 1990s, many people began predicting the demise of the console market, particularly after Microsoft heaved its bulk into the PC games arena. But, this hasn't happened. By 1998, PC games had grown to roughly one-third of the entire games market revenue. The PC, as a game platform, was good enough to be a future contender, but certainly nothing the consoles should worry about.

Much time and energy is spent debating about which box will win out as the entertainment platform of choice. Will it be the familiar console-plus-television combination that Sony, Sega, and Nintendo have capitalized on? Will it be a standard television, supplemented by some sort of additional device (called a set-top box) that may also include other capabilities, such as cable, or VCR-like recording and playback? Or, will it be a PC (whether desktop, laptop, or hooked to a network)?

The theory, in the early 1990s, was one of convergence: that all these various things we do with technology in the home (run popular software programs, watch broadcast or cable TV, receive satellite transmissions, rent videotapes, record music or images, play games) would converge in a single place, all using the same device, or set of devices. More recently, there's less certainty that this convergence will actually take place. Many people argue that the PC will never become a true entertainment device, that it will remain a tool for processing and accessing information, and that attempts to turn it into an entertainment platform will fail. Likewise, others predict that attempts to turn the television set into an interactive device (for surfing the Net à la WebTV, for playing games, or for interactive digital transactions) will fail, because that device will largely remain one for passive, not interactive, entertainment.

How this will play out remains to be seen. But we're already seeing makers of all sorts of electronic devices—whether PCs, game consoles, DVD devices (the replacement for the CD player), or cable set-top boxes—attempt to shovel more function into their respective products. Which is why the new Sega Dreamcast player has an Internet connection built in, and why it has a partnership with WebTV to combine all their common attributes: access to broadcast TV and the Internet, as well as sophisticated game-playing abilities.

Richard Miller, chairman of VM Labs, a Silicon Valley start-up, is hoping that more consumer device manufacturers want to pack their machines with potentially stunning game-playing capabilities. VM Labs has produced a set of components that create a standard game-playing platform that can be installed in any kind of consumer device, such as VCR, set-top box, or DVD player. As of press time, VM Labs had signed up just one partner, Motorola, which announced its intention to use the VM Labs technology—Miller calls it "firmware," because it's a combination of both hardware and software—in a new set-top box it was designing.

Miller is betting that more consumer device manufacturers will think game-playing capability is an essential feature to differentiate their products. "We're asking people: what does the consumer want in his living room? Where is he prepared to spend his money?" says Miller. The answer is not a PC, but an easier-to-use and cheaper device, he believes.

Is betting on a new game platform risky business? You bet. Look at 3DO. Called, among other things, "one of Silicon Valley's most spectacular flops" (by *The Wall Street Journal*), 3DO attempted to develop a new video game machine to compete with Sony, Sega, Nintendo, and the others.[1] But, in addition to being too expensive (retailing for $700), the 3DO box had trouble attracting developers. In 1998, 3DO gave up its more grandiose plans and decided to concentrate on developing high-quality niche game products, such as the well-received Might and Magic, and Army Men titles.

So, there are four conclusions to be drawn from this.

1. Console manufacturers currently competing will continue to cycle through the chicken-and-egg process of bringing out a new platform, trying to convince developers to write for it so consumers will buy it.
2. The console market will remain a highly cost-sensitive market. Any console manufacturer that can't keep up (or down) with steadily diminishing retail prices is going to be in trouble.
3. There is probably only room (and dollars) in the market for two consoles to thrive at any given time.
4. Some sort of on-line capability will be absolutely required for any game device hoping to compete in the world of on-line multiplayer games.

Other than that, everything will continue to be up for grabs.

■ GAMES FOR THE REST OF US

Along with Mattel, which rapidly turned its Barbie Fashion Designer into a lucrative series of like titles, a number of other traditional toy and game companies leaped into the computer games market in 1997 and 1998.

Hasbro took a lead by translating a number of its well-loved gaming brands, such as Scrabble and Risk. Broderbund (before being acquired by The Learning Co.) was having success with a Rug Rats series based on the children's television cartoon; Electronic Arts was having enormous success with Tiger Woods Gold, Madden NFL, and various other sports titles; Simon & Schuster Interactive tried to make magic with games of popular television shows such as *Sabrina, the Teenage Witch,* and *Star Trek.*

Then there's the granddaddy of all board games, Monopoly, which you can play over the Internet, with up to six players (and three languages) for international real estate deals. You get to use the currency of your choice—and the game automatically converts it to your currency according to current rates. Parker Brothers is celebrating the 60th-anniversary of the game with a multiplayer, multimedia version, which is being distributed by Virgin Interactive.

Let's look at Lego Interactive Media, which is moving full speed into the wired world. There's Lego Creator, a 3-D software construction tool that allows kids to design and build things with virtual Lego bricks on a computer screen. There's Lego Loco, a train-building software game, and Lego MindStorms, which allows children to build fully operational robots using software-enabled Lego bricks. With each of these virtual Lego worlds, children can use animation to do such things as plant a garden and watch the flowers grow; build a track and a town for the railroad to run through; or create a character out of Lego blocks and "bring it to life," says Gregg Sauter, director of sales and marketing for Lego Media.

Why is the venerable Lego brand getting into software games? Simple. "Kids are spending more time playing video games, which takes away from the time they spend with our traditional bricks," says Sauter. "We needed to address that." He says the fact that it's gentle fun hasn't dampened the reception from kids in the least. "Kids can't wait to get their hands on it," he says. "It proves that point that computer games don't have to be about blood and guts."

■ BREAKING THE GENDER BARRIER

Sauter also pointed out an interesting pattern in early trials of Lego software games. Although Lego has long been the number one toy for young boys (falling behind only *Star Wars* figures and games when toy makers put a big push behind that brand), Lego products have historically not done well with girls. But, says Sauter, although boys, as expected, are driving *sales* of the new Lego software products, "we're finding that girls are playing with them once they're in the home," he says. In short, girls are turning out to be much more receptive to the software than to the actual physical bricks. Reason? "Perhaps it's because it's more about solving problems, than about physical construction of objects," says Sauter. "It's more about creating an entire world, complete with characters that live and interact in that world. And girls are absolutely at home with this kind of social activity."

Brenda Laurel has been thinking about this subject a lot. As a researcher at top-secret (and deep-pocketed) Silicon Valley thinktank Interval Research, Laurel spent two and a half years investigating girls' attitudes toward technology, and the differences in play between genders. In late 1996, with Laurel as president, Interval Research spun off a new company specifically targeted toward developing games specifically for girls.

Laurel likes to point out a list of five "misconceptions" about girls and computer games that form the basis of the Purple Moon product line:

1. **Girls don't play computer games.** No—they actually play them more than they play with other boys' toys, such as trucks or guns. They found traditional "boy games" boring—not too challenging, or too violent, says Laurel, but "boring." "We thought this was very significant," she says.
2. **Girls don't like to fight.** No—although they tend not to like hurting *human* characters (unless there's

a very good reason), they don't have problems in-
flicting violence on nonhuman characters, especially when there's a strong motivation (that is,
they are defeating the bad guy), says Laurel. "Again,
they are simply bored with games in which indis-
criminate killing is the sole focus," she says.

3. **Girls aren't competitive.** Au contraire—they are
extremely competitive, just in different ways from
boys. They tend to be more subtle, more indirect,
which doesn't mean, however, that girls can't (or
won't) compete in more traditional ways, especially
as sports and business careers become more acceptable outlets for direct competitiveness. In general,
however, girls compete through asserting social influence and structuring relationships, whereas boys
think of winning as dominating and defeating. In
short, a boy's definition of competition is much
narrower than a girl's, says Laurel.

4. **Girls are only interested in the computer as a useful tool.** Just because girls tend to list activities
like doing homework, writing reports, and other
academic activities as their primary interests in
using a computer, it doesn't mean they won't play
with it, stresses Laurel. When tempted with such
things as role playing, adventure, drawing, creating,
writing, skill building, problem solving, and clue-
based games, girls are quite eager to play.

5. **Girls are too social to enjoy the computer.** Perhaps—when the computer use was primarily a solitary and immersive activity (which, in fact, is
what has characterized many societal fears about a
technology-based society)—but with the advent of
the Internet, and the emergence of e-mail, online
chatting, and multiplayer games, sitting in front of a
computer is no longer a solitary occupation. Laurel
likes to point to teenage girls' mastery of another
technological device that has been put to social purposes—the telephone—as an example that girls are

not put off by machines themselves. They simply need to find something *interesting* to do with them.

The results of this research has been Purple Moon's games series, what Laurel calls "friendship adventures for girls." The first title in the series, Rockett, revolved around a teenage girl finding her social feet at a new high school; the second title, Secret Paths, was a more fantastic narrative, involving magic stones and an enchanted forest, but it still had at its heart some very realistic relationships between realistic characters (all girls). The third title in the series, Rockett's Adventure Maker, just released at the time this book went to press, allows players to take a more active role, by creating characters and scenes themselves; writing their own adventures for the now-established cast of characters; thus using the computer as both a creative plaything *and* tool. (The first two Purple Moon titles did quite well, both making PC Data's top 20 best-selling children's software list for 1997, despite being released fairly late in the year.)

Since 1996, a number of game software companies that focus specifically on the girl game market have sprung up. In addition to Purple Moon, there's Girl Games, out of Austin, and Her Interactive, out of Bellevue, Washington (motto: "For girls who aren't afraid of a mouse"). Other, more mainstream computer game developers, such as Creative Wonders and The Learning Company, are also making a concerted effort to appeal to girls.

Her Interactive had a great deal of success with its 1995 hit, McKenzie & Co., which is set in a recognizable high school world of dating, shopping, and socializing. It followed up on that with Vampire Diaries and other titles, but at the time this book was being researched, was most optimistic about its first Nancy Drew title, to be released in late 1998. (If it succeeds, it will be the beginning of a series based on the popular teenage detective.)

Like Laurel, the executives at Her Interactive don't believe girls are inherently adverse to playing with computers; they go further, saying it's not even that girls object to shooting-type games. "Girls don't mind killing things, but they want to have a *reason,*" says Megan Gaiser, president of Her Interactive. In initial demos of the first Nancy Drew game, called Secrets Can Kill, she found girls were especially interested in problem-solving, especially if there was a clear objective. "Girls want a mission statement," she says. "They get bored by the kind of games boys seem to love, in which there are a lot of clues, and puzzles, and adventures, but where it's hard to figure out the goal."

There was one other consistent message that girls are sending to developers: they want to play in groups. This doesn't necessarily mean they want to play *against* each other, as in multiplayer games on the Internet, but that they enjoy the socialization, says Jan Claesson, CEO of Her Interactive. He points to focus groups that show girls preferred to cluster around a single computer and help solve a problem collaboratively, even if given a choice of having their own machine. And, he says, "it wasn't important to them which girl controlled the mouse or keyboard. That wasn't the point. If they could collaborate, they felt part of the game."

Others, however, caution against too-broad generalizations about either boys or girls. "Whenever you hear the phrase 'girls like this' or 'boys like this,' you are ghettoizing them," says Justine Cassell, a professor at MIT's media lab, whose research concentrates on gender differences in toys and play.

For example, it's a common truism to hear that girls prefer stories over action. "But we all use storytelling as a way to define ourselves—both boys and girls," says Cassell, who believes products like the Purple Moon "friendship adventures" are going in the right direction. She believes, from her research, however, that both boys and girls could use the computer as a playful storytelling tool without so many constraints. "Our perceptions of what children like—both boys and girls—is very narrow. We should let them tell us the stories."

"On the other hand, we *do* cheat girls when we restrict them—when we say things like, 'they don't like to construct things,' " says Cassell. She points to a research project she's currently spearheading in which children from 139 countries around the world have been given computers and Internet connections, and asked to help "define a world that would be a better place for children to live." Girls are eagerly participating in this particular "construction" project—70 percent of the responses thus far have been from girls.

Vangie Beal, editor of www.gamgirlz.com, couldn't agree more. As the editor of the on-line site for girl gamers, she warns against typing anyone of either sex when it comes to entertainment. Herself an avid Quake player, Beal says she competes against "men and women of all ages and backgrounds," and that trying to make overly broad assumptions is silly when the focus should be developing a community and having fun.

■ BREAKING THE ON-LINE BARRIER

It was supposed to be a no-brainer—using the Internet to play games on-line. It had all the ingredients for success: People could play the games they loved (Doom, Quake) at any time of day or night, against competitors from anywhere in the world. It would be more challenging gameplay, because they'd be playing against humans, not just against machines (as in the typical PC or console game). There'd be more surprises, more unpredictability, more skill, more *fun* involved.

A host of players jumped in: Sony, with The Station; SegaSoft Network, Inc., with Heat.net; Microsoft with its Internet Gaming Zone, among others. Still, on-line gaming was, at first, an utter failure. One of the main problems was finding a business model that worked. The initial notion (that on-line game companies could sell monthly subscriptions or charge a per-hour fee for playing) proved miserably false. The second thought was that advertising might provide sufficient revenues. Wrong, again. Despite the fact that people were flocking to on-line game sites in greater and greater numbers, there just didn't seem to be a way to make money at it, which kind of threw a damper on things.

At least part of the problem was that there were so many *free* game sites already out there. "So why pay?" asks Michael Evason, a business analyst for Datamonitor, a London-based market research firm, who authored a report last year on the on-line gaming market. He thinks the future looks more optimistic. By the year 2002, more than 15 million people in the United States and Europe will pay a total of $1.4 million to play games on-line—mostly by luring newcomers in with freebies, then reaping revenues from premium play services, sales of products, and (of course) advertising. In short, the key to success in on-line gaming—and by the end of 1998, it looked as through (finally) it would be a success—would be a hybrid business model that accepted revenues from a variety of sources. It sounds simplistic, but it took industry veterans like the Total Entertainment Network (TEN) several years to get it right.

Visit the funky San Francisco offices of the Total Entertainment Network (TEN), and you'll find the usual trappings of a Silicon Valley start-up: lots of small, crowded cubicles; lots (and lots) of toys, perhaps more geared toward the supernatural than is typical; and graffiti-marked posters of cultural icons such as Albert Einstein and Elvira, Mistress of the Dark. Like most on-line game companies, TEN started out by charging subscribers a monthly fee for playing. That worked to a certain extent, largely because TEN has some very strong, and exclusive, games that people couldn't get anywhere else—titles like NASCAR Online, Wizwar, and Twilight Lands, the latter two being elaborate role-playing games.

But, says Erick Hachenburg, president and CEO of TEN, it soon became clear that a subscription-only model wouldn't cut it. So, time to revise the biz plan, and come up with something new: give away the games for free, but still make money by selling advertisements. The only problem was that the number of users was too small to support an audience that would interest major advertisers, says Greg Harper, vice president of business development for TEN. "Time to move on," he says. Then, TEN hit upon the notion that they might be able to appeal to a larger audience than just the players themselves.

In 1997, TEN launched the Professional Gamers League (PGL), which is an attempt to turn on-line computer gameplay into a spectator sport. Sure, you can be one of the contestants battling for the title of best Quake II player in the world, or you can simply log on and watch via cybercast, or go to the live championship games that are held annually, usually at some place or event that gamers would naturally like to go anyway, like the 1998 E3 convention, in Atlanta.

The money opportunities for this come in several packages. First, the players themselves pay an entrance fee. Then, there are sponsors, not advertisers. The concept is broader: they pay a single (and larger) fee for the right to be the "official modem" of the PGL or the "official joystick" of the PGL. And, in the future, as TEN sets up the ability to sell products and transact business directly from the site, TEN will get a share of revenues from sales of products, as well as any kind of peripheral advertising that creeps into the equation.

So, the PGL was launched in November 1997 by TEN. More than 1,500 Quake aficionados battled it out before coming to Atlanta last summer. There was a total of 30,000 machines in the month; eight players made it to the finals. There's an endorsement deal with Microsoft. There are official sponsors: the official modem, the official joystick, the official mouse—you name it. And, the event was webcast via the Internet, and ESPN produced a cable special based on it.

The notion that you can appeal to a bigger audience than just the people actually manipulating the joystick, mouse, or keyboard is a clever one, says Evason. "You've got an online model along the lines of television football seasons or golf tournaments. It's a chance to get into the mass market, and has the possibility of interesting some important advertisers," says Evason.

Mpath is another on-line gaming service that has worked through its early woes and seems to have turned the corner toward profitability, also because of this hybrid mixture of charging for certain premium games, selling advertising space, and selling products and services from its site to consumers. (Mpath's service is called Mplayer, and can be reached on the Web at www.mplayer.com.) More than 1.5 million people had signed up as Mpath members as of October 1998, and were increasing at a rate of 50,000 new members a week, making Mplayer one of the most heavily trafficked entertainment sites on the Web.

What is the top attraction at Mplayer? Poker. That's right, good old poker. Log onto mplayer.com, and you'll find people eager to play everything from backgammon, to Quake, to Doom, to . . . classical guitar. This is one of the lessons that Paul Matteucci, CEO and president of Mpath, said was a long time coming: people weren't logging on to play games per se; rather, they were looking for a social experience. Although traditional action and sports games are attracting 95 percent of male audiences, in more classic, traditional games like bingo, Mplayer sees a full 75 percent female crowd. Most mplayer "rooms" are split evenly between male and female—largely a function of this "aha" that on-line gaming *could* be for the masses, says Matteucci.

What was interesting, says Matteucci, is that when Mplayer opened its classic games arena (that's for the poker, bingo, and backgammon crowd), it saw virtually no crossover play from its existing population. "The average user is there for the community, and they're there for one, maybe two games in particular," says Matteucci. "A poker player doesn't get tempted into Doom or Quake. It's too different an experience."

Kesmai has come to some similar conclusions. Log onto kesmai.com and you'll see a wide variety of card, board, and puzzle games, in addition to the traditional lineup of simulation, role-playing, and adventure games.

Says President Holden, "We've found a great success with the mass-market style titles. I'm convinced there is a much broader, untapped market for computer and online gaming out there than anyone ever thought." Although Holden believes predictions of a $1 billion-plus on-line games market by 2001 are "a tad aggressive," he has no doubt that on-line gaming will be a staple of mass-market entertainment within the next 5 to 10 years.

Simutronics is one on-line gaming company that is actually profitable. Neil Harris, executive vice president of Simutronics, believes the key is to keep in mind that people are interested in playing *a specific game,* not in subscribing to some service. Moreover, says Harris, building a sense of community among the people who come to the site to play a game is essential.

Gemstone is a Simutronics game that has been live online for more than eight years. A cooperative role-playing game, Gemstone is in fact an entire universe, with its own culture, currency, rules, and regulations, and its own unique population—created by the players themselves, not by company executives. It has an enormously loyal customer base, which pays a monthly subscription fee (again, one of the few to succeed at this), and in which the average player puts in 50 hours of play a month. "If you keep in mind that the average CD-ROM game gets just 40 total hours of play, you have a sense of what a dynamic environment this is," says Harris. It's the fact that it is constantly evolving—both technically, as Harris' staff churns out continual improvements, and creatively, as both staff and players invent new aspects of the on-line world.

■ CONTINUED QUESTIONS ABOUT REVENUE OPPORTUNITIES

For companies like Microsoft, Sony, and Sega—the deep pockets of the computer and entertainment industries—

"they're not concerned about making huge amounts of money from online gaming," points out Evason. The point is to get a foothold in a fast-growing market, and do cross-media marketing of a plethora of products in both entertainment and technology.

Indeed, some industry observers, such as Scott Rubin, vice president of game programming and founder of The All Games network, predict that the big money will always be in shrink-wrapped versions of the game, bought by individuals who then log on to the Internet to play with others. The on-line service will be free (or subsidized by advertising or e-commerce), but it will not be the primary profit-making aspect of the equation. Rather, the bulk of revenues will come from the retail product itself, with the multiplayer on-line feature a necessary draw.

Activision, for example, is betting on a universe of mahjongg players with its Shanghai-Dynasty product that sells for $49.95, and is hoping to hit gold with its Nine Dragons Software, in San Francisco, and its Hong Kong Mahjongg. Whereas it might be hard to get four members of your neighborhood or household together for a game, it's no problem when there's a universe of avid on-line players. Berrie Bloem's Mah Jongg—The Real Game, which started out as a downloadable Internet freebie, has turned into a packaged product that people can play on-line.

Quake, the retail version of which is sold by id Software, Inc., hosts a Quake site, but there are currently more than 3,000 independent sites where people can play with each other. The goal is to roam through mazelike corridors and kill as many enemies as possible. Who are the enemies? Whoever logs on against you.

"Every game, going forward from now on, will have some form of online, multiplayer component," says Activision's Baker. He believes that the enormous amount of information (e.g., read graphics, video, sound, etc.) that must be packed into the typical computer game will not make it feasible for pure on-line gaming anytime soon. But, if consumers buy a retail product, get local access to the data needed to run that game, and then have an on-line experience that is integral to that . . . that's a business model that might work quite well, he says.

"In the future, you won't be able to launch a game title without a related Web site," agrees Lee Roth, president of Roth Media, a Los Angeles–based entertainment studio, who believes that "transmedia" versions of everything— from games, to films, to books, to television shows—is the wave of the future.

■ BREAKING THE MOLD

A second prerequisite for computer games arousing the interest of the general public is breaking out of the "genre ghetto." Browse the game shelves at any Wal-Mart or Comp-USA and you'll see a numbingly similar lineup. And, "just thumb through an issue of any major computer games publication, and you'll be struck by the similarity of the titles, and by the unvarying look of the 'characters' and settings and so forth," admits Holden. This is because the vast majority of games in the past was created by a relatively small group of hard-core computer gamers— talented and intelligent people, but people who were building what they themselves liked to play. They weren't necessarily interested in branching out contentwise; most game designers consider themselves artists, not business entrepreneurs. By the end of 1998, however, the winds of change were finally blowing. Yes, there were indications, back in 1998, that even the gaming elite were beginning to expand their horizons a bit. Perhaps it's out of business necessity, or perhaps they're growing up (keep in mind that many of the most respected artists designing computer games today are still less than 30 years old).

Mike Wilson is the 20-something founder of Gathering of Developers, a developer-owned-and-managed game publisher (see Chapter 11), who was previously a part of the all-star teams at both id Software (Doom and Quake) and Ion Storm. There were both business and creative reasons for establishing a company that put the designers in control of publishing their own games, Wilson emphasizes. What is particularly interesting, however, is that the first titles from the GOD studios (as they prefer to be called—their headquarters in Dallas are in a former church) are a far cry from the blood-and-guts extravaganzas one would have expected from a group that had, among them, helped produce such titles as Doom, Quake, Hexen, and Mortal Kombat.

The first title released, Jazz Jackrabbit 2, was quite a big step from the founders' largely shoot-to-painfully-kill roots. A wacky green rabbit (Jazz) and his crazy brother (Spaz) take on dangerous turtles, bats, and other enemies. There's even a wedding involved (Jazz wants to get married, but his archenemy has stolen the ring). Sound too cute to be true? An early review called Jazz one of the best games to hit the PC.

Other titles on Gathering's early list might seem equally bemusing, coming from a group of such hard-core gamers. Railroad Tycoon II is a Monopoly-like strategy game in which participants try to build and protect worldwide transportation empires. Fly! allows players to virtually soar over cities rendered in striking detail with 3-D graphics. A classic flight simulator, Fly! focuses on the thrill and craft of avionics, and on sightseeing possibilities, rather than conventional fighter missions, and was already getting an advance buzz on the breathtaking graphical reality that allowed players to peep into windows in New York or Chicago.

Why these G-rated titles? Wilson shrugs. "We wanted to work with the best," he says simply. "These are great titles. Yes, they might cross over into the dreaded mass market. But if a game is good, an avid gamer will want to play it." That is as long as a game hasn't been "dumbed down" to meet the perceived needs of the mass market, hard-core gamers will buy it, Wilson stresses. But, he adds, don't expect the blood to stop flowing. Other GOD titles will satisfy the most trigger-happy gamers. "Next year, it's back to our roots," Wilson says.

Still, this yearning to begin broadening horizons is being heard throughout the halls of the most revered game design firms. Talk to designers themselves, and you hear a reverence for craft, a dedication to art; it's not unlike what you might hear from serious sculptors or novelists.

Tom Hall, president of Ion Storm, is working on a game called Anachronox, an "epic 3D sci-fi action role-playing game." It's quite a mouthful, and it's quite ambitious—both technically and creatively. Among other things, the player doesn't wander through this adventure alone, as in a typical adventure/quest game: he or she must choose a team from an existing cast of characters to help in the journey. Each character has his or her own strengths, weaknesses, and definite personality quirks. Thus, the game includes a "serious emotional story at its heart—with strong conflicts between the various characters," Hall points out. Rather than depending on a quick trigger finger, or a sure aim with a weapon, success in the world of Anachronox will involve more subtle understanding of human nature. "It's not about killing things and collecting treasure—focused on the heart of many role-playing games—but of dealing with emotional decisions and their consequences," says Hall.

Or, look at what Interactive Magic discovered with its very testosterone-driven WarBirds (an on-line airplane battle game). Log onto Interactive Magic, Inc., at www .imagiconline.com, and play its WarBirds, for $1.99 an hour, and you'll find yourself in the midst of a fanatically engaged following from around the globe that includes actual pilots, flight simulation addictees, and WWII buffs. "The draw of WarBirds is that instead of flying against artificial intelligence (the computer) he or she is competing against human opponents," says Christine Heneghan, a media relations specialist for Interactive Magic. This turned out to be significant. It turned out that players wanted more than just to fly around shooting at each other. That got boring. So they started forming squadrons, and they started meeting for impromptu conventions so they could actually shake hands with each other in the physical (rather than virtual) world. And they continuously talk to each other, both in and out of missions. Games are divided into "combat tours" that generally last a week or two, and several times a month the service recreates an historic battle for history buffs (for example, Battle of Midway or the Battle of Britain).

If it sounds like a social experience, that's right—that's the point. In fact, although players were always able to "talk" to each other via typed text (just like in e-mail messages), the popularity of the game skyrocketed when Interactive Magic introduced a "megavoice" feature that allows players to speak, and hear, each other via audio over the Web. What do they talk about? They request help, they warn squadron mates of a pending bomber, they frantically ask for a new gunner to volunteer for a mission. This ability to chat and interact has turned out to be a critical aspect of Warbirds' success.

This sort of thing doesn't surprise Rick Goodman. He may have won acclaim for designing hit computer games like Age of Empires (Goodman was given the Computer Game Developer's annual achievement award for game design and development in 1998), but Goodman says his favorite thing to do for fun is still "calling up a bunch of friends, ordering a pizza, and putting a board game on the table." Sound odd coming from a computer game designer? Not really. It's the heart of where the industry is heading. Veterans like Goodman, who now runs his own game studio, called Stainless Steel Studios, Inc., in Cambridge, Massachusetts, understand that if the play is going to be the thing, it's about bringing people together. "People aren't necessarily always interested in pursuing goals, or immersing themselves in a fantasy environment. Many are simply looking for a way to get together and interact," Goodman points out. He believes this will become more the norm as technology gets better (and cheaper), as more games have multiplayer components, and as the content of games continues to broaden. "I'm not interested in new technology because it makes my games faster," Goodman says. "I'm excited that I can make them *better.*" A faster processor should not simply mean that you can kill more things more quickly, but that you can introduce more complexities—more subtle characters, more complex interactions—in ways that enhance the fun.

"We need games that aren't so easily classified into strategy, or action, or shooter," says Goodman, who says his personal goal is to design games in which players have "a higher bandwidth of interactivity." A technical way of putting it, but what he means is covered more completely in Chapters 12 and 13: the more games are seen as social activities, the more appeal they will have to the general population.

"The games industry used to be perceived as a fringe geek-and-kids club," agrees Ion Storm's Hall. "I think we're finally starting to grow into a viable entertainment media. It's a painful process, but it *is* happening."

Part Three
Adapt or Die

Forces of Evolution for Everyone Involved

Just as radio and television shaped twentieth-century advertising, the Internet will fundamentally redefine media advertising in the twenty-first century.

Chapter

Brought to You
by . . . (Ads)

"The best magicians can make you look anywhere they want, whether you think you are willing or not,"[2] wrote Phil Hettema, about the art of staging theme park attractions. As senior vice president of attraction development for Universal Creative, Universal Studios' Recreation Group, Hettema has helped produce the kind of entertainment that keeps people waiting in line for hours for the chance to partici-pate—including *Terminator 2, Back to the Future,* and *Juras-*

sic Park. He knows how to use technology combined with good old-fashioned magic to thrill.

But, what he described applies equally well to the art of advertising. Yes, art—because the best advertisers engage our imagination, convince us to suspend disbelief, surprise us, move us, and get us to look at what *they* want, which requires the skills of a master playwright, movie director, and music video producer rolled into one. And, when it works, it is truly magical in the sense that Hettema is referring to.

Just remember these classic ads in print, radio, and television. What do they have in common? What they have in common is that we are being directed to see what the advertisers want us to see (and remember):

> ➤ Joe Camel. A cartoon with a message for kids: Camels are your friend, so, smoke.

> ➤ The radio cigarette ad memorized by a generation (even nonsmokers got the message): "Winston Tastes Good, Like A [boomp boomp] Cigarette Should." (Meaning: smoke Winston cigarettes and people will like you.)

> ➤ The 1964 presidential campaign ad televised by the Democrats, showing a little girl playing, and the mushroom cloud of an exploding atom bomb. (Meaning: don't vote for Barry Goldwater or this will happen to all of us.)

Moreover, the distinction between entertainment and advertising has become increasingly blurred:

> ➤ Using every technique they can to engage our attention and emotion, advertising has incorporated everything possible from movies and music, not the least of which is MTV, blending the cinematic with the musical experience.

➤ TV dramas often use commercial breaks as a means to sustain dramatic tension for a few minutes. If you've ever seen an hour-long TV drama with all the commercial breaks removed, it's clear that the tension across the missing ad breaks is missing.

➤ When moviemakers shoot scenes that linger on the products of paid advertisers (a Sony TV monitor, a Coke vending machine, a popular Cuban cigar), it raises a question of artistic versus commercial value. But, surely, it merges advertising with the media.

➤ When our favorite TV and movie actors, sports heroes, and even the broadcast personalities who provide us with hard news show up in advertorials and other commercial appearances, it's just another case of entertainment being used by advertising.

➤ Advertising is often a critical part of the basic entertainment experience itself. *Vogue* is a better (more desirable, from the consumers' point of view) publication because of its ads. The same can be said for the previews you see in theaters before the main attraction.

Technology is about to add even more magic to the advertisers' bag of tricks. What advertisers are going to do with technology, how *interactivity* will enable these changes, and, especially, how it will impact entertainment as we know it, is the subject of this chapter.

The most significant change is that advertisers—again, like the best magicians—are going to be able to read our minds. Not really, but it will certainly *appear* as if this were happening.

Imagine someone offering you a slice of pizza at the exact moment you yourself realize that you are hungry for a snack. Or, imagine someone offering you a very special deal on a new BMW, just as you were beginning to think you finally deserved to buy yourself that "Beemer" you'd always wanted. Or, imagine someone sending you a video clip previewing a new movie just as you were wondering what you were going to do that evening for entertainment.

All of this is about to happen. From the advertisers' point of view, an important end result of this is that for the first time ever, they are going to know *exactly* what works and what doesn't.

There's the famous quote from David Ogilvy, the founder of Ogilvy & Mather, one of the leading ad agencies in the world: "I know that only 50% of my advertising works, but I don't know which 50%."

■ LET ME TELL YOU A STORY

It's instructive to look at how advertising has evolved over the last 75 years, from its early print roots into a form suitable for broadcast media (radio and television). The most obvious difference is that the advertisers have a much more compelling way of telling us stories, or, to be precise, the story *they* want us to hear. Early print advertisements did this as well; however, the addition of sound and moving images was so striking, that it became an even more powerful way to influence our emotions.

Erik Barnouw is now 90 years old and lives in rural Vermont. He spent the first years of his career in broadcasting and advertising, then accepted an academic position at Columbia University, becoming a prominent media scholar. He is Professor Emeritus of Dramatic Arts at Columbia University, and he organized, founded, and headed the Writers' Guild of America. His book, *Tube of Plenty,* is a must-read for anyone interested in the history of broadcast media.

Barnouw grew up along with early efforts in television and radio, just as the new media was growing up itself. In 1931, in his first position at an advertising agency, he recalls how excited everyone in the business was about the commercial possibilities of advertising over radio. "The attitude was: 'This is a new and powerful force and we have to use it,'" he recalls, because, unlike print advertising "which was cold," radio had "a human voice behind it, and had the emotional power to remind us of, and thus represent, someone we love or respect."

Barnouw stresses that listening to radio was an inherently *social* experience. Until TV became a fixture of the average household, sometime in the 1950s, radio was considered a social event, something to be shared with others. Families and friends would sit around the radio, as if around a fireplace, and listen to something together. "There wasn't a radio in every room of every house," Barnouw explains. "So the radio was the family meeting ground." Of course, that gradually changed. As more radios were brought into a household, and as stations proliferated and choices expanded, the former group audience broke up.

But, alone or together as a group, the advertisers had captured our attention in a way they never had before. This is at the heart of how advertisers began to use technology effectively. They learned how each medium could be used differently to influence our emotions.

"Most decisions are made on emotion. Which is what advertisers appeal to," says Bill Ryan, the engaging chairman of Niehaus-Ryan-Wong (NRW), the first major public relations agency to focus on the Internet as a vehicle for getting its clients' messages across. "Technology helps us amplify our voice. It's a theatre of the mind."

Our imagination seduces us into believing what we're telling ourselves: *Good sex starts in the mind.* "With radio, you eliminate the visual component, and you can appeal to a different side of the brain," says Ryan. This gives you the opportunity to elicit a response from the listeners' imagination, he stresses, because each medium has a different way to engage our mind.

So NRW, like all good ad agencies, exploits what each medium allows. NRW is extraordinarily savvy on how to use technology most effectively. Its very impressive list of clients includes Apple Computer, TCI's @Home Networks, Cendant, The Well, Virtual Vineyards, Woman's Wire, and Yahoo!, as well as a number of the cutting-edge start-up companies we've covered in this book (AT&T's a2b music, CyberGold, Imagine Radio, Personify, and reel.com, among others).

When Ryan refers to using technology to "amplify voice," he's not talking about simply saying things louder; rather, *voice*, in this context, is used as one of the three main elements of building brand, as advertisers view it. The other two elements are *vision* and *positioning*. If *voice* is equivalent with personality (think Tony the Tiger, for Kellogg's Frosted Flakes), then *vision* refers to the trust the consumer has in your ability to deliver what you promise to deliver. Kellogg's products are good for you because they'll make you healthy, vibrant, and happy. Finally, *positioning* refers to how your brand compares with the rest of the world. How do we view Tony the Tiger as opposed to Toucan Sam of Froot Loops?

This notion of brand comes down to reinforcing images in the consumer's mind, often repeatedly, even endlessly. When branding succeeds, consumers are unable to disassociate the images and related emotional implications from the product or service in question. When we see Tony the Tiger, we think of Kellogg's, and we think of wholesome, good, cheerful, and safe.

Ryan himself cheerfully admits that "advertisers have obviously done a job on me over the years." For example, Ryan found himself shopping in a local Japanese supermarket (not uncommon in San Francisco) looking for Head & Shoulders shampoo. Because all the products were labeled in Japanese, he was looking for the logo.

"Through continual education and bombardment, I've come to assume that if I have dandruff, I need Head & Shoulders," Ryan says ruefully. Branding is very powerful stuff when it comes to the emotions it manages to attach to the images in question. "If I'm considering the purchase of a new luxury car, branding actually helps me choose between the alternatives," he points out. After all, a Mazda and a Lexus cost about the same, have the same features, and even look a lot alike, but "I'll buy the Lexus because our friends and neighbors will know I drive a Lexus." We've been told a story by Lexus that associates quality and prestige with that automobile. Our neighbors will envy our wealth and style if we own one.

■ THE RIGHT INFORMATION, TO THE RIGHT PERSON, AT THE RIGHT TIME

So what does all this have to do with emerging technology such as the Internet? That's simple. The problem advertisers have always faced is that the "continual education and bombardment," required for effective branding is expensive. (A single 60-second spot for *Seinfeld* went for $1 million, and a full-page ad in *The New Yorker* costs $25,000.)

Perhaps worse, it's extremely inefficient. Most ads don't get seen by most people they are intended to reach. Fewer than 1 percent of people who see a magazine advertisement will respond to its message. Yet, how much an advertiser pays is based on how many people see the ad, not how many people do something because of it.

So, advertisers are always on the lookout for the means to make their efforts more effective. Of course, the best measure of effectiveness is that the more ads they place (display, broadcast, mail out), the more sales they ring up. "The advertisers' wet dream is to make a sale to everyone who views the ad," says Tom Morgan, president and founder of N-Volve, an on-line service for children that wants to become the America Online for Kids. The problem, as Ryan sees it, is that with a few exceptions, "advertising has largely been simply blasting it out and hoping someone reacts. And this is a very inefficient form of communication."

The biggest exception to what Ryan calls the *blast-out* method is, of course, direct mail, in which the mailing is made selectively (for instance, to those people who subscribe to a certain magazine). If you subscribe to *Folk Guitar* magazine, you may be more likely to respond to an offer for the collected works of Gordon Lightfoot. Such directed mailing can achieve very high response rates, sometimes exceeding 50 percent. That's cost effective. I mostly pay for ads that are most likely to result in actual sales.

Yet, the Internet is making it possible to get even closer to this advertiser's ideal of "one ad, one sale." "It's now possible to get closer to this dream than anyone would have thought just a few years ago," says Morgan.

What is the key? It is not only getting the right information (advertising) to the right consumer, but getting it to him or her "at the right time," says Ryan. The issue is one of psychological readiness. Consider someone who loves tennis. She loves to watch tennis, she loves to play tennis, she loves to talk about tennis. Yet, a postcard advertising a sale of tennis rackets at the local sporting goods store might come at the wrong time—when she's paying the monthly electric bill, or viewing her latest mutual fund statement. It might be more effective to show her a Wilson tennis racket ad when she's watching the U.S. Open, or (better yet) surfing through a web site that sells tennis equipment.

The power of the Internet, only now being realized by advertisers, is in the ability to direct information to the psychologically ready, even eager, consumer. For starters, this seems to be what advertisers call *considered* purchases (i.e., items or services that the consumer is already considering buying), which is why the more generic banner ads you see on the typical Web page are less than effective, and why Internet advertising is much less effective for purchases of such things as shampoo, soap, or deodorant, rather than items such as books, CDs, or automobiles. The ideal recipient of any advertisement, in other words, is "someone who is predisposed to want to hear it," says Ryan.

➤ Love Potion Number 9

Presenting ads to us at exactly the moment that we're most psychologically receptive (not to say vulnerable) is not really magic, of course; however, the combination of new media technologies and the Internet together make it possible to significantly increase the advertiser's ability to do the following:

- ➤ Place an ad so the *right person* views it.
- ➤ Tailor it so it contains the *right information* for that person.
- ➤ Present it to that person at the *right time* (the point of greatest receptivity).

➤ The Right Person

We've already seen one way the Internet lets advertisers find the right person. Back in Chapter 3 ("Let's Get Personal"), we examined the attractive deal (or Faustian bargain, if you prefer) that advertisers offer on-line consumers: Give us as much personal information as you're comfortable doing, and, in return, we'll deliver an entertainment experience that's customized, personalized, and enhanced for precisely *your* interests.

The weak side of this method is twofold. First, people might not tell the truth, or the whole truth; whether in the interest of protecting their privacy, or for some other reason, they may provide misleading information about their age, interests, or habits.

Another possible downside to asking people to tell you things is that they might not know. That is, consumers might not know they have the ability to be avid fishers, or that they would love mystery novels. If they don't know—are not self-aware on this particular point—they won't be able to tell you. So, you miss out on an opportunity to sell them fishing tackle or the latest best-selling thriller.

As Morgan points out, there are certain incentives to be truthful. "If you're really a girl, you'll get Barbie ads instead of GI Joe ads. You're going to get better deals and pro-motions, discounts, incentives, so it's in your best interest to be truthful."

As far as trying to understand what people might like when they're not aware of it themselves, there's another tactic: depending not on what they say but on what they *do*, which, not surprisingly, isn't always consistent with what they say.

This may sound like *1984* all over again, but get used to it. This is the future of advertising. So, paranoid people need to prepare themselves. Ultimately, advertisers will know a lot more about us than we know about ourselves. They'll know we lingered over an image of a shiny, new red sports utility vehicle for 27.6 seconds longer than we looked at the blue subcompact, despite our stated inten-tion of buying an economy car; they'll see we visited Ama-zon.com's paperback nonfiction best-seller list 35 percent more often than we looked at hardcover, literary fiction; and they'll see that we are willing to pay 9.5 percent more for the same basket of groceries than our next-door neigh-bor if it comes from a market with a more upscale image, and so on. They (advertisers) will be watching literally everything we do on-line, and will thus have access to the soft inner belly of our individual psyches.

They'll know, in short, that they are getting to the right person. Whether we consciously tell them will ultimately become irrelevant due to technology.

▶ The Right Message

Eileen Gittens is chief executive officer of Personify, whose technology and services allow its customers to learn more about *their* customers' true behavior than had ever been thought possible. Her clients include a number of technology leaders (Intel, Novell), as well as decidedly low-tech household names (The Gap). Her business is based on the fact that most advertisers, no matter what media they are using (print, radio, television), have always been in the dark as to the precise reaction any one consumer has to any particular ad.

Personify's tools are able to capture and effectively analyze the data of what a consumer does (which is quite different from what they say they do). Early Web pioneers were just as clueless, says Gittens. Mostly, "they just don't know," who is visiting their sites, or buying their products, she says about on-line advertisers. "It's a-wing-and-a-prayer marketing," she says.

This is ironic, because the Internet is the one place where advertisers can see the precise result of their efforts. Take one of her clients, an on-line store called Virtual Vineyards that sells wine over the Internet. "They thought their market was wine snobs. So they created a site that's a wine connoisseur's dream come true," she says. This included recommendations from top sommeliers, such as Paul Prudhomme, and unique travel packages for wine tours in France.

But, when Personify came along and analyzed the log files for visitors to the Virtual Vineyards site, Gittens was able to tell them that 80 percent of their sales were to wine novices, or people who didn't know much about the art of winemaking, and they were totally uninterested in all the bells and whistles built into the Web site.

The implication for advertisers is enormous: Once you understand who your customer is, and what (generally) he or she wants from your product or service, you can tailor the message accordingly. What technology does, in short, is it allows advertisers to tailor the message more precisely.

A television commercial aired during the Super Bowl must be constructed to appeal to as many viewers as possible. The mass media requires a one-to-many construct: one ad for many potential viewers.

Ideally, an advertiser would like a one-to-one ratio: one message for each individual consumer, designed to appeal to his or her individual taste. Because this is not (yet) possible, says Gittens, on-line advertisers are using what she calls the "one-to-some" model. The reason this works fairly well, she says, is because "People tend to aggregate according to interests and needs." So, although for a client like Novell, which has 100,000 visitors a day to its web site, one-to-one marketing is not an economical option, "we can group Novell site visitors by factors such as whether they value convenience, price, or usability," she says. Different messages are then targeted toward these different groups.

Once you have differentiated your consumers by broader categories, it's possible to drill down even further. Says Ryan, "once you have them in the boat, then you can work on selling them one-to-one." The trick, whenever possible, is to manage the complex mass of information advertisers will increasingly have on individuals, and turn it into usable information, he says. If the 1980s and 1990s were about database mining, the next generation of advertising tools will focus on recognizing more subtle patterns within a much larger and more complex mountain of consumer information.

Data mining let a company know, for example, that 36.8 percent of its customers responded to certain ads, but it did not help them understand the expected behavior of any individual customer. This is what Personify does, in effect: create a "predictive" model of customer behavior derived from how that consumer behaved while on-line, even if there's no direct link. For example, a Personify analysis might discover that consumers who browse the Peapod.com site, shopping for their groceries, are more likely to purchase hand lotion while viewing information about bananas. "We convert a firehose of data into the pearls that are meaningful from a business perspective," she says.

➤ The Right Time

In addition to trying to find the right person and send them the right message, advertisers also spend a great deal of time and effort attempting to guess when a person is ready to buy their product or service. Interestingly enough, the higher the price of a product or service under consideration for purchase, "the shorter the period a person can bear the stress of that situation," observes Morgan. So, understanding when a consumer is in this "mode" is critical.

Advertisers are well aware that people surfing the Internet can be either on a mission or on a ride. If they're on a mission, then they know just what they want, and sometimes are even ready with a product order number before they log on. When they're on a ride, however, they're hoping for serendipity. Surprise me.

This isn't to say that the two forms of surfing can't co-exist. Often, people go to a bookstore or a grocery store on a mission (to pick up a specific item), but end up being on a ride (buying things they didn't intend to buy), which is just what Amazon.com is doing with its recommendation engine. Whenever you show interest in a book, they suggest several other books that might also match your interests. In short, they are trying to convert your mission into a ride that results in more profits for them. In brick-and-mortar retail, this is called the "impulse buy," and infinite amounts of research have gone into promoting it.

The best ads are often informational, especially for a subject matter you are personally interested in. If you subscribe to a skiing or stereo magazine, chances are good that the ads in that magazine can contain valuable information for you, often as valuable as the articles themselves. You are psychologically ready to receive those ads when you open the magazine.

One of the prime reasons that on-line advertising, thus far, has missed its mark is that there's been little attempt at figuring out your state of psychological readiness. On-line advertisers, however, are just beginning to understand how this concept might work in cyberspace.

Personify helped another client, the Computer Literacy Bookstore, determine the profile for which customers were ready to buy, and for which customers wanted a lot of information before they'd be ready to buy. Personify helped Computer Literacy redesign their entire web site so that customers who are ready to buy are immediately taken to the page to do so, while other customers are presented with book reviews, reader comments, and links to related information. These customers see an entirely different structure to the Computer Literacy site than do customers who know the book they want to purchase. Because they know which customer will be most receptive to the pitch, they use that information to present the offer *only* when that customer is ready. There is no wastage, and it's better for the customer (who sees no ads when he or she really doesn't want to).

■ GETTING MORE RESPECT

This brings us back to the Faustian bargain (the exchange of personal information for enhanced service), which can be used to give us more of what we want, but can also be misused to take advantage of what we don't even know about our own behavior. Ryan points out how the Internet has a unique opportunity to engage us positively. "We can stop treating the advertisee, like a scene from *A Clockwork Orange,* and treating them as an informed, intelligent, consumer," he points out. If the advertiser thinks of the consumer less as someone who needs to have products and services forced down his or her throat, and more like "someone who needs an appropriate amount of information to make a decision," something very good could happen in the advertising world. For example, the Saturn car salesperson, instead of following you around the lot like a used car salesperson, is available to answer your questions when you're ready to know. "We now have the ability to treat the consumer with more respect," says Ryan.

■ AS LONG AS IT RESULTS IN MORE PROFITS

As we will see in Chapter 11 ("Family Feud"), not every entertainment business uses advertising as a source of revenue. TV and radio broadcasters, newspapers, and magazines do, but record companies, book publishers, video game makers, and movie studios don't—at least, not yet.

Advertisers will adopt new technology as long as it's profitable. In the end, it comes down to the total cost to make each sale. If they can do it for less, that's good business. And if the Internet can deliver a far more efficient way of making sales, then broadcasters had better pay attention.

They don't want to repeat what happened to radio when the TV audience exploded. RCA (the Radio Corporation of America) completely supported NBC (its wholly owned subsidiary, the National Broadcasting Company) financially for almost three decades before NBC would have been able to operate on its own income. In effect, radio built the gallows (television) that eventually was used for its execution.

Erik Barnouw explained that the reaction to TV was originally very mixed. "Some people were very eager to get into TV and thought that radio was finished, and others saw that radio was subsidizing TV. Radio subsidized its own destruction." No one wants to subsidize their own destruction. If advertisers follow the eyeballs (and ears), then broadcasters are sure to follow. They will follow the money.

Significantly, the Internet offers advertisers something that a broadcast medium can't. It can customize what each viewer sees. Anyone watching tonight's episode of *Frasier* on WNBC (NBC's owned and operated affiliate in New York) sees exactly the same program and ads at the same time as anyone else who is watching.

All of this means that advertising efficiency and effectiveness can be considerably higher on the Internet than in traditional broadcasting. If they can spend less and get better results, advertisers are going to jump at this approach. Advertisers won't dump TV, just as they didn't dump radio or newspapers, but they will spend an increasing percentage of their total ad budgets on the Internet.

■ BROAD OR NARROW

This brings us to the raging debate over whether Internet advertising will *ever* be a successful business and, therefore, whether the Internet will *ever* become a truly mass-market broadcast medium. The issue revolves around the question of broadcast (to a mass audience) versus narrowcast (to a smaller audience). Is there ever going to be enough income potential to survive for sites with just a modest amount of traffic? Naysayers think not.

Here's the view of the doubters, as voiced acerbically by Rich Wood, director of WOR-FM, in an Internet newsgroup discussion, "In web-casting everything is a first. Never been done before. Going to revolutionize life on the planet. Going to wipe out media as we know it. I can't find a video site where the mouth movements match the audio, but, I guess, that's not important when something's a 'first.' "

Their view is that not only is current on-line media quality questionable at best, but that even if it ever reaches broadcast quality, it still won't significantly displace current broadcast media, because it isn't a self-supporting business. The problem is that the way broadcast ad sales are made doesn't work well on a global network.

On the other hand, Martin Nisenholtz, president of *The New York Times New Media,* sees how it *will* work. *The New York Times* operates on both sides of the advertising equation—advertisers pay to place their ads in *The New York Times,* and *The New York Times* places its own ads in other media to bring in subscribers. Nisenholtz says that the most loyal ad customers for their on-line edition are the ones who already do business in the digital world (such as books, PCs, movies, and travel services). "They see the fate of their business in how well they execute their on-line marketing campaign. As compared with companies that sell packaged goods. Records, books, and movies are all shifting their sales online." Entertainment is already moving on-line.

Nisenholtz knows the advertising business from both sides. Way back in 1982, as a senior vice president at Ogilvy & Mather, one of the world's top ad agencies, he launched their interactive marketing efforts, *O&M Direct*. He says that makes him "either a pioneer or a very silly person," but he knows the value of advertising, and how to use it. He says that *The New York Times Online* does place some ad inventory with Yahoo! (the top Internet portal), but that will never outperform the inventory they place with *Slate* (a high-brow, on-line magazine).

They measure productivity by the number of loyal, re-turn customers, not by click-throughs. "Click-throughs are meaningless by themselves," he says, "if I put the word 'sex' in a banner ad, I can get a 50% click-through rate, but that had no relationship to what I'm after. Loyal cus-tomers." *Slate,* a niche, outperforms Yahoo!, the top Inter-net portal. It's clear to *The New York Times* that niche has value for them. In fact, Nisenholtz says that they "get their highest productivity where they don't get the highest click rate at the outset. Though this may sound counter-intuitive, it's true." *The New York Times* sees on-line adver-tising as extremely cost effective, when used properly.

■ STOLEN STREAMS

There's an interesting problem associated with consolida-tion and Internet advertisements. That is, even as all dif-ferent kinds of media *consolidate* to create this new kind of entertainment content on the Internet—after all, whether it's audio, video, images, text, it's all just digital bits and bytes—the media content is also starting to *separate* from the advertising that subsidizes it.

To put it more simply, one of the advantages of the Internet is that you, the consumer, don't have to worry about where your entertainment content is coming from. You don't have to consult the electronic equivalent of the *TV Guide*, or consult a radio programming schedule. Click on what interests you, and your browser takes you there—whether it's to a video clip of a new movie, or an audio clip of your favorite rock star, or a photographic image of whatever is in the news that evening.

But, there's a problem—a big one. Advertisements are stored in separate files from the media clips themselves. If you are pointed to a media clip from a different web site, you don't necessarily get the related ads. It's as if *Frasier* episodes were broadcasted by one TV station while the related ads were broadcasted from another, sister station: you are supposed to get the two broadcasts together (that's what makes this particular business profitable). But, if it were possible to watch just the "content-only" station, everything would break down economically.

Now, you begin to get the idea of the problem, because (as we've discussed before) there's no such thing as a free lunch. If you are being entertained, then someone is paying—either you are forking over some money to cover all (or part) of the experience, or you've agreed to allow someone else to subsidize you in exchange (usually) for your time and attention.

What's at issue is whether any one web site should be able to point you to another web site that contains good entertainment content that you are also likely to enjoy. You might be surprised to learn this, because that's something virtually all web sites have in common. It's even considered to be one of the major strengths of the Internet. But, when a web site is pointing to a media object (an Internet radio station, a comedy show, CNN's news, the JenniCam), and allows you to jump there, pronto, they can, in effect, steal the ad revenue from the media owner.

Notice a key difference between outright stealing of content and just pointing to it: a web site that wouldn't dream of posting a CNN video clip (that would be stealing) on its site would think nothing of letting people jump directly to that clip using a hot link—not incidentally collecting the related ad revenues as you pass by. You are, in effect, depriving CNN of its rightful revenues.

Take it a step further, and say a single web site was savvy enough to provide pointers not only to a single CNN video clip, but to all of CNN's televised news, all WOR radio shows, and all of *The Wall Street Journal* on-line newsclips. It would be able to sell progressively more ads as it accumulated viewers, and with such terrific content, it would be gaining a great deal of revenue without doing a bit of content creation or broadcast. Perhaps worse still, the original content providers (CNN, WOR, WSJ) would have costs associated with every one of the additional viewers in the form of added Web servers, network connections, and so on. Naturally, they'd consider this theft.

This issue is only now beginning to get some publicity. But, keep an eye on what is one of the sharpest thorns in Internet advertising's sides.

■ A PLACE FOR EVERYTHING, AND EVERYTHING IN ITS PLACE

Rather than predicting any sort of all-or-nothing result of media wars, we believe that the Internet will have a place in consumer advertising. As with similar struggles over the differences in effectiveness between print, radio, and television, there will turn out to be complimentary uses for these otherwise competitive media outlets. So, we'll see increasing use of cross-promotion in all media segments. Advertising agencies will have yet another bucket to take their clients' advertising dollars—each bucket (print, radio, television, Internet) having its strengths as an advertising medium. We're already seeing this happen:

➤ E-Trade, an on-line stock-trading company, announced that it intends to spend two-thirds of its entire 1999 operational budget on marketing. Yet, recognizing that it is difficult to build an on-line brand solely with on-line advertising, E-Trade is doing aggressive cross-media ad placement using TV, radio, newspaper, magazine, and direct mailing promotions. Expect to see E-Trade bulletin boards on a freeway near your town, E-Trade radio spots, E-Trade television ads, and of course, E-Trade Internet banners whenever you browse an investment-related site.

➤ Reel.com, the video rental operation run by Stuart Skorman, offered the *Titanic* video for sale at a promotional price of $9.95, thus losing almost $6 on every sale. They advertised this special on-line-only deal . . . you guessed it—on Howard Stern's syndicated radio show. It was a classic loss leader, brand management strategy, and it worked, because enough people who logged onto the reel.com site to snatch up *Titanic* at this bargain price ended up buying other videos as well. More importantly, reel.com's traffic skyrocketed overnight, and they were on their way toward building a brand.

Not to mention that virtually every media conglomerate is increasing its on-line operations, and heading toward selling on the Net. They can't afford not to.

This is why Tom Morgan says we're going to see entirely new kinds of media companies. "Media companies now participate in direct transaction, even though they're not a retailer. America Online takes as much as 65% of transaction gross. You've never seen a direct marketing media company, you've never seen a transactional media company, you've only seen an advertising media company. But on the web, we have all 3 kinds of media companies, or 3 steps where one company can follow all the way through—some of the revenue of the media will surely be transactions."

That is exactly what we talk about in Chapter 11 ("Family Feud"). All the entertainment businesses are moving into everybody else's businesses, and advertisers are in the new media mix as much as any industry.

Competition between networks offers the promise of broadband entertainment, and the threat of another closed network.

Chapter

Brought to You
by . . . (Networks)

"What in the world is a former FCC chairman doing predicting the possible demise of the broadcast business?"

—REED HUNDT, FCC chairman, 1993–1997[1]

"The all optical network will succeed in the future for the same reason the integrated circuit triumphed: it will be incomparably cheaper than the competition."

—GEORGE GILDER, author of *Telecosm*

"When I look at the Internet, I see the future of communications. When I look at our aging switched networks, I see the Valley of Death."

—a senior telecom executive[2]

"If you're not scared by this, you don't understand."

—JOHN SIDGMORE, chief operating officer, WorldCom/MCI

There's an old joke told by folks who live deep in the countryside: A traveler stops to ask directions to a large city, and one of the locals replies that "if that's where you want to go, I wouldn't start from here." That's often the way it is with technological advancement—the current state of affairs isn't usually the best place to start, especially for aging telecommunications networks. In a perfect world, as new network technology emerges, telecom networks would simply replace older technology. But, when hundreds of billions of dollars have been invested in the current way of doing things, it's not economically practical to simply start over, which is why existing telecommunications providers are in such a state. What this has to do with entertainment—what the plumbing of the digital age has to do with the average consumer—is a story that begins in our homes.

Here's a safe bet: just about every reader of this book currently possesses at least one TV, an antenna, cable TV service, VCR, radio, stereo system, CD player, telephone, PC, and Internet access. Why is this a safe bet? Statistically (as of the time this book went to press), 98 percent of U.S. homes had all of the consumer devices named, and more than 50 percent already had PCs and Internet connections. A significant number of households also subscribe to a digital satellite TV service (such as DirectTV), and own and use at least one cellular telephone (which are increasingly digital rather than analog). What will happen in the first few years of the twenty-first century is, in a sense, more of the same—more TVs, more satellite TV subscribers, and many more people who choose to connect to the Internet.

There is, however, a different kind of change under way, a change most of us will only be peripherally aware of: that's how the *delivery mechanisms* for these various products and services will change. In other words, it's not that we won't have the same sorts of options in terms of networks that can provide us with entertainment and related communications services. We will—but even more so.

What will change is *which* networks will bring us *which* services; already, all the boundaries have begun to blur. Eventually, they will disappear entirely. Consider the following:

➤ Today, most cable TV subscribers think of their cable service as a way to get broadcast and cable TV networks and pay-per-view movies. Several cable systems, however, have already started to offer high-speed Internet access, and some even offer local and long-distance telephone service. Cable isn't just for cable.

➤ Today, most people think of the telephone as something they use for voice calls, fax, and Internet dial-up access; however, technology to offer movies, television, and more has already been proven in early trials. Telephone networks aren't just for telephone.

➤ Today, people think of the television as a device that does nothing but deliver video entertainment; however, digital television will deliver Internet access and will become something we'll be interacting with (at least while we surf the on-line television guides).

We will have ever more choices of how we get our entertainment: broadcast television (antenna, cable, satellite, analog and/or digital, Internet), cable networks (cable, satellite, Internet), telephone service (wireline, wireless, cable, satellite, Internet), Internet access (wireline, wireless, TV, cable, satellite), not to mention video games, recorded music, newspapers, magazines, books, and more.

Choice is good, and although consumer behavior is very slow to change (i.e., we don't think of our local telephone company as the place to rent movies and listen to records), in the end, consumers will continue to seek out the best value in price, availability, service, reliability, simplicity, and bandwidth. This is what matters most to most consumers, and what will ultimately decide how we get our entertainment. So, let's take a look at how service providers will do at each of these (because they all dream of providing all of our services).[3]

■ TELL ME—OH, WHAT CAN I DO?

Once you get over the shock of the big new idea, it's sometimes not all that strange. Okay, I can get my telephone service from my cable TV company. But, where do I hook my telephone into my TV? You won't. In a decade or two, we'll think in terms of the service we get, more than in terms of who delivers that service. The service is what we can each do: receive network TV broadcasts, receive cable and satellite TV networks, receive radio broadcasts, make phone calls (local, long-distance, mobile), access the Internet.

One of the biggest differentiators between these services is whether they are one-way today (the broadcasts), or if they are inherently two-way (telephony and Internet access), which makes it clear that a service provider needs a two-way technology to provide more than broadcast services. Thus, today's one-way broadcasters (TV, cable, satellite) will need to either enhance their systems with two-way capabilities, or partner with some other service provider who offers consumers a way to communicate back to the broadcaster (sometimes called *back channel,* or *upstream*).

Cable services are already upgrading to two-way. Satellite providers are about to launch two-way services (Motorola's Iridium global telephony services and Teledesic's data services), but most satellite companies offer two-way service via a different back channel (via telephone or cable). Because no consumer would even consider putting a digital TV transmitter on his or her home (even if priced to sell at just $500,000), only telephone and cable are suitable for two-way communications.

The point of which is that if digital TV and satellite broadcasters want to offer us the full gamut of interactive services, they'll need to have a solution that involves some other network's back channel. As we'll see, that's potentially a big competitive disadvantage.

Grade: Telcos and cable get an A; TV and satellite broadcasters get a C.

■ EASY ENOUGH FOR EVEN DAD TO USE

Let's see which kind of network has an advantage in the ease of use required to build a mass market. Why we watch so much television can be attributed, in part, to the fact that it's easy to use (turn it on and go limp on your couch) and free to use (after you buy a TV set). Although every time we hook something up to it, the setup and connections get just a little bit more complicated—VCR, cable, stereo, satellite DSS, DVD, not to mention connecting all the TVs in the house to a single cable set-top or satellite receiver. As much work as that sounds like, it's nothing compared with the astonishing technical annoyances we bear when we change any of the software on our personal computers. Computers are something only a mother could love. Here's an anonymous story that makes the point.

> *The computer industry loves to brag about the truly remarkable improvements in performance and function that they've brought to market. And it's not uncommon for senior technology executives to compare the improvements in PC speed with the automotive equivalent: If GM made cars the way we make PCs, the average car would go 25,000 miles an hour. They're right, of course. But for no reason whatsoever, it would randomly crash twice a day. Occasionally, executing a maneuver such as a left turn, would cause your car to shut down and refuse to restart, in which case you would have to reinstall the engine. Everytime manufacturers introduced a new model car buyers would have to learn how to drive all over again because none of the controls would operate in the same manner as in the old car. You'd press the "start" button to shut off the engine.*

Building a mass market depends on making it transparently easy to use (including installation and upgrades). If it's easy enough for your average five-year-old to use, then that's about right for a mass market. And, despite the marketing hype, this is *not* something that the PC industry has yet been able to accomplish.

TV, cable, and satellite broadcasters have all succeeded in deploying entertainment systems that virtually anyone can use without significant training. Although it can be argued that telephone companies (local, long-distance, and cellular) have also succeeded in creating systems easy enough for most people to use, they have not widely deployed *entertainment* services.

What does all of this mean? It means that today's broadcasters have usability as a home-field advantage over the telecom companies for the raw broadcast of entertainment. There's no such advantage, however, for interactive entertainment, because no one has shown the ability to do this for a mass market. And, although two-way interactivity enables all the new, possibly wonderful forms of entertainment we've discussed, it opens Pandora's Box to all the bothersome technical issues we experience with PCs, which is not for everyone. It's too soon to say which kind of network has an advantage with interactivity.

Grade: Broadcasters get an A for broadcast-only usability; telcos get a B.

■ AVAILABILITY

It doesn't matter how cool, useful, or usable a service is if most people can't get it. Not surprisingly, the one-way broadcast systems (terrestrial and satellite TV) are far less expensive to deploy than two-way systems (cable, wireline, wireless). The dramatic difference in cost will translate into how quickly they can deploy, and how much it will cost us.

Terrestrial broadcast is the easiest and most cost-effective means to reach a massive audience. TV broadcasters estimate the cost of upgrading to digital TV at something on the order of $3 million, which, with roughly 1,500 commercial stations in the United States, puts the industrywide upgrade cost at $4.5 billion.[4] That's a lot to invest, but it's still just 2 percent of the industry's revenue over five years. Once the system is deployed, there is no cost for each new user who taps into that network. This is a key economic advantage for terrestrial broadcast. Marginal cost (for the broadcast network) per user is zero; the consumer pays for the TV set, antenna, and any converter.

Digital broadcast satellite (DBS) is also a rather cost-effective means to reach a large geographic audience for broadcast. The deployment cost for each satellite broadcaster is very roughly $1 billion. (The cost is hard to estimate because it depends on the price that the orbital slot was auctioned for, and that depends on the competitive bidding for that slot.) Then there's considerable latitude (no pun intended) in the system design for how many satellites need to be deployed. It's probably a good generalization to say that each DBS system can be upgraded to HDTV for $1 billion. And, as for terrestrial TV broadcast, the consumer picks up the tab for the converter set-top.

Telephone networks and cable TV systems require the most expensive system upgrades. AT&T estimated that for the entire system upgrade, the average cost per household would be $750. Thus, with 100 million households in the United States, the system cost is roughly $75 billion—an order of magnitude, or more, expensive than the TV and satellite upgrades. And, because the system is two-way, there are additional costs for every user who is added to the universe of all users: switches, servers, routers, backbone bandwidth, billing and accounting software, technical support operations, and so on.

These costs are viewed by the various networks as investments—system upgrades that enable the entire array of telecommunications and entertainment services that we've outlined. Despite the considerable expense involved, there's simply no alternative to this. It would be competitive suicide to let the other networks do it all. So they're all doing it—or, at least, saying they are. After all the highly publicized failures in the early 1990s, everyone is taking their rollout plans with a heavy grain of salt.

And, then, there's the FCC, which is part Dudley Do-Right, part Snidely Whiplash, depending on one's point of view. The FCC is eager to have all these services deployed—yesterday, please—but not as eager to relax all the many regulations that bind these networks to old and inefficient technologies and business models. This is too good a melodrama to summarize in a few pages, but it's along the lines you might expect. All parties involved in this are acting in their self-interest; all decisions are debated and many are taken to the courts for resolution; there's politics in everything, and a lot of posturing. Suffice it to say that the high stakes mean that this is going to play out over decades. It would make a terrific soap opera, if only most people could understand what was going on.

When Congress passed the Telecommunications Act of 1996, they thought that, having legislated deregulation, there'd actually be considerably less regulation. They had better be patient. Looking ahead 10 years:

➤ Digital TV is very likely to be fully deployed with total U.S. coverage.

➤ Cable systems are very likely to be fully digital, but with less than complete national coverage (probably 70 percent).

➤ Telephone systems are very likely to be fully deployed broadband access, with complete coverage.

➤ Satellite systems will surely upgrade for broadband, able to reach more than 90 percent of U.S. homes.

Grade: Terrestrial TV, satellite TV, and telcos get an A; cable gets a B for incomplete coverage.

■ BANDWIDTH

The facts are pretty clear. *Theoretically,* the coaxial cable coming into your home today offers the greatest possible bandwidth by an order of magnitude. Cable can deliver up to 300 megabits per second (Mb/sec). Wireline connections, the pair of copper wires that comes into your home for each phone line, have the ability to reach as high as 30 megabits per second. DTV's downstream capacity of 20 megabits per second per channel is high bandwidth for commonly shared content, but low bandwidth for non-shared content. The same can be said for satellite. Even with radical improvements, wireless bandwidth will not be a serious bandwidth contender.

Grade: Cable gets the only A; telcos, TV, and satellite TV get a B; wireless gets a C.

■ RELIABILITY

No one has a clue. It's all about the difference between a TV and a PC. TVs can work for decades, but we usually reboot our PCs several times daily. This *is* something that the consumer electronics industry has achieved. A television set from the 1950s could work today when connected to an antenna or cable system. This durability is not incidental to the success of the TV networks. If early owners of TV sets experienced the same upgrade path that's required for PC hardware and software, it's doubtful that the TV would ever have become a mass market. Most people won't voluntarily put up with that kind of abuse, though PC owners seem to. You don't need to worry about system upgrades to your TV set making your VCR inoperable.

Until now, that is—as soon as these living room products are enhanced with a heavy dose of interactivity, they'll become as general purpose as the PC and as unreliable. Prepare to reboot your life.

Grade: Everyone gets an "Incomplete."

■ LAST, BUT NOT LEAST, PRICE MATTERS

Television is free, they say. Sure it is, once you buy a TV set; a VCR (98 percent of U.S. households have); and now maybe a DVD, too, as a replacement for our CD player. That was okay for more than 18 million consumers who have purchased home theatres, at more than $3,000 a pop. That's an investment that will last them for a decade or more—well, maybe not.

Once we start converting *all* the home entertainment systems we have to digital TV, the bill starts to get much larger. Let's look at what it will cost us if we want to enjoy high-definition TV, as opposed to just standard-definition digital TV. Otherwise, why would we upgrade to high-definition? Then we'd need a digital tuner/decoder, a digital antenna, a digital VCR, a digital DVD, a digital cable modem (or set-top), and a digital video game console, and a digital WebTV (if we have one). It could cost the average household $2,000 for all this. Dear Santa, please help. No wonder the consumer electronics industry is eagerly awaiting this.

If the consumer electronics industry actually succeeds in getting most households to replace all of this equipment, that surely makes them one of the big winners in the coming decade (with $200 billion in new equipment sales). That is assuming, of course, that most households care enough about high-definition to shell out that kind of cash. This is a questionable assumption.

Then, there's the ongoing cost of the services we use. Let's look at the average costs. Broadcast TV is free, cable TV is $40 per month, satellite TV is $60 per month, local phone service is $20 per month, long distance is $60 per month, cellular is $40 per month, and Internet access is $30 per month. That totals about $250 per month (or $3,000 per year). Combined, there's $300 billion at stake in the U.S. market.

It's hard to compete against a free service (TV network broadcast), but cable and satellite companies do so successfully today, mostly because subscribers have a broader selection of shows. There will always be an audience for free content, almost regardless of how bad the content is.

Here's the key to price: if your network is more than 20 percent out of line with the price of other network services, your network will fail to win a mass audience. So, everyone's network prices need to be in line with other networks (including all consumer device and installation costs).

Grade: DTV gets an A, and everyone else gets a B.

■ AND THE WINNER IS . . . ?

The winner is the consumer. All of these networks are engaged in what they believe is a life-and-death competition to bring us all of these services, at price points that most consumers will find attractive. Within the next decade, at least one of the networks will likely succeed in doing so.

So, why bother comparing all the network alternatives? The reason is that it illustrates many of the important issues that need to be addressed, and the relative strengths and weaknesses of each of these alternative service providers. Table 10.1 summarizes the comparison that we've imagined for the year 2008. Possibly, Table 10.1 is most helpful in clearly marking each network's weak spots:

TABLE 10.1 Imaginary Comparison of Network Alternatives in 2008

	Services	Simplicity	Availability	Bandwidth	Price	Reliability
Cable	A	A	B	A	B	?
Wireline	A	B	A	B	B	?
DTV	C	A	A	B	A	?
Satellite	C	A	A	B	B	?
Wireless	A	C	C	C	B	?

➤ Cable TV has the best shot at deploying all of the services, but it probably will not reach everyone.

➤ Wireline also has a good shot at deploying all services, but the telco track record does not suggest that they've got the entrepreneurial ability to deploy widely. What's more likely is that they'll partner with another network for entertainment. Telcos have the technology, but do they have the will?

➤ DTV broadcasters have the best price (free), and they have a good clue at what people want (content that draws the largest audiences, devices that are trivially easy to use). But, for truly interactive services, they'll need to partner with some other network for the back channel (upstream from the consumer). They can't do it alone.

➤ The same can be said for satellite TV services. Although there are two-way satellite services about to be launched for telephony (Motorola's Iridium) and data (Bill Gates' and Craig McCaw's Teledesic), there's no promise that these will ever be broadband services capable of delivering entertainment.

➤ Wireless will be a constructive partner to several of the other networks, but it has no chance of going alone to offer all of these services.

■ OPEN AND CLOSED

Along with the bragging rights for bringing all of these cool services to as many people as possible, goes the right to control something that we want no one to control. In the movie *Citizen Kane,* when Charles Foster Kane states, "They think what I tell them to think," he means it. His power crosses all media.

It's not altogether different in the world of TV, cable, and radio. Although no one has that kind of über-control over the totality of our entertainment choices, there are choke points that do limit what we can watch. Each of the networks is essentially, a scarce resource that the network controls to maximize its profit.

The four commercial TV networks control all of the material we watch on the only broadcast network that reaches everyone. There's no Gutenberg press to help the independent video producer. The four networks are the only way to reach that audience; therefore, they are the only way to reach the advertisers who want that mass audience.

Cable is similar, except that it's dominated by two companies: Time Warner Turner, and Tele-Communications, Inc. (TCI). If you want to have carriage on their systems, not only do you have to pay these operators for carriage, they will first have to approve your content.

Then, there's the Internet, a truly open network with no limits on what can be shared across the world. Anyone can be a publisher, anyone can be a broadcaster, and one can view whatever they want. The Internet is the most open network ever devised.

Think about it. If *you* profited by controlling a scarce resource, such as access to a large number of cable TV households, what would you think about the possibility of a network that no one can control and with no scarcity. Some pundits have already begun to question whether today's closed networks will be able to control the world's only open network. If they can convert the Internet to a closed network ("Pass through us if you want to publish."), then it's probably in their economic self-interest to do so. Scarcity equals power. "Carriage is no big deal unless the network is a closed, scarce resource," says Tom Morgan.

This is why it matters who wins the war of the networks. If the networks remain separate, sometimes com-

petitors and sometimes partners, then the Internet remains open. If any one of the networks wins the war, then
sooner or later they'll find an excuse to close the network
("We're just protecting the public."). The ghost of Charles
Foster Kane continues to haunt us.

How everyone in entertainment is messing around in everyone else's business. Or, "There's a little bad in everything good that happens."[1]

Chapter

11

Family Feud

"General Electric and Time Warner announced yesterday that NBC and Turner Broadcasting are moving toward the creation of a new professional football league."

—CNN/SI, May 27, 1998

"There is no education like adversity."

—Benjamin Disraeli

What do you see when you connect these dots?

➤ Disney (species *Michaelus Rodentus*) is evolving into something, uh, new. Disney.com, the company's main web site (until that's superseded by its go.com web site) has links to every corner of Disney's worldwide entertainment empire. Listen to Disney Radio live, play on-line games, book a holiday on Disney's new cruise ship, check out previews of upcoming Disney television series episodes, link to the ESPN sports site, check out the news on ABC.com, or enter The Store to buy something (and Disney has a lot to offer). Everything connects to everything. Watch, listen, subscribe, buy. And, Disney intends to profit from every revenue opportunity, whether advertising, subscription, or sales.

➤ MSNBC is the love child of the two companies with the highest market capitalization in the world: Microsoft (number 1 at $267 billion) and General Electric Co., the parent of NBC (number 2 at $256 billion). Together, they've created what they call "the only news organization to embrace broadcast, cable, and the Internet." You can watch on network TV (NBC), cable TV (CNBC, MSNBC), and go on-line for more information on MSNBC.com. Watch, subscribe, interact. How do they make their money? They make it from both advertising and subscription. It won't be long before there are direct sales, too—and we're not talking about MSNBC T-shirts, either.

➤ British Interactive Broadcasting (BiB) is the child of four powerful conglomerates. British Sky Broadcasting (BSkyB) is the world's largest satellite pay television operator (part of Rupert Murdoch's worldwide media empire, News Corp); BT is one of the world's largest telecommunications companies; Matsushita is one of the top two consumer electronics companies; and British Midland is one of the world's largest banking and financial services. When it's launched in early 1999, BiB will offer these interactive services to its subscribers in the United Kingdom: shopping, home banking, travel and entertainment ticketing services, on-line games, and more. Because it will be received on the same digital set-top device that BSkyB subscribers use to view movies, on-screen guides, television, and radio, it will be used to provide interactive advertisements in the commercial time slots. Watch, listen, interact, buy. Advertising, subscription, pay per use, sales. You name it, they're going to do it.

What we see when we connect these dots is nothing less than the future of entertainment: new kinds of entertainment, new business models, and new industry structures. What the aforementioned examples show above everything else (business savvy, technological innovation, chutzpah) is that, just as in other industries (retail, manufacturing, consumer goods), digital technology is wreaking glorious havoc in the entertainment sector. "The computer and communications explosion is *totally transforming* industries that move and process information, such as media, entertainment, communications, and business services,"[2] proclaimed *Business Week* in one of many articles on the topic published in the past two years. So, for example, BiB is an example of a satellite TV broadcaster moving from advertising and subscription into sales.

Possibly even more dramatic than the wholesale changes *within* each of these entertainment industries are the massive changes starting to occur *between* them— record makers are moving into the territory formerly controlled by radio broadcasters; radio broadcasters are encroaching on the fields of their TV brethren; TV broadcasters are starting to incorporate the sorts of things found only in video games; and so on. For example, while you're playing a game at Disney's Blast, you can be listening to Disney Radio (on-line), watching Disney TV previews, and even engaging in live on-line chat with famous personalities—all at the same time, if you can bear it (or should that be *mouse* it?).

As we've seen, the Internet and related technologies have made it possible—perhaps even necessary—for existing entertainment providers to compete in new ways. When we're watching a video newsclip, while we're reading related articles, while we're engaged in heated debates with people we've never met—what *is* that experience? It's not quite like the radio, television, newspaper, and interactive entertainment we've ever had before. In short, we're increasingly watching our radio, listening to our newspapers, playing our television.

What's happening is that all of the media that have always been separate are being joined into something entirely new and unexpected. And, in the process, they're blurring many of the distinctions to which we've long been accustomed. Welcome to the twenty-first century, where you won't need those outdated notions anymore. Walt Disney's CEO, Michael Eisner, predicted that when the smoke clears, there will be an entirely new entertainment medium, one that blurs all the distinctions we've ever made between TV, radio, movies, games, and records, not just in the experience itself, but in the business models underlying each formerly separate segment. It's the biggest new game in the business, and it really is a family feud. Are you friend, or foe, or maybe both? Whichever is most profitable.

■ BEFORE AND AFTER

This book is about upcoming changes in the ways we play—changes not only in the experience of being entertained, but also in the *business* of entertainment. To see just how striking these changes will be, take a look at how these industries are likely to look before and after digital technology ground zero hits (see Table 11.1). Everything is shifting, both within—and between—industries.

Radio and TV broadcasters will shift away from advertising-based revenue, and toward revenue generated by direct sales and subscriptions. Record makers will shift from making their money on sales and subscriptions, to collecting advertising dollars, and to selling new kinds of music-related products and services, as will video game publishers, and so on.

■ THE ENTREPRENEUR FORMERLY KNOWN AS PRINCE

If you want to shatter the fundamental relationships within a particular industry, it doesn't hurt to be famous

TABLE 11.1 Changing Business Models in Entertainment Media Segments

	BEFORE			AFTER		
	Advertising	Sales	Subscription	Advertising	Sales	Subscription
Movies		100%		←	→	←
Radio	100%			→	←	←
TV	100%			→	←	←
Cable TV	50%		50%	→	←	→
Records		90%	10%	←	→	→
Games		100%		←	→	←
Gambling		100%		←	→	←
Magazines	55%	20%	25%	→	←	←
Newspapers	80%	10%	10%	→	←	←
Books		90%	10%	←	→	←

Sources: Adapted from Veronis, Suhler & Associates, and Silicon Valley Virtual.

and successful, and have a large and loyal following. Prince, right around the time he morphed into The Artist Formerly Known As Prince, had a strong idea about the way he wanted the future of the record business to play out: without middle people. In late 1997, The Artist Formerly Known As Prince (TAFKAP) issued a press release that announced, among other things, his "xperiment in truth." This "xperiment" would contain "no charts, no royalty disputes, no returns, no arguing over product placement, no singles and video budgets, no egos, and, most of all, *no* middleman!" he continued.

Now, whether this "xperiment" succeeded—and that's debated by music industry analysts—what is not debatable is that all the problems TAFKAP complained about are endemic throughout entertainment. No matter the media, in every kind of publishing, whether music, books, games, TV and radio syndication, magazines, or newspapers, publishers and authors/artists are engaged in an endless tug-of-war over who gets paid what.

Typically, a first-time recording artist can expect to receive an advance against royalties somewhere in the range of between 10 and 15 percent of net revenue ($0.50 per CD sold). The more famous you are, the better your track record, the more clout you have. "Everything is a negotiation," says Albhy Galuten, senior VP of technology at Seagrams' Universal Music Group, the largest record company in the world.[3]

One of the best examples of the power to negotiate was the $18 billion licensing deal that CBS and Disney's ABC agreed to with the NFL. The NFL had been able to nearly double the terms it had previously offered the television networks for the rights to broadcast NFL games, even though it was clear to everyone, including those two networks, that they could not possibly recoup all of that expense simply with advertising revenue. They thought they had no choice. And, just three months later, Time Warner and NBC announced that they were going to form their own football league. They thought they had no choice. So, be famous and hire good lawyers.

"When you're an unknown act, you simply have to accept the contract the label offers you, or you don't get published and promoted," agrees David Kessel, chairman of IUMA. "It's piracy; and they get away with as much as they can."

Artists have always tried to bypass the system, either to maintain creative control, or simply to distribute content that commercial enterprises felt wouldn't be profitable. Lewis Carroll self-published *Alice in Wonderland;* John Sayles finances his own films; and the mavericks at id Software (the makers of Doom and Quake), among others, have figured out ways to get their art out, and find their respective audiences—often to wide acclaim.

But, just because a new distribution channel (the Internet) makes it easier to create, publish, and distribute their own material, it doesn't mean that they still won't need what a good publisher offers: namely, skill during production and edit, investment capital for production and marketing, and expertise in cost-efficient distribution. It is the best opportunity to be heard, and to reach your audience. So for every element in the recorded music value chain, the labels will no longer be the only ones adding the value at every step. Artist and Repertoire (A&R) executives are starting agencies to help independent artists, thereby shifting the power away from the labels. And, just as these changes are already happening in the record industry, similar changes are also playing out in computer games, radio, and television.

■ WE WANT OUR RIGHTS. AND WE DON'T CARE HOW. WE WANT OUR REVOLUTION, NOW![4]

In the video game industry, an organization called Gathering of Developers has taken on a pioneering role in reshaping the intra-industry food chain. Gathering of Developers intends to be a new kind of game publisher. Gentler, kinder,

formed and owned by very successful game developers, it offers game developers just about the best publishing deal
they can find anywhere. Better royalties, more ownership of
their artistic intellectual property, and generally more
rights all across the board. And, it can also help with development, marketing, and distribution (which means access
to limited shelf space). In a market in which less than 5 percent of titles are profitable, any of these can be barriers to
success and will stymie all but the most tenacious independent developer. By all means, it wants to be profitable—just
not over the bodies of its developers.

"Gathering of Developers is not about any one developer," said its founder, Mike Wilson. "It's about an excellent group of developers who are looking to unite and
create drastic change in the way they deal with their retail
publishers and distributors."[5]

From traditional broadcasters' (both radio and television) points of view, the Internet creates at least as many
problems as opportunities, thanks to intra-industry tur-
moil made possible. Internet broadcasts will totally aggra-
vate and disrupt current advertising arrangements, on
both the national and local levels, in a variety of ways:

➤ It disrupts the relationships between the network,
   its affiliate stations, and their advertisers (it's all
   about national versus local advertising revenue).

➤ It raises questions of how to make a successful business with niche audiences (versus the traditional
   mass audience required by broadcasters).

➤ It's Bad for the Network, Their Affiliates, and Advertisers

Take the case of CBS' syndicated show, *The Howard Stern
Show*, for instance. In 1997, CBS revised its radio affiliate
contracts, disallowing any of its syndicated content to be
broadcast live on the Internet. You will find none of CBS'
syndicated shows on the Web, anywhere. You will not find
Howard Stern live on the Internet. You will not find Don

Imus live on the Internet. No radio station that carries them as an affiliate can put their signal live on the Internet. The reason CBS is not allowing their programming on the Internet is because they want to avoid competition with their affiliates' advertisers.

Each local station fills the time slots it gets with ads that they've gone out and painstakingly sold to pay for the $300,000 a year that Howard Stern costs them. David Lawrence said, "I can't think of one general manager who would say 'Oh sure. Go ahead and listen on the Internet. You don't need to listen to our commercials. You don't need to support our advertisers. Let me just give that to you for free.' " So, in support of their affiliates, CBS won't allow their programs to be heard on the Net.

But, once they figure out how to insert commercials on the broadcast network feed, the next trend could be even worse for the affiliates. When you listen to radio on the Internet, you'd be hearing commercials inserted in the local positions that are Internet-only, and that will cause a furor with the local affiliates.

Here's what David Lawrence says would happen if the local affiliate is being bypassed. "Let's say you're listening to *The Howard Stern Show* on the Internet in Kansas City, and the Kansas City radio station is paying $300,000 a year for Howard Stern. Since that local station is going out and selling spots, they don't want you to hear a feed that was prior to them acquiring it and adding their own spots, in the chain, they don't want that to happen. The advertiser doesn't want that to happen. The advertiser wants you to hear the local affiliate's version of the show with the local commercials intact."

➤ It's Small Potatoes

The business of radio and television advertising is based on large audience reach, and media buyers are used to audience-reach size of hundreds of thousands and millions of listeners. So, today, when the subject of Internet ad sales comes up, they often quickly lose interest because most web sites have dramatically smaller audiences. A local station broadcasting over the Internet might have 10,000 listeners and really feel good about that. No one has a million listeners today.

David Lawrence makes this point clearly "There's an audience for niche, but advertisers are absolutely disinterested in tiny niches. They are used to delivering millions of eyeballs, millions of ears, and millions of page views.

"I see an incredible lack of good content coming down the pike. We're diving deeper into the barrel of crap to put stuff on the air. Now there are sometimes incredible creative bursts of genius, but from the audience standpoint, it's what the heck am I going to watch on these 500 channels? Nobody is banging on the door of these studios with incredible quality stuff they can't get on the air."

Television broadcasters will eventually have to address the same issues of local versus national (or global) advertising, and broadcasting versus narrowcasting. But, the key enabler of widely deployed broadband consumer access is still a few years away, and so it's just too early for the television networks to do more than the leaders (NBC, Disney, Time Warner) are already doing.

■ SO, WHAT'S THE STORY?

Although there's no question in anyone's mind that traditional radio and television broadcasting will be around for decades (and arguably forever), there is clearly a great divide over the just how great this Internet broadcast opportunity is.

Here's the heart of the debate: traditional broadcasters may not think—yet—that they face serious competition from Internet broadcasters, but new media broadcasters think it's a no-brainer. Thomas Edwards, president of The Synch, a pioneering Internet video broadcaster, describes the compelling reasons that "Internet broadcasting is a no-brainer for all broadcasters. The Internet is the biggest new market in the world, the fastest growing mass communication medium of all time, with global, personalized content, interactive one-on-one sales and marketing, new advertising channels, and new sources of revenue." Remember that Premiere Radio Networks is succeeding with both traditional and Internet broadcast opportunities, and sees them as completely complementary.

But, if you think that these industries are going to have a hard time sorting out the new rules of competition, that's nothing compared with the blur of media that consumers and advertisers are going to have to figure out. After all, the Internet interregnum opens the market to everyone and anyone, which means that all entertainment industry segments not only have to worry about changes within their traditional structures, but are finding themselves open to disintermediation from other entertainment media segments. This is a polite way of saying that it's damn foolish to be complacent—and to think that, because you are a radio station, your competition consists solely of other radio stations, or because you're a bookstore, your competition on-line is of the Amazon.com variety.

Let's take a look at how several industries are already starting to spill over into the territory of their neighbor industries: record makers moving into the radio business, radio broadcasters moving into TV, TV broadcasters moving into interactive video games, and video gamers turning into broadcasters and franchisers of talent—much like the NFL.

➤ Let's Tune In to the Record Channel

We've seen how the record industry and radio broadcasters have long depended on one another. But, if you think of radio as the marketing division of the record industry (as two halves of the same industry, separated since birth), then it becomes obvious that the marketing division is keeping more than the rest of the industry would like.

With royalties from radio generating just 7 percent of the record makers' revenue, the record makers see a lot of upside to entering the radio business. The reason is that 80 percent of the ad revenue that the radio broadcasters make is from playing music, and the music makers just get to keep 7 percent of the money the broadcasters make. They can do better than that by doing it themselves. And because, as we've seen, the absence of regulation on the Internet allows anyone to broadcast as much as they'd like, the record makers are starting to inch into that role.

The only question is *when,* not *if,* the record labels will become full-fledged broadcasters with the broadcaster's business model (aggregate audience and sell ads). There's no downside for the labels to try this, and it's certainly worth a try with the lost costs of Internet and e-commerce operations, most of which they're doing already. The only issue at all is whether they'll choose to play (and, in effect, promote, if not actually sell) material from other music labels (as Warner Brothers Online chose to do). Expect this sooner, rather than later.

So, if you were a radio broadcaster what would you do? Good question.

➤ Let's Watch Some Radio

Sounding like a contradiction in terms, the future of Internet radio includes the addition of other media (video, text, graphics, and 3-D animation). We've seen that on the Internet, it's all just bits. And, there's nothing to prevent an Internet broadcaster (of any type) from distributing every kind of digital media possible. Already, radio station web sites have text (transcripts of interviews, full-text news stories, links to related information, on-line chat rooms for the audience to meet and talk about whatever they want).

Of course, this isn't new. Don Imus, Howard Stern, Dr. Dean Edell, and Rush Limbaugh have all had their syndicated shows broadcast via both radio and cable television networks. What is new, is that on the Internet, there's very little reason to *not* include video and text and so on. The marginal costs are low, and there's a big disadvantage to not keeping up with your competitors. Log on to Xfm, *http://www.isis.ie/xfm/*, alternative radio live from Dublin, Ireland, and watch their *radio* shows. Or, watch the video clips of clips that they created originally for radio. Or, log on to Tu ½, live radio from Monterrey, Mexico, and watch interviews and music videos while listening to the live performances. Or, log on to Virgin.Net, and follow their news headline links ("All the news that's fit to print out") to video clips from related newscasts. Or, log on to KPIX's Web page (San Francisco's CBS radio station), and check out their Traffic-Cam to see just how bad tonight's commute home is likely to be.

➤ Let's Watch Some Video Games (Video Games Broadcast As TV)

In 1997, the San Francisco–based on-line game service Total Entertainment Network (TEN) launched the Professional Gamers League (PGL), which is an attempt to turn on-line computer gameplay into a spectator sport. Sure, you can be one of the contestants battling for the title of best Quake II player in the world. Or, you can simply log on and watch via cybercast. Or, perhaps you caught it on CNN, or ESPN?

The notion that you can appeal to a bigger audience than just the people actually manipulating the joystick or mouse or keyboard is a clever one, says Michael Evason, an analyst with Datamonitor, who authored a report on on-line gaming. "You've started thinking like a football franchise, or golf tournament, as having an entertainment product that can be broadcast."

➤ And Listen to the Newspaper, and Read the Radio, and . . .

What is happening? What's happening is this—all the media that have always been separate are all being joined into something entirely new and unexpected, and in the process, they're blurring many of the distinctions we've long been accustomed to. Welcome to the twenty-first century, where you won't need those outdated notions anymore.

■ LIMITED TIME, LIMITED MONEY, (INCREASINGLY) LIMITED CONSUMER ATTENTION SPANS

So what are the consequences of this? Now, more than ever, every entertainment industry segment is battling with every other. This has always been more or less the case, of course. Although we can do several things at the same time (for instance, listening to radio while we work or play), we usually choose between alternatives. So while we're surfing on-line, we're not usually watching television. Or, when the TV is tuned to *The Simpsons,* we're not playing our favorite Mario Brothers game, or reading the local newspaper. Each entertainment media competes against every other for the eyeballs (or ears, or joystick fingers) of consumers.

Coupled with this limited attention span are limited entertainment dollars to spend. We make choices: buy this CD, not that one; subscribe to this magazine, cancel that one. Only the very fortunate (or perhaps the very foolish) can afford to buy everything they want.

Of that entertainment delivered to us "free"—radio and television, for example—the same model holds true. Someone is always paying—in these cases, advertisers. And advertisers are making *their* choices, which ultimately determine yours. They choose to sponsor Jay Leno instead of David Letterman, or to withdraw advertising from TV entirely and place their budgets in radio, because that's how they can reach their customers, they think.

There's only so much discretionary money to spend on entertainment—both from the consumer's and the advertiser's points of view. Figure 11.1 shows how Veronis, Suhler

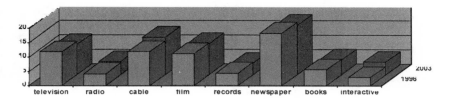

Figure 11.1 Consumer media 1996–2001.

Source: Veronis, Suhler & Associates, *Communications Industry Forecast 1997–2000,* and Silicon Valley Virtual.

& Associates sees the consumer media entertainment revenue pie changing between 1996 and 2001. Not much of a change? We will still be spending most of our time at the television (1,551 hours per year), the radio (1,072 hours per year), perhaps a little more time surfing the Web (39 hours per year), and playing video games (37 hours per year).

Whether you believe that these changes will amount to something truly momentous all depends on whether you look ahead or backward. It's true that all of the changes we've described amount to less than 1 percent of every entertainment business. But, and this is a very big *but,* in the first five years of its existence, the same was true for the television, the videocassette recorder, the personal computer, and the Internet; initially all had little *visible* impact on the stats. In the end, their individual impact was profound.

We believe that the *possible* changes we've discussed are largely inevitable, the forces are irresistible, the barriers have been torn down (like the wall that separated East from West Berlin). Do you really think that it's all going to remain as it was?

Welcome to the twenty-first century. You won't need those ideas where you're headed.

The natural tension between
interactivity and linear will lead
to a whole smorgasbord of
choices in digital
entertainment.

Chapter

So, What's the Story?

"The greatest magician would be the one who would cast over him-self a spell so complete, take his own phantasmagorias as au-tonomous appearances . . . We (the undivided divinity operating within us) have dreamt the world. We have dreamt it as firm, mys-terious, visible, ubiquitous in space and durable in time; but in its ar-chitecture, we have allowed tenuous and eternal crevices of unreason which tell us it is false."

—JORGE BORGES, *"Avatars of the Tortoise"*[1]

"We cannot control what goes on in our dreams."

—BRUNO BETTELHEIM, *Uses of Enchantment*[2]

"We like to know that there is a ruling power in control of an imag-inary universe, and it makes us uncomfortable if the author seems to abdicate the role."

—JANET MURRAY, *Hamlet on the Holodeck*[3]

Say you're one of the more than 3.5 million people (and counting) who bought a copy of the blockbuster computer game called Myst. You install it on your computer, and are instantly enthralled with its shadowy, spooky, immersive world. It's like being plunged into a particularly vivid stage set—one with overtones of both horror and fantasy genres. You know something's about to happen. There's

229

that eery music, those evocative sound effects, the menacing graphics. But, what's going on? What's the story? There happens to *be* a story, a fairly involved one, involving hidden treasure, two captive brothers begging to be released, and a good and powerful wizard.

But what's different about Myst is that, unlike a traditional play or movie, which would inexorably draw you through a linear plot (first, this thing happens, then *this* thing happens), you won't find out what's going on in Myst unless you *act*. To change the emphasis slightly: unless *you* act, unless *you* begin exploring this strange and hypnotic world that the computer masterminds at Cyan Inc. concocted for you. Once you begin to act—click yourself a few steps to the right, for example, toward this . . . *thing*—puzzles and clues are dropped in front of you, and a story begins to unfold. And, you'll probably spend dozens of hours over the next month (if you're anything like the average Myst player) following the story to its bitter or bittersweet end, depending on the choices you make.

Interactivity, as defined by Webster's, is "acting or capable of acting on each other." In other words, if you take an action, you will see a result of that action. If you choose to free one of the evil sons in Myst, for example, you will need to deal with the other evil son. Your actions have repercussions.

Interaction is at the heart of most computer games. The very first commercial game, Pong, involved fairly simple hand-and-eye coordination in the interactions between player and computer. The player reacted to small white blips that resembled Ping-Pong balls, hitting them using a virtual paddle, a white line that appeared on the screen, and which the player manipulated using a joystick.

The popular video arcade game Frogger involved helping a cute little green critter over a number of natural and manmade hurdles. SimCity allowed players to build virtual cities, complete with housing, power stations, roads, and shopping centers—and to take charge of their communities by acting appropriately if threatened by overdevelopment, crime, earthquakes, and—yes—even Godzilla.

Interactivity is even at the heart of recent hits like Barbie Fashion Designer, and Deerhunter, in that the player gets to *control,* to some extent, the kind of experience he or she has.

■ A NATION OF CONTROL FREAKS

Indeed, at its most basic level, interactivity is about control. In linear forms of entertainment, such as novels, films, or television shows, someone else is in control: the writer of the novel, the playwright, the director of the film or television show (along with a creative, technical and administered supporting cast, of course). Someone else has decided *what* you will experience and *how* (in what order) you will experience it.

You can, of course, reject the experience entirely (close the book, turn off the television set, walk out of the theater). But, if you choose to stay, you have, in effect, relinquished control. (You can always close your mind, but that's another issue altogether.)

Interactivity is what has historically distinguished computer games from other kinds of mass entertainment media. But, as we'll see, there's an increasingly blurred line between traditionally linear forms of entertainment, which take you through a story, or narrative; and new forms of digital entertainment, which are experimenting with giving consumers varying degrees of this thing called *control.*

Myst was unusual for a number of reasons, not the least of which is its staying power (it's still on games best-selling lists, more than five years after its debut). What was particularly unusual was that Myst also represented an interesting mix of interactivity and narrative. People are still mulling over just why it worked. After all, hard-core gamers who thrive on the notion of gratifying responses, or "gameplay" (a synonym for great interactivity—see Chapter 8), point out that Myst is slow, sluggish, and that in the interest of serving its rather convoluted story, true gameplay is largely sacrificed.

On the other hand, people accustomed to more linear forms of narrative, like movies or books, point out that Myst ultimately lacks a strong narrative thrust. The Myst plot depends on the player's actions and initiative, rather than the creator's skill with pacing, suspense-building techniques, or scene construction. So, when a player is not skillful enough at negotiating physical hurdles, or not clever at solving riddles, the story comes to a dead stop.

Tom Hall, president of game maker Ion Storm, says that for any interactive entertainment provider, this balance between narrative and interactivity always requires delicate maneuvering. "You can create a world like Myst, and allow people to wander around and—hopefully—bump into things, but even if it's a wonderful and beautiful and well-crafted world, most people need a little more structure than that," he says. "You have to lead the player sometimes without letting them know you're leading them." *Structure*—another way of saying that many of us prefer someone else to be at least nominally in control.

■ SIX DEGREES OF INTERACTION

Although most forms of mass entertainment, especially in the broadcast or print media, are based on linear narrative and require the audience to be a relatively passive recipient of the entertainment, it's important to acknowledge that there are subtle *degrees* of interactivity in many of the ways we play. Some forms of entertainment, as we've pointed out, are almost totally passive (hence, the "couch potato" label given to those who do little more than recline on a sofa and occasionally press a button on a remote control.)

Other kinds of entertainment, however, edge closer toward interactivity. A good word to use is *participatory* rather than passive.

Going to Wrigley Field and rooting for the Cubs from the bleachers is an example of a participatory experience: you are a part of the spectacle, even if you aren't swinging the bat or pitching the ball. The attractions at most theme parks, such as Universal Studios or Disneyland, are participatory rather than interactive in nature. Or, as researchers at Evans & Sutherland point out, "active-passive," because although things are being done to you, nothing you do can affect the outcome of the experience (see Chapter 1).

"It's not necessarily interactive, even when you are being slammed around on a motion platform with sub-woofers pounding your ears, and wraparound images everywhere you look," says David Cole, president of Aquathought Labs, in Fort Myers, Florida, a maker of immersive virtual reality machines for scientific and academic institutions. That is, you may well have extreme physical reactions—scream and sweat and otherwise react—and "you might even consider it entertaining, or fun. I'm not slamming that. But it's not 'necessary interactive,' " he says.

Phil Hettema also makes the distinction between participation and interactivity in his business, that of designing theme park attractions. (Hettema is head of new development for Universal Studios' theme park business.) "If you're in a vehicle, or sitting in a theater, you are being lead, in a linear fashion, through a story," he says. "Although King Kong may pick you up and shake you, and although you might be shot at by bandits passing by, you have absolutely no effect on the drama that is unfolding."

234 ◄ PLAYING FOR PROFIT

You are perhaps participating, especially if you're with others, but you're not interacting. "The experience is the same whether you are there or not," says Hettema.

Hettema, who has a background in traditional puppetry, points out that audience *participation* in live dramatic events is an ancient and honored tradition. Moreover, participation in live entertainment could often move closer to true interactivity: hisses, boos, catcalls, and cheers can even affect entertainment, by changing the nature of the experience for others in the audience, as well as subtly affecting the performers themselves, even in a scripted work.

But, that's hard to do in an age when most of our entertainment is delivered remotely (i.e., via radio waves or television broadcasts). And, it's hard when that entertainment is being delivered (using technology) to a mass audience: how does an individual affect the outcome of entertainment designed for a group of people? Whether it's the millions who tune in for the Super Bowl, or the other 50 people along for the roller-coaster ride, allowing the individual to have any sort of control over the experience is a difficult technical, as well as creative, question.

What digital technologies are finally enabling is an explosion of possibilities along this passive/interactive spectrum for mass-media entertainment. It was previously impossible for a single viewer of a television program to affect the outcome of something designed for the masses.

You couldn't demand, for example, that Seinfield and Elaine get back together at the end of an episode. The story (or narrative) will unfold as it has been scripted, acted, taped, and broadcasted. And, there are many arguments in favor of letting ourselves go—letting ourselves be pushed into an immersive experience that we wouldn't have the imagination—or the skills—to create for ourselves. As the writer Robert Stone says, what an artist is always trying to do is "crowd the reader out of his own space and occupy with your own, in a good cause. You're trying to take over his sensibility and deliver an experience that moves."[4]

Yet, as new media experiments emerge, we will see more diverse ways that entertainment providers can play with the degrees of interactivity, or control, within a particular work, both in relinquishing it and taking it back when necessary for artistic purposes.

For a more precise example of these varying degrees of interaction, compare rewinding your copy of *Star Wars* and replaying the Death Star destruction scene on video, with riding the Star Tours attraction at Disneyland. Thinking about the difference between the largely passive experience (watching, and watching again) and the *participatory* experience (waiting in line at the space port, boarding the spacecraft with other passengers, and having the visceral feel of the ride through hyperspace) is quite dramatic.

Now, compare those degrees of interaction (or noninteraction) with the newer kinds of digital fun found at such places as DisneyQuest (see Chapter 13). You not only ride a roller coaster, you *design* the roller coaster. You decide whether you're being hurled past mountain peaks and ravines, or through space, or through ice caps. You determine the nature of experience personally. Now, *that's* interactivity.

Another example of the way this is playing out in mass media could be found in a cybercast preview of the popular rock band Aerosmith's new album in October 1998. The band played excerpts from the album *A Little South of Sanity* live from a concert hall in New Jersey. You might think that it's just another rock concert.

But wait, there's more. Fans who tuned into the concert via the Internet got treated to a new kind of mass-media broadcast experience—one edging closer to interactivity than was previously possible.

For anyone who viewed and listened to the concert via the Web (yes, you could both hear and see it, via live audio and video feeds) could, in effect, "direct" their personal view of the concert. Seven separate cameras were set up on the stage in New Jersey, each capturing a different aspect of the show; seven separate video feeds were broadcast over the Internet. And, Web watchers got to switch back and forth between the various cameras—live—however they chose. They chose what they wanted to look at at any given time and swapped between the different cameras at will, creating their own unique concert experience.

Now, it wasn't truly interactive in the sense that viewers in front of their PCs could do nothing to affect the concert (unlike actual concertgoers, who could yell, jump up, or do things that actually impacted the performance). But certainly they could do more to personally control the entertainment they were viewing than would previously have been possible in a mass-broadcast event.

And here's another interesting interactive angle: prior to the concert itself, the band members participated in an on-line chat on America Online, responding to questions e-mailed in from interested fans, in real time. That part of the evening's entertainment was truly interactive.

■ BUILD YOUR OWN MOVIE

Log onto www.monsterhome.com, and you'll see another example of entertainment experimenting with this balance of interactivity and narrative. The basic story is one of the staple plots of B horror films (done with sly campiness): members of a family are invited to return to their ancestral home at the bequest of their rich and supposedly dying grandfather. They are warned that if they do not show up they will be cut out of the will. Not surprisingly, they all show up (the opening sequence is of the doorbell to a spooky mansion being rung).

Due to limitations of the technology, Monster Home has the feel of an extremely low-budget movie—the images are grainy, the motion blurred, and the sound scratchy. But you *are* immersed in the story, and you are watching it on your computer screen, not on TV or in a theater. And then there's the biggest difference of all: after the opening video sequence, *you* choose which scenes to watch, and in which order. There are a total of 76 scenes, and depending on the choices you make, you will see different aspects of the plot. And, choosing some scenes will preclude you from being able to watch other scenes. "There's a certain element of risk, in that the choices you make will have repercussions," says Geoffrey Shea, president of Image Business, the small Canadian firm that created *Monster Home.*

Shea is the first to admit this isn't a new concept. He recalls going to a "participatory" theater experience in Toronto years ago, in which the audience wandered from room to room, and at will decided which scenes of the play in progress to view or not view. "It was boring," he recalls. Why? A lack of causality, a lack of *tension*. If it doesn't matter what order you view scenes (or witness a story line), it follows that that story line can't be terribly compelling.

And this was the case with Monster Home, Shea cheerfully admits. His team is primarily made up of visual artists, designers, and people with film backgrounds who also possess sophisticated technological skills. Most of Image Business' revenue is derived from developing Web applications for corporate clients. But, Shea was intrigued by the possibility of a marriage between narrative entertainment and the Web. Monster Home was a tongue-in-cheek experiment.

Shea is also quick to state that the "interactive" aspect of Web-based entertainment in general, and Monster Home in particular, is completely "overemphasized," for all the reasons explored in this chapter. "I don't necessarily believe you want the role of the author or artist to be that dramatically diminished," he says. "An audience comes to a piece with certain expectations. They are looking to be guided through a vision of the world as created by this other person, this artist. At the end, they hope to be satisfied emotionally by that experience. You don't necessarily want to take control away from the author, and place it in your own hands, or the hands of the other 300 people in the audience."

Not surprisingly, any entertainment provider who wanted to play with this line between narrative and interactivity is going to face certain challenges. Chief among them are the following four challenges:

1. How do you make the basic story line coherent if the audience may or may not witness any particular segment of it?
2. How do you make it *interesting,* given that traditional suspense- and tension-building techniques are ineffective. Imagine if Hitchcock couldn't control when you viewed the shower scene in *Psycho*—before or after you knew about the specific nature of the Anthony Perkins's character's derangement—and you get a sense of this problem.
3. How do you calculate the exact right mix of narrative (what aspects of the story to force upon the audience) and interaction (what actions the audience can take on its own) to create a satisfying emotional experience?
4. How do you calculate the amount of *effect* the audience should have on the proceedings? Can they decide if the Janet Leigh character gets killed or escapes? Can they decide not to open that door on which the basic plot hinges? In short: on what part of the continuum between passive consumption, participation, and true interaction, does your entertainment fall?

This is the problem facing Warren Spector, a senior games designer at Ion Storm. Spector has thought a lot about the differences between interactivity and narrative—naturally—he comes from a film background (is just shy of completing a doctorate in film studies), and spent his early professional life designing board games, before moving onto computer games. He points out that the video clips showing the history or "backstory" of a game often flop—especially if a video clip (or section of narrative) intrudes into the gameplay. "I love interactivity, and as soon as you start rolling a video clip, it's impossible to interact," Spector says. He insists that computer games are a different media than film or television. It's a unique mix of story and interactivity.

In the game Spector is currently designing, called Deus Ex, he's trying to tell a "really cool story." He's trying to craft a large and completely immersive fantasy world for this role-playing game—yes, Myst does come to mind— but he doesn't want to depend upon the player luckily stumbling across the right things in the right order so the story keeps moving along in a coherent manner.

So, Spector has created a series of what he calls "controllable modules," or narrative boxes. Every player must move from one module to the next, in a straight and predetermined line. Within each module, however, players have multiple ways to solve or not solve a problem. In other words, the players have control. "I want overall control of the narrative," says Spector. "But I also want to give the player a sense of control. So, sure, someone can go around killing everything he sees. But then he'll miss some important clues, and will be forced to solve the key problems in another way."

In other words, the player makes choices that have consequences. "If you walk into the hotel, and shoot the hotel owner, his daughter is not going to talk to you. On the other hand, a different character, an unsavory one, might be attracted by your behavior, and give you information that you wouldn't have gotten if you'd behaved in a less bloodthirsty way," says Spector. In this way, the player who kills everything, and the player who talks to everyone first, can both solve the Deus Ex mission—but will do so in different ways.

Fiction writers have long experimented with this notion of nonlinear narrative, usually by asking readers to "choose" a branch in a story line, and then telling them to flip to the appropriate physical page in which the text can logically continue, given their choice.

More recently, cyberfiction writers, such as Mark Amerika and Michael Joyce, have constructed hypertext narratives on the Web that do this same thing, but in electronic form: you choose where you will wander in the story, and so, in effect, you have control over the experience. So log onto Grammatron.com, and you'll be plunged into an interactive novel on the Web. There's no conventional plot; there are just chunks of text, and you choose the order in which you will experience those chunks. The novel is not finished, and may never be; it bills itself as "a public domain narrative environment."

Critics have pointed out (and they're right) that in many of the ways we judge a work of fiction, Grammatron is a failure. It lacks tension and is full of inflated language and grandiose abstraction. (One early line, "he is him and I would be her if only she'd let me be," is representative of what is often truly appalling writing.) But, as a first step into testing the waters of a new media, it's a valiant effort. As Janet Murray points out in her excellent book-length treatment of this complicated subject, *Hamlet on the Holodeck,* the fact that an artist has yet to appear who has full mastery of the new technological tools doesn't mean the media itself is fatally flawed. We're just waiting for the Shakespeare of the form to emerge from the current chaotic state of the art, Murray correctly says.

The "Holodeck" recreational device in the new *Star Trek* television series is often held up as a vision of the ultimate high-tech playground, one that successfully combines narrative with interactivity. The Holodeck concept allows players to assume certain roles within a given scenario, or story, and to act freely within the world created for them. For example, the android Data often chooses to become Sherlock Holmes, and act out stories in which he is the famous detective. The world in which he is immersed to act out this fantasy is correct in every sensory detail to the fictional world originally created by Arthur Conan Doyle.

The worlds that the Holodeck creates for the *Star Trek* characters are completely interactive: the stories the characters find themselves in are utterly dependent on choices made by them; their actions and decisions when faced with the fictional events are often humorous, always entertaining, and always have happy endings (even when there's some technical malfunction). No wonder we all long for a Holodeck of our own.

The irony, of course, is that it is *all* scripted, all carefully controlled, by the *Star Trek* writers. The technological and creative tools do not yet exist that would allow people to immerse themselves in a imaginary narrative world *and* also remain in control (have the interactivity) *and* also have it guaranteed to be an entertaining experience. It's far more likely to be like life: fully interactive, sometimes thrilling, often mundane.

It takes more than simple craftsmanship to create a truly compelling novel, play, or film; it takes artistic sensibility and expression to turn the experience into something transforming, something magical. This is why we turn to these immersive experiences (entertainment) to begin with, to take us out of the world we normally inhabit.

"A good experience is about a series of cues (whether visceral or emotional). The same set of cues arranged in a different order might result in no response whatsoever," explains Phil Hettema, senior vice president of attraction development for Universal Studios' theme parks, which means to say that if the player indeed gets full control, the response may well be . . . dull.

It can be argued, therefore, that seeing interactivity as the ultimate "good" in entertainment—taking the stance that giving the audience more control is always a better thing—is just as limiting a view as demanding that all truly good entertainment must be linear in nature. For example:

> ➤ Would our experience of da Vinci's art be greater if we were allowed to walk around a 3-D version of the *Mona Lisa?* Pinch her and watch her react? Would we be as intrigued as we've been all these centuries if we had more than simply the mysterious and restricted glimpse of this woman that da Vinci has chosen to give us?

> ➤ Would our enjoyment of the films of Alfred Hitchcock be increased if we could wander through the scenes at will? Affect what choices the characters made? Avoid the hair-raising suspense sequences by making the hero (or heroine) take different courses of action at critical moments?

> ➤ Would a performance of Beethoven's Ninth Symphony be more emotionally satisfying if we could banish the conductor and interact with it ourselves? (Stop in midmeasure, instruct the horns to play louder, the violas softer?) Granted, there's a certain population of music aficionados who would jump at the chance to conduct this piece, even in front of just a virtual orchestra. But many of us prefer to have a skilled master give us his or her interpretation, to surprise and delight us and take us out of ourselves.

So, it's not a question of whether straight narrative (linear control) or interactivity is better. Both satisfy certain human needs for entertainment, which is why we might not necessarily want to interact with our favorite television programs, or choose the outcomes of the movies we watch, or write our own ends of novels. We might want to have a broad smorgasbord of entertainment offerings that run the gamut between truly interactive and truly passive.

■ THE NOTION OF TRANSMEDIA

What is more likely, as media analyst and designer Celia Pearce has observed, along with others, is that new technologies will enable a hybrid mix of *complementary* entertainment offerings that span several types of media. An interactive version of *Cheers* wouldn't replace the witty, well-crafted, and painstakingly rehearsed traditional version. But, it could supplement it. After watching a particularly enjoyable episode, you could wander into the virtual bar, and do some verbal sparring with Sam or Woody. It would be fun, and it might add to your enjoyment of the show itself, which you still avidly wait for every week.

At the E3 conference in 1997, Tom Brokaw gave the keynote address, noting that he had realized decades ago (actually, during the Watergate era) that television was simply not capable of delivering the entire story. More recently, Brokaw said, it was becoming clear that a *combination* of media—the Web, with broadcast TV, with cable, was the way to go, points out Lee Roth, president of Lee Roth Media, in Santa Monica, California, a new media studio. As evidence of this conclusion, Brokaw said that two out of three MSNBC viewers are actually logged onto the Internet at the same time they are watching the television broadcast. "Entertainment experiences that cross media are the future," declares Roth.

Some veterans of the computer game industry, like John Baker, vice president of corporate development of

Activision, believe that interactivity and narrative are inherently separate, that a game will either be a linear or interactive experience, and "that they will never truly come together." "I would say the vast majority of entertainment is linear, and will remain so," says Baker.

The one place where this distinction begins to blur is the Internet, Baker admits. But he believes it's a mistake for linear entertainment companies to try and get into this business without understanding the inherent differences between the two kinds of experiences. And, like Roth, Baker is convinced that the two forms will be "increasingly complementary to each other." "As the interactive entertainment business begins to mature, linear media companies will revisit it with a new perspective, and see it as complementary to their business," says Baker. "They'll also probably be more successful at creating content that works in this space," he says, referring to the hitherto disastrous efforts of Hollywood companies to successfully build computer games.

■ FINDING A FORM THAT SUITS US

"To find a form that accommodates the mess, that is the task of the artist now," the Irish playwrite Samuel Beckett said, in conversation with John Driver in 1961.[5] Conversely, consumers of entertainment are eager to find the form that accommodates them. When they choose, they want the pleasure of bouncing up against viewpoints, perspectives, creative imaginings they wouldn't encounter otherwise. People will continue to want to be stretched by others' ideas, visions, and imaginations. And, conversely, sometimes they will want more control. Sometimes they will want to take a more active role.

What technology increasingly offers them is a broader choice. They can still get passively immersed in others' creations—if they choose. Technology doesn't preclude that. The good news—the truly good news—is that technology can only increase our choices of entertainment along the passive-interactive-narrative spectrum. And, choice is always a good, if sometimes frightening, thing.

Entertainment providers are out to prove that technology doesn't have to have an isolating effect—especially if you have to leave the house to play with it.

Chapter 13

New Playrooms

"You could read Kant by yourself, if you wanted; but you must share a joke with someone else."

—ROBERT LOUIS STEVENSON, *Virginibus Peurisque*

"Bits are bits. Fads come and go. You don't want technology for its own sake. Eight years ago, simulators were going to be everything. That died quickly. What really matters is whether you can provide an immersive and emotional experience, enough to make someone say, 'I've been someplace I've never been before.'"

—PHIL HETTEMA, senior vice president of attraction development,
Universal Studios

*All who joy would win
Must share it—Happiness was born a twin.*

—LORD BYRON, *Don Juan*

It's Saturday night at Dave & Buster's, in Chicago's hip Near North neighborhood. The elegant marble-floored and white-linen dining room is full of all sorts: young parents with toddlers, young people on dates, groups of 30-something men and women who look like they came straight from professional jobs in the nearby Loop. Dress is casual, but definitely not grungy. Clean (even pressed) jeans and corduroys and cotton button-down shirts dominate among the diners, although the wait staff is formally, even elegantly, dressed. There's some light rock playing softly in the background, not enough to distract from conversation. It looks like any other casually upscale restaurant you might find in the neighborhood. The menu contains everything from plain burgers to grilled mahimahi.

You wouldn't think you're in one of the few success stories of high-tech location-based entertainment (LBE). That's right—Dave & Buster's, a national chain that now boasts more than 14 locations nationwide, is one of the few pioneers in LBE that has figured out a formula for actually turning a profit.

Just a short walk from this elegant and spacious dining room is the heart of a massive entertainment complex—50,000 square feet, or the size of a professional football field—that contains the very latest technological toys available. There's Rapid River Rafting, which lets you paddle down a virtual river. There's a virtual golfing game, which lets you try your luck at simulated versions of world-class courses like Pebble Beach. There's laser tag in which teams combat each other with high-tech guns.

You might think it sounds suspiciously like any other video game arcade. True, there are some similarities, but disabuse your mind of those dark dingy corners found in malls or cineplexes. Neither is there any trace of those loud, ominous groups of teenage boys. Dave & Buster's mission is to provide wholesome fun for all types. And, all types are having a ball: grandmothers are helping five- and six-year-olds shoot basketballs through hoops; a team of elegantly dressed young women is challenging a group of equally fashionable young men to a game of Ground Zero laser tag; and the people observing the fun seem to be enjoying themselves as much as the ones actually playing the games.

Buy a ticket at the counter with $6 worth of gameplay on it, and wander through the offerings. Sure, you'll see the typical shoot-em-ups so dearly loved by young (and not so young) boys, but there is also traditional billiards on elegant handcrafted tables, shuffleboard, and Mystery Theater performances on weekend nights.

Think of it as a calmer, more organized Disneyland or Disney World without the trip to Florida or California, Vegas without the sleaze, a state fair without the pigs, or a sort of Planet Hollywood–style theme restaurant, but one in which the exhibits are there to play with rather than just be looked at.

And the results speak for themselves. Headquartered in Dallas, and founded by old buddies Buster Corley and Dave Corriveau in 1982, Dave & Buster's is the undisputed leader in this growing market niche. The average size of its facilities is 500,000 square feet, or the size of a football field. The average annual revenue per facility is $13 million; the average number of visitors per year is 700,000; the average amount spent per visitor is $17.50. And an astonishing 47 percent of revenues come from the games themselves, rather than the food and drink.

That's not bad for a company that bet the farm—well, the restaurant—on the appeal of technology in a brightly lit, family-friendly setting. And, Dave & Buster's has really managed to break out of the teenage ghetto: the average age is 33 years old; the clientele is 40 percent female (extraordinarily high for digital amusement centers); the average annual income is $61,000. Dave and Buster are certainly doing something right.

■ GET OUT OF THE HOUSE!

They've succeeded in teaching the entertainment world a valuable lesson. What high-tech playrooms, like Dave & Buster's, contribute to the future of digital fun is the notion that technology doesn't have to be a socially isolating experience. Forget notions that computer-based entertainment is solely for those individuals who don't mind being hunched alone over a keyboard, or transfixed in front of a screen with joystick in hand. It can be something you do with others—not just virtually with others (as in on-line multiplayer games that we've seen in other chapters, like Chapter 8), but actually, *physically* with others, especially when you have to leave your home to play.

Thus, new venues that include recently opened LBE sites like GameWorks, Entros, DisneyQuest—and, of course, the increasingly technologically sophisticated amusements found in traditional theme parks by Disney and Universal Studios and the like—have at their core the notion that the technology itself isn't the point. The point is the social experience.

"We don't care at all about the technology. It's all the same to us. We use it only to foster social interaction," says Stephen Brown, president and founder of Entros, a Seattle-based LBE playground.

This "aha" has been a long time coming, for there's a litter of dead bodies in attempts to cash in on the concept that technology can be used for fun in group, as well as solitary, settings. And, the basic idea—to get people out of their homes, and engaged with each other while they're involved in structured (or semistructured) fun activities—is hardly new. Bingo at the church hall every Friday night was precisely for the same purpose.

But somehow, in the technological age, we seem to have lost that sense that social interaction and technological innovation don't have to be mutually exclusive events, which is why we've seen such spectacular flops in virtual reality and LBE in the past. "The emphasis used to be placed solely on the play environment, on the type of expensive, large-scale simulations you couldn't do at home," says John Latta, president of Fourth Wave, Inc., a technology consulting firm that tracks site-based entertainment venues closely. "They ignored the social context, and because of that, most of them failed."

The new arcades have a different goal: to use technology as the enabler, but not let it become the focus, of the experience. Yes, the toys themselves are high-tech in nature. But—and this is key—they are easily accessible, even to the most phobic of technophobe. Think of it as going to the Atlantic City or Santa Cruz Boardwalk, or to the County Fair (depending on your geographic location). You don't need prior knowledge or skill to join in on the rides or games. They're fairly intuitive or extremely easy to learn. You don't have to have world-class skills acquired during hours of practice with a joystick and a quick trigger finger; you just need to try (and part of the fun is trying).

Perhaps most important, you're not alone. You're there, playing, with others. It's a social, not a technical, experience.

■ THE GAMES PEOPLE PLAY (TOGETHER)

Here's a sampling of some of the site-based entertainment venues that are starting to show what can be done with technology—and profitably appeal to a broad spectrum of well-heeled clientele.

➤ Dave & Buster's

The granddaddy of the new generation of LBE venues, this steadily growing (and consistently profitable) chain has steadily refuted all the naysayers. As the most mainstream of these kinds of venues, Dave & Buster's has made a concerted effort to stave off any attempts of being taken over by adolescent crowds. No drinks are served to anyone under 21 (despite whatever local drinking laws allow), and there are strict rules that children under 18 must be accompanied by adults at all times. In addition, no children at all are allowed on the site after 10:00 P.M. These rules are strictly enforced—to good effect. Big beefy guards are friendly, but closely observant, to make sure that everyone from elderly grandmothers to five-year-old girls feels comfortable at all times.

"We wanted to build a place for people to be able to get out, get great food, and have great fun," says Dennis Paine, vice president of marketing for Dave & Buster's. In many cases, he says, the games are beside the point, other than enabling social interactions. One game, Ground Zero, is a case in point: it splits participants up into teams to play highly competitive bouts of laser tag, and although the game itself is fun and intense, "much of the fun is derived from interactions outside the game itself—you hear people talking before they go in, and laughing as they come out."

What has made Dave & Buster's succeed where so many have failed? Among other things, "superb execution," says Latta. Security is actually quite pervasive (to prevent the place from turning into a teenage hangout), "but you'd never know it." In fact, says Latta, there are fairly rigid rules of behavior in terms of dress codes, curfews for underage children, and staff training. The public doesn't necessarily see this—but they feel the effect, in that it's a great place to go. "Dave & Buster's management pays close attention to the very fine details," says Latta.

➤ GameWorks

GameWorks is another high-tech playroom that has gotten a lot of press since opening its first site in Seattle in 1997. A joint venture of DreamWorks SKG, Universal Studios, and Sega Enterprises, the Seattle site was such a success that at least 100 more GameWorks sites are planned to be opened by 2002.

What is GameWorks' motto? *Get out of the house!* And, it has loaded up its immense spaces with just about every technology-based temptation that will conceivably achieve this goal. Every high-tech toy from virtual car racing (a staple of most LBE venues) to BattleTech—a fighter pilot game in which players sit in fully equipped, podlike battle stations—is here, but also an impressive roundup of good old-fashioned video arcade games like Pong.

Although if you wander into GameWorks on a typical Saturday night it seems to be doing booming business, a closer look might convince you there's a fairly narrow following. The space, although large, is loud and boisterous. There are few women, and even fewer conversations going on. It's too loud, and the games are too immersive. Instead, people are intent on the games themselves.

For these and other reasons, it's not for the general public. It's not the place to take your elderly parents for an evening out, even if they want to be stimulated. Certainly, it's not suitable for a toddler's birthday party (whereas a full 13 percent of Dave & Buster's revenue comes from private parties of that sort). Instead, Game-Works is more an upscale version of the arcade you'd find in the mall. Certainly, there are bigger, fancier, more expensive machines, but it won't be to the taste of too many people who aren't already addicted to their Nintendo. (If you're already an avid gamer, there's a distinct attraction.) But, GameWorks probably won't convert anyone to the notion of digital entertainment who isn't already halfway there.

➤ Entros

This is what distinguishes Entros from the pack. Another Seattle-based venue (what do you expect from Microsoftland?), it first opened its doors in the early 1990s, and has proven such a success that it opened its second site in the trendy SOMA (south of market) section of San Francisco in late 1998, and plans to debut at least another dozen sites by 2001.

Entros has a slightly different flavor to it than other sites. True, technological toys abound, as in Dave & Buster's and in GameWorks; however, there's a decided attempt to avoid *solitary* immersions in these toys.

And, whereas Dave & Buster's and GameWorks provide the games—many of which are single-player—and hope the social niceties take care of themselves, the owners of Entros have a more structured approach. "We had a very distinct goal: to create a setting in which the isolating effects of the Technological Age will be dispersed," says Stephen Brown, president and founder of Entros. Ironically enough, this is done with the ample help of technology. There are team events, such as scavenger hunts (which involve multimedia clues hidden in digital places); there's a high-tech version of blindman's bluff; and there are completely wired versions of Jeopardy-like quiz shows.

"Technology advances have all been in search of greater efficiency, and to eliminate as much messy human contact as possible," says Brown. But, although this means that you might have extra time at the end of the day, it has its negative side effects, he maintains.

A decade ago, you'd have routine daily interactions with bank tellers and gas station attendants—and, as trivial as they might have seemed, "they would help ground you in who you were, and how you fit into society," says Brown. Automation has replaced many of these human interactions, and so Entros was born to give people a place to go out and enjoy interactions with people again.

But, instead of just creating an environment where they *hope* this will happen—like Dave & Buster's does—"we *force* it to happen by designing activities and events that create a vibrant social interaction," says Brown. One example: a game show that everyone plays at once—no matter if there are 30, 50, or 200 people involved, everyone is plugged into the action. Questions are presented on huge screens that provide sound, images, video, as well as spoken words. Players divide up into teams, and use handheld remote devices to key in answers. Most significantly, the questions are designed like everything at Entros, to get groups of people playing together and *collaborating*. "So one question will be about the Beatles, and a 40-year-old Baby Boomer father will know the answer; the next question will be about Smashing Pumpkins, and his 16-year-old daughter will be able to help," says Smith.

➤ DisneyQuest

DisneyQuest is another recent LBE entry that made its appearance with a splash that would make a tsunami proud. A scaled-down version of the massive Disneyland and DisneyWorld theme parks, DisneyQuest bills itself as an "out-of-home entertainment center" that can be the focus of a day's outing, rather than a full-scale vacation destination. Four years in the making, expect to see dozens of DisneyQuest sites opening over the next five years.

DisneyQuest is divided into zones, or different ways you can play. Unlike Disneyland, you don't pay admission, but instead buy a ticket (individual or group) that contains digital units for engaging in the various activities. The price, or number of units required to participate varies from attraction to attraction.

For starters, there's the *standard arcade game* zone, just as you would find at GameWorks, and there are more than 100 of these games, ranging from simulated air fights, to simulated skateboard racing, to simulated car racing. There are also the classic arcade games for the nostalgic at heart—games such as Pong, Frogger, and Pac Man that capture the look and feel of arcade games from the 1970s and 1980s.

Then there is the *ride* zone, which includes such attractions as the Virtual Jungle Cruise, which takes four riders on a simulated ride down a river. It's interactive in the sense that the riders themselves select the route, and must work together to steer, stop, speed up, or go in a different direction as they travel down the river. Likewise, a CyberSpace Mountain ride allows riders to design their own roller coaster, specifying such attributes as speed, or whether they get whipped through ice, fire, or space.

Finally, a *create* zone focuses on high-tech skill building, and craftsmanship, showing children how to design animated figures, build characters, and dabble with other aspects of digital art.

LBE observer Latta says he very much approves of what he's seen of DisneyQuest thus far. Although there are the inevitable technological and logistical glitches that come with any new venture, "Disney has the right idea: to focus on the experience within the facility rather than the individual games or rides," he says. And the best thing about DisneyQuest is its interactive nature: guests themselves are allowed to define the experience.

"It's a very ambitious extension of what Disney has done before, and provides a whole new dimension to what we think of as entertainment," says Latta. Note the phrasing: not a replacement, but an extension. Not a substitution, but an *addition* to what we call entertainment.

■ CHALLENGES ABOUND

Despite the long-term success of Dave & Buster's, and the optimistic prognosis for other fledgling LBE sites, numerous business (and sociological) challenges abound for would-be LBE entertainment providers.

The biggest problem is keeping the entertainment offerings fresh. After all, the toys in these new playrooms do not come cheap. And, they need to be updated—or changed completely—on a regular basis or customers will get bored and stop coming.

One LBE site that didn't make it provides some valuable lessons. Called Virtual Worlds Entertainment, and based in Chicago, this firm still manufactures the popular BattleTech pods that are a big draw for avid fighter-pilot simulation junkies in Dave & Buster's and GameWorks.

But, Virtual Worlds failed completely when it attempted to open its own dedicated sites around the world. "Frankly, the locations didn't have a lot of appeal for repeat visits. It provided pretty much the same experience every time," says Ted Keenan, vice president of business development for Virtual Worlds. At the height of Virtual Worlds' attempt at creating dedicated sites for its games, it boasted 22 stores around the world (seven were company-owned, the rest were franchises). And, although there was a dedicated and loyal core of repeat customers who genuinely enjoyed playing the BattleTech game over and over, the stores simply couldn't support the kind of continuous (and very expensive) product development that would be required to bring a larger audience into the stores. Now, says Keenan, "we're a firm believer in the 'smorgasbord' approach," meaning locations that can offer a wide variety of attractions so that repeat visitors don't get bored.

One interesting hindsight: when it owned a single store, also in Chicago, Virtual Worlds was doing quite well financially. It had a strong niche market—male customers 18 to 35—who repeatedly spent sufficient funds to keep the site profitable. But, in its attempt to attract a broader audience, the site was renovated and redecorated—even though the games remained the same.

The idea was that creating a more elegant decor might attract more women into the store, says Keenan, and in fact there was a lot of traffic when the site opened up because it was truly a showplace "sort of like Jules Verne meets Victorian England," Keenan says. Unfortunately, the initial interest quickly died down, and in retrospect, Virtual Worlds might have done better to stick to its knitting. At the time, only about 7 percent of arcade players were female. When it revamped its premises, Virtual World managed to get that up to an 11-percent female audience. "But now we ask ourselves, to get that extra 4 percent female audience, how many men did we turn off? How much revenue did we turn away from the door from people who didn't like the 'hybrid' approach?" asks Keenan, who shrugs and says, "It's a puzzle."

XS New York is more of a nightclub, with 20,000 square feet of virtual reality–type gaming equipment. "It's essential to keep constantly refreshing and updating your games if you want people to keep coming in," agrees Jay Berkman, president of Skyline Entertainment, which runs XS New York, a high-tech nightclub located in Times Square that contains 20,000 square feet of high-tech games and simulation gaming equipment. Unlike Dave & Buster's, XS is not a restaurant, but depends on the games as well as live bands to draw the crowds. "Cyberhosts," adept in serving drinks as well as manipulating joysticks, make patrons feel comfortable, which is also essential, stresses Berkman, who currently sees his guests as 60 percent male, 40 percent female, mostly between the ages of 18 and 35.

"It's absolutely necessary that the training and quality of your staff is of the highest quality. No matter what kind of technology you're employing, you are primarily in the entertainment business, and you must make sure that the staff is friendly, responsive, proactive, helpful, and courteous," he says.

■ PORTENTS OF THE FUTURE

Concepts that will be useful in other LBE sorts of locations are being spotted at other venues: in museums, at corporate training facilities. Scott Jochim, founder and CEO of Digital Tech Frontier, a designer of high-tech machines for entertainment, training, and medical use, has also spent a great deal of time studying how the needs of the individual can be balanced with the entertainment of the crowd as a whole.

Jochim built a group-interactive product for AT&T, called "The Training Theater," which was installed in AT&T's Basking Ridge, New Jersey, facilities. AT&T employees being trained on international product offerings are put in a small room—it holds just six people—that contains a large video screen at the front of it. Each seat is equipped with handheld wireless keypads. After a 10-minute training presentation, the students participate in a quiz show: a live presenter asks questions related to the training, and the students respond by hitting their keypads. After that, a Q&A session allows individual students to key in questions and get personal attention without feeling as though they are drawing attention to themselves, or wasting the group's time. What this interactive theater allows, in effect, says Jochim, is to give each student a sense of being individually tutored; although this particular site only has six seats, there is nothing that would prevent there being 20 or 200 seats, and which would give a fully wired teacher a sense of a reaction from a large group that he or she would otherwise miss. "People are often afraid to speak up, afraid to ask questions, and teachers aren't always sure what is getting through, what is not being understood," explains Jochim. This kind of technology begins to deal with both issues.

It comes down to the attempts of Evans & Sutherland (see Chapter 1) to figure out the correct balance between the needs of the individual, and the needs of the group, in a social entertainment experience. "Allowing members of an audience to vote on what direction an experience should take is a very very primitive form of interaction," insists Stanley Walker, vice president and general manager of Evans & Sutherland's Digital Theater Division. Why? "At least a part of the audience is going to be voted down, and probably frustrated," he said.

So, what the team at Evans & Sutherland is trying to do is work with the notion of collaboration that gives the sense of *true* interaction, one in which the group experience doesn't override the individual's sense of satisfaction. It is better that a more sophisticated form of interactivity gives the group "tasks" they can only accomplish together, such as navigating a submarine through a lunar valley, and successfully avoiding dangerous objects in that valley. In a hypothetical case like this, "A group would be working with

260 PLAYING FOR PROFIT

each other, shouting to each other, trying to make this thing happen," says Walker. Voting won't do that—"it won't get you working cooperatively with the guy sitting next to you," agrees Rick Hinton, creative director of Evans & Sutherland Digital Theater Division.

Another challenge for LBE sites is just sheer economics. Unless you have the size and breadth of a Dave & Buster's, it might not be possible to support the high cost with a single entertainment venue. That is why the Irvine Spectrum Center, in Irvine, California, is catching the eye of many LBE entrepreneurs. It's like a DisneyQuest, only there are multiple vendors, and one doesn't get the feeling one is trapped in a self-contained world.

As of late 1998, the Irvine Spectrum Center boasted 500,000 square feet of entertainment that included traditional movie theaters, an IMAX 3-D theater, a Dave & Buster's, and a live-show amphitheater called Sing-Sing, which has at its heart two pianists sitting in a pit. Other high-tech games abound. Latta featured it in his *Wave Report* as a sign of good things to come: "It makes it possible to draw huge crowds and still host numerous entertainment facilities that would be a drag on a conventional mall," he writes. People come for the entire evening; they wander around the various entertainment offerings; entrance is free, and part of the fun is just being there. (If this were an Internet site, it would be called a portal.)

Indeed, even veterans of site-based entertainment venues such as amusement parks say that the technology itself is clearly less important than the overall experience. Phil Hettema is senior vice president of attraction development, Universal Studios' theme park division. Of all the rides he's helped design, he's most proud of such big draws as *Back to the Future,* and *Terminator II,* in which "we provided experiences that were immersive in a new way," he says, largely through more sophisticated uses of sensory cues, such as wraparound visual presentations, and higher-fidelity audio experiences, and other "prompts" that were visceral in nature and that shook and swayed participants.

But it's wrong, Hettema insists, to put too much emphasis on the technology. "Our goal is always an emotional one—to take you somewhere you've never been before," he stresses. It's more than just the notion of "suspension of disbelief" required of any art form. Rather, it's "pushing the audience to forget where they are, they are so totally engaged in the experience."

It's not necessarily a question of rendering things more "realistically" either, Hettema argues. "A great work opens the door to your imagination, and doesn't necessarily fill in all the blanks," points out Hettema. "An attraction that uses technology to fill in every sensory detail for you might not be nearly as compelling an experience as one that leaves something for you to imagine, because then you don't have to do any of the work, and you are less engaged."

If you ask Hettema, a leader in his field of location-based entertainment, what the future has in store, he's quiet for a moment. These things will become more immersive, no doubt about it, he says. Displays will become larger, sounds higher fidelity, a more visceral experience. But that's not really the point.

The key, he says, will always be the social aspect of the experience. "Am I doing this thing by myself, or is someone else in proximity? Am I, in some way, feeling connected to others? Is my experience affected in some significant way by others' human and emotional response?" These are the key questions, insists Hettema—and he also believes that what he calls "this shared intimacy" will probably not be achievable over the Internet.

"We, as humans, are very very sensitive to the behavior of others," he says. "When we're in their proximity, we pick up all kinds of cues—not just visual, such as seeing what they are doing, or audio, such as hearing what they are saying. There are so many other kinds of cues," says Hettema.

True, with technology improving so rapidly—and becoming easier to use—just about anyone "can do a cool streaming audio site, or display images on the Web," continues Hettema. But, ultimately, true entertainment is something else—something that requires craft, and is magical in its effect, and which gets people involved with each other. "Bits are bits," shrugs Hettema.

Epilogue: Expect the Unexpected

"The empires of the future are the empires of the mind."
—Winston Churchill

"You can observe a lot by just looking around."
—Yogi Berra

"You can't direct the wind, but you can adjust the sails"
—Anonymous

It's never too late for a good, sincere apology. So, here are two.

■ PREDICTING THE FUTURE IS A DUBIOUS ENTERPRISE, AT BEST

Sometimes, it's hard to remember just how fast the world is changing. Let's remind ourselves.

On July 1, 1863 (the day before the decisive civil war battle at Gettysburg, Pennsylvania), predicting who would ultimately win that war would have stumped even the

263

most astute observers. Yet, just three days later, the many reasons that the North was absolutely bound to win (its much larger fighting force, industrial capacity, financing, capacity to endure) began to be clear. And now, in grand hindsight, we can see that the seeds of victory for the North, and defeat for the South, had been sown decades earlier through complex economic and social decisions whose ultimate outcome was hazy, at best.

The same can be said for the winter of 1942 during World War II and the end of hostilities in 1945. At the end of 1942, the outcome of WW II was a toss-up at best, for the allies. The fascist forces were winning and advancing nearly everywhere. The U.S. fleet had not been reconstructed from the disastrous loss at Pearl Harbor, the Russians were in rapid retreat in their own land, and things seemed fairly hopeless. Yet, just three years later, when hostilities had ended, it was clear, again, that the allied victory was a good possibility, and even likely.

We forget how quickly things can change when in the midst of a battle, even though they may seem ludicrously obvious in retrospect. Today, most companies in most industries rarely try to plan further ahead than five years. Most will settle happily for three years, and in Silicon Valley, it's not uncommon for new business plans to be revised every six months or so. (It's been repeated so often that it's become a cliché, but many people insist that "Internet years" go faster than dog years.)

Here's another example. In 1993, just four years before we began work on this book, the first Internet browser was still in development. Also circa 1993, the inevitable "digital convergence" of media, communications, and technology was beginning to be whispered in corridors of money and power. Of course, that was before a number of multi-million-dollar failures of interactive TV and broadband service experiments were each dubbed, in their turn, "the deal of the century." It was before Apple and IBM got married (you guessed it—that was also the "deal of the century") and spawned two children who, sadly, didn't live past adolescence, but who were supposed to help lead us to the nirvana of convergence. It was before Bill Gates noticed this little thing called the World Wide Web. *That's* how fast things change.

So what about that thing called digital convergence? We're all still waiting. And yet, all these people and companies had it right, in a sense. Sometimes it *is* clear that we're on the verge of something different. It's just not clear how the changes will play out, or what technical or sociological or cultural factors they are dependent on, or even *why* they're happening. It just becomes apparent to some key people that the old world order is, well, old.

Those who fail to sniff the possibility of change in the wind are left behind. When IBM failed to acknowledge the changes heralded by the PC—and, simultaneously, how Microsoft intended to dominate that platform's software operating environment—it put its future at risk. The problem wasn't that IBM didn't correctly predict the future—as we've pointed out, even Bill Gates didn't see the Internet coming. The problem was its complacency, its refusal to sense a change coming, and to be prepared to act swiftly, however that change played itself out.

So, even if some, or even most, of our predictions turn out to be false, we think it's a no-brainer that the Internet and related digital technologies will continue to wreak havoc with the structure of today's entertainment industries. If predicting the future is risky business, complacency is a riskier one.

■ COVERING TOO MUCH TERRITORY IN ONE BOOK DOES EVERYONE A DISSERVICE

Our second apology centers around the fact that we've tried to cover so much territory. Certainly, the prospect of writing, much less reading, a book that attempts to cover 10 industries is rather daunting, especially because each respective entertainment industry segment is at a different state of technological evolution. So, trying to explain computer games (console, PC, on-line, location-based), radio (terrestrial, Internet, satellite), recorded music; television (terrestrial, cable, satellite, Internet, wireless), gambling (local, and virtual), and the alternative networks that carry them (telephone, cable, satellite, wireless) within the context of the book is an ambitious project. We admit that. And, so, this isn't an encyclopedia—you can tell.

But our conviction is that a few basic themes run across each of the aforementioned industries. By now, you know the chorus: Wild West (lack of regulation), personalization (it's interactive, and it's directed at the individual), and the challenges that arise from a technology that enables both global reach and local specificity (puts a new spin on the phrase, "Think global, act local."). We think that examining the massive changes occurring throughout these entertainment segments in light of these three factors is not only a useful, but illuminating, exercise. We think it's at the core of how we're going to play in the digital age.

■ WE LEAVE YOU WITH A QUESTION

Our attitude, even as we're positing possible scenarios, has been: Question the status quo. Avoid complacency. Call us revolutionaries or call us fools, but we are aiming our puny flashlights a little bit up the road, and we think we can discern the outlines of specific shapes ahead.

So here's the question that drove us to write (and rewrite) this book, and it's something you can also ponder: If *this* isn't what's going to happen, then what will? The possibilities are certainly exciting.

Notes

CHAPTER 2

1. *Wall Street Journal* Technology Summit, New York (October 1998).
2. See Erik Barnouw, *Tube of Plenty,* 2nd edition, New York, Oxford University Press, 1990.
3. Erik Barnouw, *Tube of Plenty,* p. 57.
4. Kevin Werbach, *Digital Tornado: The Internet and Telecommunications Policy,* Working paper no. 29, FCC, Office of Plans and Policy (March 1997).

CHAPTER 4

1. Hal Vogel, Entertainment Industry Economics.
2. Source: *Webnoize News* (July 10, 1998), http://news.webnoize.com/media-mix/2582.html.

CHAPTER 5

1. Peggy Miles, *Mecklermedia Internet World's Guide to Webcasting and Internet Broadcasting,* New York, John Wiley & Sons, 1997.
2. FCC Mass Media Bureau, Policy and Rules Division, *Review of the Radio Industry, 1997,* MM Docket no. 98-35.

CHAPTER 6

1. DavidBowie.com.
2. *Webnoize* (July 8, 1998), http://news.webnoize.com/business/2569.html.

3. DavidBowie.com.
4. Edgar Bronfman, Jr., keynote speaker at R&R Convention 1998, Los Angeles, www.rronline.com/convention/news/text12b.htm
5. Harold Vogel, *Entertainment Industry Economics, 4th edition,* Cambridge, UK, Cambridge University Press, 1998.
6. National Academy of Recording Arts and Sciences Conference on Downloadable Music, Los Angeles (July 23, 1998).
7. Richard Feyman, *The Meaning of It All, Thoughts of a Citizen Scientist,* Reading, MA, Perseus Books, 1998.
8. It is first because it's the foremost problem the record industry is vocal about, and most actively working to resolve.
9. J. William Gurley, *Data broadcast: The new frontier,* C-Net News.com Perspectives (December 22, 1997). http://www.news.com/Perspectives/gurley.html Perspectives.

CHAPTER 7

1. George Gilder (speaking at the Telecosm98 conference in Squaw Valley, CA), *Forbes Bandwidth Blowout* (Sept. 15, 1998).
2. For another view of the rationale behind the FCC's interest in digital TV, see Joel Brinkley's *Defining Vision,* New York, Harcourt Brace, 1998, in which he discusses how digital TV was cynically promoted as a last-minute, political means to avoid the redistribution of broadcast spectrum.
3. Hal Vogel, *Entertainment Industry Economics, 4th edition,* Cambridge, UK, Cambridge University Press, 1998.
4. UltimateTV press release (Sept. 10, 1998).
5. iQVC on-line, http://www.qvc.com/hqttour.html.
6. *Webnoize News Service,* "NBC Buys Into Intertainer. Will Provide Programming" (August 3, 1998).

CHAPTER 8

1. Don Clark, "3DO CEO's Game Plan Is More Modest," *The Wall Street Journal* (May 28, 1998): p. B1.

CHAPTER 9

1. Norman Douglas, *South Wind,* chap. 7 (1917), cited in *The Columbia Dictionary of Quotations.*

2. Phil Hettema, "Adrenalin by Design," chap. 24 in *Digital Illusion: Entertaining the Future with High Technology,* edited by Clark Dodsworth, p. 373, New York, Addison Wesley, 1998.

CHAPTER 10

1. Wall Street Journal Technology Summit, October 1998.
2. Total Tele, www.totaltele.com.
3. We've made it nearly all the way through this book and we've been able to keep industry jargon and babble to an absolute minimum, and we're not going to let loose now. This will no doubt annoy some readers who would just as soon have us dump all the euphemisms and analogies and dive right into techno-babble. But, we don't believe that the technology issues that dominate industry discussions—as important as they are to these industries—are really what will determine the future of entertainment. Thus, we focus on what matters to consumers. Consumers will decide what happens, by deciding where they spend their time and money.
4. There is considerable debate about the forecasted costs.

CHAPTER 11

1. Boris Badenov, *The Rocky and Bullwinkle Show* (Jay Ward, producer).
2. Michael J. Mandel, "You Ain't Seen Nuthin Yet," *Business Week* (August 24, 1998). www.businessweek.com/1998/35/covstory.htm.
3. NARAS Conference on Downloadable Music, Los Angeles (July 23, 1998).
4. Judy Collins, *Marat Sade.* Original German-language version of the text by Peter Weiss; English version by Geoffrey Shelton. Verse adaptation and lyrics by Adam Mawgus.
5. Erica Smith, Gamecenter.com, "Mike Wilson Speaks About GOD," C-Net GameCenter Interview (December 18, 1997).

CHAPTER 12

1. Jorge Luis Borges, "Avatars of the Tortoise" (essay), in *Labyrinths: Selected Stories and Other Writings,* p. 202, New York, New Directions Publishing Corp., 1962.

2. Bruno Bettelheim, *The Uses of Enchantment: The Meaning and Importance of Fairy Tales,* p. 37, New York, Alfred A. Knopf, 1976.
3. Janet H. Murray, *Hamlet on the Holodeck: The Future of Narrative in Cyberspace,* chap. 7, Cambridge, MA, The MIT Press, 1997.
4. Interview with Robert Stone from *Writers at Work: The Paris Review Interviews,* Eighth Series, edited by George Plimpton, p. 326, New York, Penguin Books, 1988.
5. Deirdre Bair, *Samuel Beckett, a Biography,* New York, Harcourt Brace Jovanovich, 1978.

Index

About the Authors

Alice LaPlante (Woodside, California) is an award-winning computer industry journalist. Formerly the news editor for *InfoWorld*, her technology and management articles have appeared in *Forbes ASAP, Business Week, ComputerWorld,* and *PC World*. She teaches writing at Stanford University and San Francisco State University.

Rich Seidner (Woodside, California) is an international media consultant with more than 30 years' experience in technology and business development in computer game and digital entertainment industries.